THE CHRISTIAN FAITH
AND SECULARISM

THE
CHRISTIAN FAITH
AND SECULARISM

Edited by

J. RICHARD SPANN

KENNIKAT PRESS/PORT WASHINGTON, N. Y.

THE CHRISTIAN FAITH AND SECULARISM

Copyright 1948 by Stone and Pierce
Reissued in 1969 by Kennikat Press by arrangement with
Abingdon Press
Library of Congress Catalog Card No: 70-86062
SBN 8046-0589-0

Manufactured by Taylor Publishing Company   Dallas, Texas

ESSAY AND GENERAL LITERATURE INDEX REPRINT SERIES

FOREWORD

THE GROWING WORLD INTIMACY CREATES AN INCREASING AWARENESS of a malady in our civilization. The authors of these 1947 Evanston Conference lectures associate this sickness with "secularism." Part I defines secularism as an evasive, often unconscious, philosophy which does not deny but ignores the presence and ethical influence of a living God. Secularism depends upon education, science, personal aggressiveness, and organized power, while ignoring the spiritual and ethical forces of Jesus Christ.

Part II discusses some of the influences of secularism upon the creative forces of our contemporary culture. Part III is a study of its impact upon political life, and Part IV evaluates the effects of secularism upon some of our economic and social issues.

The last, and largest, part of the volume presents the importance of "Christianity's Witness in a Secular World." Christianity can and should be the most creative force in our civilization; however, it has also felt the blighting influence of secularism. The aggressive proclamation of the Christian philosophy is held to be the one means of transforming the secular forces into the forces of righteousness.

Christian ministers and laymen must be alert to differentiate between the purely secular and the distinctively Christian. This volume is designed to help make this distinction clearer and to give power to the preaching that meets the needs of people living in these difficult days.

J. RICHARD SPANN

CONTENTS

Part I

INTRODUCTORY

Part II

SECULARISM IN CONTEMPORARY CULTURE

Part III

SECULARISM IN POLITICAL LIFE

Part IV
SECULARISM IN ECONOMIC AND SOCIAL ISSUES

Part V
CHRISTIANITY'S WITNESS IN A SECULAR WORLD

Part I

Introductory

THE NATURE OF SECULARISM

Leroy E. Loemker

SECULARISM IS NO LONGER, AS IT WAS A HUNDRED YEARS AGO, AN intellectual revolt against theological domination. It has become the supporting atmosphere of our culture. To describe it is like describing the air about us. No logical knife can dissect it; it is too pervasive and fluid to be captured in the net of any system of ideas. We are so completely adjusted to it that we do not mark it, but only those salient traits of our culture for which it is the permanent foundation. It is not surprising, therefore, that the secular temper is less noteworthy for what it affirms than for what it excludes.

Secularism is practical atheism. A classical analysis of it is found in Plato's *Laws*, though this was written at a time in which secularism was more discernible through a cultural atmosphere which itself was religious. Though Plato's account was intellectualistic, the suggestion of a more deeply rooted attitude and practice filters through the analysis of the Athenian stranger.

No one who, in obedience to the laws, believed that there were Gods, ever intentionally did any unholy act or uttered any unlawful word, but he who did must have supposed one of three things: either that they did not exist (which is the first possibility), or secondly, that if they did, they took no care of man, or thirdly, that they were easily appeased and turned aside from their purpose by sacrifice and prayers. (*Laws*, 885.)

The more dangerous impiety, Plato recognized, is not the intellectual act which denies God, but the pattern of life which neglects him or abuses his holiness. Secularism is our failure to let God be God in our lives. Its nature is neither to affirm nor to deny religious faith, but to live indifferently to it. Neither reverence nor blasphemy does it know. Saint and devil alike are no secularists, for both fear God, though one rejoices and the other trembles.

Secularism is thus not a philosophical position. It is not primarily an interpretation of life in terms of the sensual, the changing, and the

11

material, though some philosophies have, as we shall see, both encouraged and exemplified it. The typical modern secularist indulges in little interpretation, for our age is given less to reason than to the coercion of opinions, and we reserve our intellects for the expedient quest of our narrower interests.

Secularism is irreligion, but it is not synonymous with iniquity; often it is strengthened by the moral protest against the intolerance, the otherworldliness, the inhumanity that have marked much religion. It might be well today if tragic India had more of this critical secular spirit. It is only an exclusive secularism which dries up the springs of culture and the creative resources of man. Secularism is not immorality, but a shift in the conception of moral powers and moral ends. As its best-known modern advocate defined it, it is "the doctrine that morality should be based solely in regard to the well-being of mankind in the present life, to the exclusion of all considerations drawn from belief in God or in future life." [1]

Nor is it to be confused with indifference to the church. In lands predominantly Roman Catholic, secularism does indeed assume the guise of anticlericalism. But to Protestants a confusion between the neglect of God and the neglect of the church is itself a sign of the growth of the secular spirit. Its roots lie far deeper in the pattern of human life than does mere devotion to an institution, so that, aside from merely external habits of behavior, secularism within the church is scarcely to be distinguished from that without.

Secularism, finally, marks the contemporary culture, not merely of nominally Christian lands, but of every region to which the modern emphasis upon man's ability to achieve his salvation through his own efforts has been extended. To understand it one must therefore first grasp the essential nature of religion.

How Religion Operates

Religion is the surrender of the person to God, and the commitment of life's goods to God's will, or God's plan, or the course of God's activities. The center of its reference is objective and ultimate; it calls forth reverence and worship. There are many forces in contemporary life which have the effect of blunting man's sense of his dependence upon anything, whether on nature, on the community, or on God.

[1] G. J. Holyoake, *Secularism, the Practical Philosophy of the People* (1845).

There are also, increasingly felt, forces compelling him to a greater awareness of his dependence upon the first of these without the last. The secular spirit thus moves with little stability from self-reliance to the surrender of individual integrity, not to God, but to natural and social pressures.

Religion may operate in either of two contrasting ways upon the attitudes of men. Salvation may be regarded as a supreme good apart from all other values of life, the pearl of great price for which man, the trafficker in goods, will sell all he has. But it may also be considered as the release of the whole man, and all of his valid interests and needs, from evil. Both trends are found in every great religious tradition— the exclusive and the inclusive, the will to dwell with God by renouncing all other values, and the will to enhance and unify all other true ends through their divine source. For example, religion in the West created the modern quest for law in nature, and then warred with it. It is, as Hocking has said, the mother of the arts, but it also destroys its offspring.

The reason for this paradox is to be found in the dynamic quality of human life and interests. A dominant purpose provides any man with power either to exclude from his life other aims which conflict with it, or to enlarge his personality by swinging into its field and imparting new radiance to those other loyalties which may be made to cohere with it. Which of the two occurs depends upon the fruitfulness and meaningfulness of his dominating purpose. Men may thus be of single minds about religion or some other great challenging loyalty, or, like Plato's democratic man, they may be many-minded and fluctuating, or their great loyalty may provide a unity within which a plurality of lesser and related ends may harmoniously be attained. They may seek that Kingdom of God unto which all other things worth seeking will be added.

Christianity differs from other great faiths, not only in the uniqueness of its revelation in Jesus Christ, but in the unique spiritual process which that revelation launched in human history—a process in which God seen at last as both just and loving, as at once universal and yet present to men, effects his ends through a particular type of human character and a particular type of new social community. But to the fundamental dilemma between the inclusion or the exclusion of life's values in this character and this community it has given no unambiguous answer. If, for example, Kierkegaard is right about the Christian life, a vast leap separates it from other great human experiences— aesthetic, moral, and intellectual. And this is indeed true in Christian experience; it is but one of the symptoms of our secularism within the church that we so easily confuse aesthetic indulgence with worship, a provocative sermon with an experience of the living God, and a moral resolve with the saving power of that God. Yet Kierkegaard was wrong when we consider, not religious experience itself, but those accumulations of experience which comprise personality and sustain the Christian community. For the test of valid Christian experience is its power to regenerate character. Ugliness, falsehood, and narrowness of social vision are all barriers against the spirit of God. A Christian is one who, in common with like-minded persons, finds in the historical influence and present action of Christ's spirit a channel by which divine power is mediated and his life unified and given purpose. A Christian society is one in which such persons, living in communion with each other and with God, impart to social structures the spirit by which our common life is infused with justice and love, the power of science is directed toward human good, and art and other creative human efforts are given a content ennobling to men.

Modern Aspects of the Secular Spirit

Modern secularism is the repudiation of God as the source of such spiritual unity and power. It builds upon a twofold foundation: the withdrawal of religion from the issues of this world (as described above), and man's unavoidable concern with them. Plato's three classes of atheists reveal the resulting stages to which secularism gives rise: first, the repudiation of a God whose providence is no longer understood to affect life; then the confusion which results from the denial of such a unifying providence; and, last of all, the turn to magical and superstitious controls for the values we seek.

The secular spirit shows itself most clearly in the effort to achieve full personal and social growth through some other dominating interest than loyalty to God. Among recent expressions of such a hope, one by Robert S. Lynd may be quoted.

Religion, in its traditional forms, is a dying reality in current living. And yet no culture can live vitally without a central core of emotionally resonant loyalties widely shared by the mass of the people. . . . Our culture, in its headlong preoccupation with individual money-making, has been reckless of the fate of common values and loyalties; and as a result these have been disastrously dissipated, notably in the increasingly prevalent pattern of urban living. . . . American culture, if it is to be creative in the personalities of those who live it, needs to discover and to build prominently into its structure a core of richly evocative common purposes which have meaning in terms of the deep personality needs of the great mass of the people. Needless to say, the theology, eschatology, and other familiar aspects of traditional Christianity need not have any place in such an operating system.[2]

It is important to note how much Lynd has already set aside as lost. We must have a living faith, but it is probably too late for Christianity to provide it.

Here is reflected our confusion of Christianity with its theology, because our faith as Christians is not alive; our confusion, too, between the truth of such a faith and its social effectiveness, because we can no longer recapture a unified conception of truth and of human destiny. Hence the achievements of science and technology, of the arts, of national power and world-wide economic structures, being more conspicuous than is the experience of God, offer themselves as tempting substitutes for him. Our language is better fitted to discuss them. We can serve them without first being reborn. The cults of state or of a vague "humanity," of science or of beauty, of social reform or of revolt, tempt us as sources of moral inspiration and human betterment in which every just interest shall have its place. And under limited circumstances, for a limited time, and involving a restricted social range of values, such loyalties do in fact arouse a personal and a social response which leaves no value untouched, and which gives power, and even some unity and plan to life.

Yet in the outcome all such idolatry turns out to impoverish rather than enrich, and to reduce life and culture to mediocrity. In the first place, the faith is not inclusive enough to absorb into it all of man's valid interests and hopes. In the second, its true nature is derivative and merely instrumental; it cannot supply the fullness of power which enlivens man's full being. Social revolution as an ideal, for example, cannot evoke the full power of art (for it recognizes only the art of revolt), nor of truth, nor of character. Great human talents

[2] *Knowledge for What?*, pp. 238-39. Used by permission Princeton University Press, publishers.

and consecration, given to the service of any end less than the one God, tend themselves to be debased. Art becomes trivial, character labored, and truth for its own sake pointless and without unity. Profanity itself, as T. S. Eliot has with much wit observed, degenerates into a reflection of our sense of practical futility. Self-reliance is transmuted by a necessary internal development into self-centeredness. Cultural promiscuity is mistaken for cultural universality, and indifference for tolerance; and the false hopes which have given goals less than the highest to our efforts end by perverting our science, debasing our taste, and weakening our moral zeal. Man cannot gain his full stature in the service of any half-god. Mediocrity is the first fruitage of the secular spirit.

The second stage, also characteristic of our times, is at once less fruitful and harder to overcome. It is the aimless pluralism and confusion in values which appears when the secular idols have lost our loyalty. It is what Plato has described in his picture of the democratic man, enslaved to every passing appetite. It approaches what Nietzsche described as nihilism. Man and society dissolve into a patternless collection of interests and allegiances, each of which is threatened by the others. The louder and more successful the forces which coerce us, the more distracted and impersonal become our lives, and the more rapidly shift the objects of our tastes and loves. This is the plight of countless numbers of men, if not of our civilization itself. It is war in its widest human sense; there is no more peace whereby we may restore the internal unity of our selves. And until the Christian Church succeeds in providing for distracted men a refuge and help in restoring the spiritual meaning of their life through worship, it will make little headway in its struggle against the forces of decay and disintegration. The second fruits of secularism are disunity and conflict, both within man and in the social order by which he and his fellows live.

There is a third stage in irreligion, most dangerous of all because it is outwardly so near to religion itself. Yet it is at the opposite pole, for its interest is selfish and its effect is to deny that God is God in the very act of calling upon him. As Plato saw, we believe that we may easily appease him and turn him aside from his purposes by sacrifice and prayer. Magic retains the form and activity of religion but surrenders its spirit. It begins when our will outweighs God's as we manipulate the forms of religion to our own ends; it ends by our forgetting God's holy nature in our exclusive concern with the formula which is to achieve our ends. Within the church this magic assumes the form of collecting merit through regular loyalties; it may even be debased into the use of the institution as a means of conserving other social processes to which we are greatly attached. Jesus' harshest words were aimed at the magic of scribe and Pharisee, who trusted in vain repetitions and deified the institution and the practice of religion.

The growth of magic in the common relations of modern life attests man's insistent demand for a providence of some kind. A scientific and technological age has not satisfied man's deepest hungers —for the recognition of his own worth, for social participation, for triumph over evil and the attainment of good. The very historical tradition to which Christianity has contributed so much has intensified this emphasis upon expediency and immediate results. The seventeenth century discovered the power of science and its applications; the eighteenth, the possibility of distributing political sovereignty; and the nineteenth, new visions of social and economic justice. But all these attainments together, reinforcing each other in modern secularism and growing independently of their religious sources, have failed to help man achieve his goal. Thus he has resorted to the desperate application of formula after formula to extend his powers beyond their natural limits. Superstitions abound where the church has lost its power; the cult of luck draws more and more worshipers and creates an increasing dislocation of our economy, and the great isms propose magical short cuts to the fulfillment of men's hopes. Science has not made us less credulous in human affairs, and beyond the limits of technology our faith reaches far past our valid knowledge when we fix it upon national power, Marxist dialectic, or worldly success. Whether crude or philosophically refined, the superstitions of our day are a measure of the failure of scientific rationalism to satisfy our whole nature.

Protestant liberalism, it may be pointed out in passing, contains its own peculiar temptations to encourage the secular spirit. The liberal church movement invites a dependence upon organization, upon moral effort, and upon socially relative goals which, in itself, is not religious. When the church overlooks the depth of tragedy in human life, the extent of man's dependence, and the universality of God's justice, it too is caught in the currents of our secular order.

The fruits of secularism are thus mediocrity, disorganization, and superstition. History becomes a succession of circles as the quest for salvation moves from the failure of one worldly myth to the construction of another. Life becomes confined to horizons within which man was not made to operate, so that creativity withers and our culture is debased to a worship of what Toynbee has called "ephemeral selves, ephemeral institutions, and ephemeral techniques." The very human power to build, to love, and to enjoy is lost when it seeks to stand alone, without the life-giving powers of God.

The Arguments of Secularism

Though not merely a philosophy, secularism is not without its intellectual interpretation and defense, which must be understood and refuted if men are to be re-educated to religious attitudes. The theoretical supports are to be found in that uneasy mixture of empiricism and naturalism characteristic of so much nineteenth-century thinking, to which the utilitarian and positivistic interpretations of religion, and the romantic conception of human nature, have imparted the quasi-religious accents of humanism. The secular arguments are an eclectic compound of subjectivism, materialism, scientism (as a philosophy of value which holds generally that facts point to evaluations), and optimism. Carried out consistently these would refute each other at crucial points, but together they have effectively strengthened man's conviction that he knows the good, that the mastery of nature gives him the power to achieve it, and that he possesses a stature big enough, by himself, to attain it. These trends can be illustrated in certain areas of recent thought where their failure is discernible.

The appeal to science and its applications has been the most important intellectual stimulus to the secular attitude. Science has always been driven by a double motive—the desire to understand and the desire to control. The former has often supported religion; indeed it was from the quest for the cosmic lawgiver that the modern concept of natural law derived. The latter motive is analogous to magic; where it predominates, it increases man's inclination to regard himself as self-sufficient. Modern thought has not sufficiently portrayed the affinities which exist between the scientific and the religious attitudes. Meanwhile there are three different ways in which a one-sided or exaggerated emphasis upon science has supported irreligion.

The first is by emphasizing the adequacy of human intelligence, using the scientific method, to solve its own problems satisfactorily. According to this opinion, which has been the basis of great reforms in American education and politics, man's redemption is delayed only by man's failure to press his objective, analytic approach into the social and cultural spheres. When intelligence succeeds in breaking down a few more barriers—the irrational resistance to reason within man's own being, the distinction between the human and the sub-human in nature, the wall between questions as to *what is* and questions as to *what ought to be*, and the resistance which national and other superindividual organizations of power offer to human freedom—then, it is held, man will need no other savior than his own intelligent will. The infamies made possible by man's recent technological triumphs, and the terror which they have created, have put this philosophy on the defensive; and we now have dramatic evidence of the great breach between knowing the solutions to human problems and doing the things which these solutions demand. We have recently heard atomic scientists and military leaders, loudest in voicing the cry of human need for moral regeneration and religious redemption.

A second tendency of science has been the effort to show that nature, including man and his associations, is a self-explanatory process, and that there is therefore no need and no possibility for a further explanation that is supernatural. The old-fashioned mechanism of the eighteenth century has now proved inadequate in virtually every science; since Hume it has been hard to consider causality as explanation. But mechanism has now been expanded to include part-whole patterns functioning as a unity, radical discontinuities, and temporal advances from simpler to more complex entities, so that as scientific analyses have become more refined, the concept of nature has itself grown to include human values and purposes, and even, in the thought of many contemporary thinkers, a cosmic creative process. There is at present a serious effort to retain and reinterpret the insights of Christian orthodoxy—the doctrines of sin and redemption, of atonement and sacrifice—in terms of such an immanent God. Yet these naturalistic revisions all tend to reduce religious experience to some relation less personal than the communication and communion of God with man created in his image. The dialogue of worship is lost, and religion does not call forth the full spiritual power of man's responses. Such naturalism still offers false encouragement to an exclusively secular spirit.

The applications of science are material, and it is this influence which has most of all affected the popular creed of secularism. Science has helped commerce to exaggerate the role of gadgets, of physical efficiencies, of things, in making men happy. The radio and the automobile still loom up so large in man's notions of the good that he forgets the state of his soul and the effect of these gadgets upon it. Thus while philosophical materialism is refuted, practical materialism remains a decisive human factor which will probably be altered only with the economic order upon which gadgets depend.

A second area is that of the scientific study of human nature itself. There have been prolonged efforts to find the foundations for a non-religious ethics in psychological theories which reduce human nature either to structures of feeling and perception—in which pleasurable contents should mark the good and painful the bad—or to patterns of response—in which successful adaptation should mark the good, failure in adjustment the bad. The attempt to understand man and his powers by such a reductive process—whether that of "mental chemistry," as Mill called associational psychology, or that of applying biological categories—has often resulted in an arbitrary practice of systematically translating human experience into another set of terms, in the course of which the distinctively human and creative is lost. Thought becomes association; ideal purpose becomes biological response; religion and morality are tested by survival value. Psychology could never have hoped, by means of dead bones such as these, to find living answers to the problems of man, had it not been for the illusory glow of life imparted to them by the romantic tradition whose lights tranformed biology itself, feelings and instincts themselves, into the good.

But of recent years psychology has been driven, by its own failures and the clearer perceptions of others, to re-examine and re-adjust its principles of analysis. Both psychiatrist, within a naturalistic framework, and theologian, studying the human barriers to salvation, have dispelled much of the fascination which the romantic view of man once evoked. Philosophical historians have shown the conditions under which the abstract psychologies arose, and psychological critics themselves have pointed out the empirical inadequacy of many of the old positions. We are aware of the discontinuities in mental life, of the enormous perversions and sins of which feeling is capable if caught by the coercions of an evil society. Man does not appear either so mechanical or so self-sufficient as psychology once considered him.

A third intellectual factor in the justification of secularism has been the emphasis upon social reform which arose in the nineteenth century and has since affected our political and economic life so conspicuously for both weal and woe. Convinced of progress in history, and convinced that it is measured by material change, we have worked doggedly to prove our faith. It is true that the theories of how reform shall come have varied to the point of becoming main sources of conflict among us—nationalist against internationalist, capitalist against socialist, and libertarian against determinist. Yet ultimately it is this hope of reform which alone gives plausibility to a secular ethics.

A critical judgment upon these diverse philosophies of social reform may well begin with the contemporary need for universality in our ethical and social thinking. The relativism concerning human goods which underlies our philosophies of action—whether violent or in the gentler spirit of legality—is inadequate for a world which must become one or none at all. The "cold war," in which our journalists say we are already engaged, is the clash between two incompletely rational and opposed systems of class reform, each of which claims universality—capitalistic nationalism and Marxist internationalism. Reason itself demands a more ultimate basis of judging both, a basis involving both cosmic and moral principles corrective of their imperfect ones.

Because of its explicit atheism, Marxism is itself one of the most prominent secular philosophies. Certainly there is much evidence in current civilization of the partial truth of the Marxist generalizations The extent to which the concern with physical necessities and wealth has determined human thought and institutions is obvious to any thoughtful observer. But that Marx should generalize this observation to a revolutionary absolute is itself an instance of the error of secular thought. His diagnosis is correct in many essentials; his proposed solution involves the secular confusion of what is with what ought to be, of power with right. Marx's criticism is a naturalistic derivative from the Augustinian vision of God's plan in history; and to correct Marx's error we must return to the Augustinian doctrine that the spiritual life, though time and space are its field of action, derives its essential nature, its true fulfillment, and its hope of redemption from God. If the Christian Church can establish its independence from the practical materialism of Western culture, it may be able to fulfill its obligation of restoring social criticism, and the half-truths of both Marxism and capitalism, to their Christian setting in the divine judgment upon all history and society.

Examined together, these intellectual challenges to religion show that the secular spirit has produced chaos in the intellect as well as in the tastes and loyalties of men. Men's conclusions are valid only within the framework of the assumptions with which they begin; the postulates which we use in our system of thought often limit the human value of the truth we seek. We outgrow secularism as a way of thinking only as we correct the principles with which we start. As our failures become apparent and we understand better the nature of man and the depth of his needs, thought itself will provide wider and more reverent intellectual perspectives for our life and culture.

THE WAY OUT

What, finally, are the paths out of our contemporary secularism and the frustrations in which it involves the spirit of men? It is difficult to change the air we breathe. The way out can be found only as many individuals, by unified and concerted practices and responses, alter the spiritual quality of their own interests and obligations. The answer to the secular spirit is a more effective human medium for the spirit of God. This is the role of the true church.

First of all, man needs to regain his sense of humility. The events of our time are such as to impress us with our sense of failure and of need, but in many respects the molders of our opinions still operate to shut from us the vision of our own inadequacy. When they no longer do so, our danger will be the spirit of nihilism in place of that of humility. By any truly human sense of values our failures and brutalities are indeed such as should awaken the sense of our guilt and the divine judgment. About this the church must speak in complete boldness and truth.

It needs also to instruct its people in the foundations of their faith and its applicability to human values and social order. We cannot become bearers of salvation if we are not clearer about the conditions, the cost, the scope of salvation. The religious illiteracy of church people is not decreasing with education. Where doctrine is taught, it is too often as a dead language. Understanding of the conditions of world order is not keeping pace with the rapid movement of decisive world events. The dilemma of our century crowds upon us daily more firmly—not merely one world or none, but one loyalty, great enough to unite us all, to inspire us all, to save us all, or the chapters of our era of moral leadership and achievement must end in suffering and death. To grasp the Christian message concerning man, God, and salvation is to have a protection against the ways of thought which reinforce secularism. In particular, we cannot teach the worth of man in the divine plan, and the limits of catastrophe or achievement in history, or push back the naturalistic limits of men's hopes without a return to the central doctrine of human immortality.

Most of all the church must lead men to see the narrowness of their daily loyalties, and the triviality and impermanence of much that they live for. It is our own treasures that betray us in the end. American life can achieve greater substance and durability only through a widespread transvaluation of values. We need to return to the golden standard, to reorder our hopes and our faiths, to reweigh our habits and our obligations by the moral demands and the spiritual promises of the Christ. The church must hold aloft the glory of the gospel; it must enlarge our vision of the possibility of salvation, so that even now men's hearts may be strengthened and their resolves to live together in God's spirit clarified by a vision of the will and the power of the living God.

HISTORICAL INTRODUCTION
TO SECULARISM

John T. McNeill

THE WRITER OF DEUTERONOMY ASCRIBES TO MOSES A SONG IN WHICH the Israelitish nation is personified as Jeshurun. The name means "upright," but Jeshurun's uprightness has departed. He has been spiritually victimized by worldly prosperity. Bloated with the products of the field and the flock—butter, milk, the fat of rams, and the blood of the grape—Jeshurun, we read, "waxed fat, and kicked: . . . then he forsook God which made him, and lightly esteemed the Rock of his salvation" (32:15). Now Jeshurun, alias ancient Israel, is much like other people in similar conditions. A few short years of relative ease and security usually suffice to bring to expression a like insolent recalcitrance against God's moral law. The history of secularism is a phase of the human story through every era and generation, but especially in those times in which the physical goods of life have been abundant. It is less likely to appear, though it does sometimes appear, in economic scarcity, when material wealth is inordinately desired. Secularism is, then, no merely modern phenomenon. It is a disorder endemic in humanity, which, from time to time, passes to an epidemic stage. Wherever the rich earth presents her fruits in plenty, creating confidence of worldly security, and where some leisure is attainable, we are likely to see the upsurge of human nature in revolt against the underlying realities of existence. Indeed a lusty, unruly, and irreverent arrogance lurks not far below the surface even in professedly devout souls and in nations committed to a high mission. Man's behavior, when this malady or intoxication is upon him, has its amusing side. Viewed from the elevation of philosophy or of religious faith, or merely in the broad light of history, it assumes indeed a weirdly comical aspect. We understand why a psalmist was moved to say, "He that sitteth in the heavens shall laugh." But the results of it are not amusing; they are unendurably disastrous. The divine utterance suitably directed to a secular society is rather: "Turn ye, turn ye, . . . for why will ye die?"

Many are the biblical rebukes of this spirit of secularity. We read that a mighty king caused to be erected splendid edifices, monuments of his success, and boasted: "Is not this great Babylon, that I have built . . . by the might of my power, and for the honour of my majesty?" But while the word was in the king's mouth, the stroke of judgment fell. There was another ruler who, in pride of achievement, made an oration and received an ovation; but "he gave not God the glory: and he was eaten of worms." We know the terrible miscalculation of the man in the parable who said unto his soul: "Soul, thou hast much goods laid up for many years; take thine ease." We should remember that leading minds of the ancient pagan world took an attitude similar to that of the scripture writers. When this proud reliance upon temporal wealth or power appeared, it was subjected to reproof as a thing perverse or sacrilegious. That divine penalties await it is a frequent theme of the Greek tragedies. Aeschylus, in *The Seven Against Thebes,* has a chorus declare:

> The eager cry doth rend my breast,
> And on end stands every hair,
> When I hear the godless vaunting
> Of unholy men! May Até
> Fang them in her hopeless snare.[1]

Cicero, who skimmed the cream of the classical moralists before him, was persuaded that a secular spirit brought social ruin in its train. When piety, reverence, and religion are gone, he says, "there follows turbulence and great confusion of life." And if this should happen, "very likely good faith and social unity among men will also be taken away, together with justice, that most excellent of virtues." [2] He approves a saying of Chrysippus the Stoic to the effect that it is "insane arrogance" for man to assume that he has no superior in the universe. The letters of Seneca and the preachments of Epictetus abound in similar warnings, and Plutarch echoes the judgment of Cicero. The men of the ancient world often disregarded these admonitions; and when they did turn to their gods, they failed to discern in them a moral splendor that would satisfy the aspiring soul. Even while the Greco-Roman society was sinking under the weight of its offenses,

---

[1] J. S. Blackie's translation.
[2] *De Natura Deorum* I. ii.

the pagan spirit was not wholly secular. Men clutched at new religions, sometimes no doubt merely that they might gain secular advantage, sometimes in a sincere hope that in the religious realm, if anywhere, relief might be found from the inhumanity and insecurity of the world.

Meanwhile the Kingdom of God was proclaimed and the Christian community inaugurated by Christ and the apostles. Witnesses to the God whom Jesus had revealed were a growing minority spreading through the provinces of the empire and beyond its borders. They felt themselves called to be different from the children of this world and were regarded with disquiet and resentment as a new genus of mankind. There had been many cults and saviors, but none that produced such a transformation in the life of its devotees; for the Christians lived as those whose affections were set upon things above, whose spirits were sustained by a power with which worldly motives could not compete. Whatever their defects, the early Christians were the reverse of secular-minded. At the end of the period of the Roman persecutions one of their persecutors was forced to admit the impossibility of crushing them because very many of them were willing "to suffer all kinds of death" for their convictions.

This did not mean, for most of them at least, a denial of the realities of the present world or an indifference to its duties and opportunities. Even in the early days of apocalyptic expectation we observe among them an insistence on practical ethics as related to "them that are without." When apocalypticism gave place to the prospect of a lengthened period of the world's continuation, the Christian ethic was adequate for the new outlook. Christians from the first had been taught to be industrious, honest, thrifty, and charitable. They cared for the economic needs of their fellow Christians and frequently extended their charities beyond their own ranks. The fact that they prayed *for* the emperors while they refused to pray *to* them is an index of their positive but uncompromising attitude to secular affairs in general. "What the soul is in the body, that Christians are in the world," said a second-century protagonist of Christianity. Even while they were harried by persecution, they sought to fulfill the words of Jesus: "Ye are the salt of the earth, . . . the light of the world."

Yet the very firmness of their devotion led to their being exposed to an unforseen peril. It brought them toleration and the patronage of imperial power. Suddenly the church was presented with an almost undreamed-of victory. Jubilant was the celebration, as contemporary Christian writers affirm. But Jesus had warned his followers: "Woe unto you, when all men shall speak well of you!" Not only had the Christians gained the good will of the government; they had property and prosperity. The church statistics were suddenly swollen, and, as one historian remarks, "there was an unholy rush into holy orders." Therewith the secular spirit entered the church, and it has never since been entirely cast out. What remained of the heroic devotion of earlier Christianity passed largely into the rising monastic movement, leaving the ordinary membership of the church on a relatively secular level. Where the profession of Christ costs little or nothing in terms of odium and discomfort, where it even gives community status and worldly security, there will be nominal Christians who in the ranks of Christianity seek and obtain their secular reward. The church carries them as a liability—though she may mistakenly regard them as an asset—unless and until their souls awake to higher things. So it has happened that secularism has often found a safe refuge in the quiet recesses of the ecclesiastical institution, or even disported itself among the eminent clergy.

The great upheaval of Western society in the fourth and fifth centuries and the long era of instability that followed were marked by the spread of monasticism but not by the increase of lay piety. I have referred to prosperity as the occasion of outbreaks of secularism. But secularism may be embraced also where there is little worldly security and only a great desire to obtain it. The secularization of the Western church in the feudal age has been the theme of many a historian. The feudal concept of possession with obligations to a superior came to dominate the church itself, so that ecclesiastical offices were associated with the holding of landed property in feudal tenure. This involved for the clergy a variety of secular activities in fulfillment of feudal obligations. The system of the *Eigenkirche* or *ecclesia privata*, by which the heirs of the original donor of the church property nominated the incumbent, was widespread in the Middle Ages and productive of a host of abuses. Bishoprics and abbacies were bestowed on men of secular talents rather than on men of spiritual gifts. Many churchmen, without consciously embracing secularism as a principle, entered into the general competition for possessions, in which lay, as they supposed, the hope of security amid the eddying tides of feudal strife. History provides countless instances of the general rule that while large possessions firmly held do bring a temporary security, the contest to obtain them produces a general insecurity, and the effort to hold them against those whom the process has left dispossessed or dissatisfied in many instances proves too great to be maintained. The medieval period exhibits ceaseless and ruthless contention for property and worldly position on the part of laymen and ecclesiastics as anxious for security as they were ambitious for power. At the same time it was the period of sharpest criticism of the property motive on the part of religious men. In the mind of Francis of Assisi property itself was the cause of the prevailing wicked strife and must be quite abandoned by the religious for the sake of peace. "Signor," he said to his bishop, "if the day comes when we have property, we shall need arms to defend it. Then will follow disputes and lawsuits and the hindrance of the love of God and our neighbor." Francis imparted to his followers a new spirituality. But the loathsome atrocities of the Italian wars, reported by Salimbene a generation later, warn us against the assumption that the Franciscans achieved a transformation of society by their testimony to the spiritual life. They were but few, and violence was rampant and well-nigh universal.

Francis lived in a time when feudal power was beginning to give place to the power of an aggressive merchant class, and his movement began in an uncompromising rejection of the acquisitive spirit of mercantile life as represented by his own father. The rising bourgeois of the later Middle Ages exhibited the phenomena of secularism in a degree hardly surpassed anywhere in history. In the fifteenth century men of great wealth and business enterprise—such as Jacques Coeur of Bourges, Cosimo de Medici of Florence, and Jakob Fugger of Augsburg—played great roles in public affairs through the acquisition and adroit manipulation of money power. They paid their respects to the religious system, but the fear of the Lord was not in their hearts. It is well known that Cosimo patronized letters and art, and it is said that he died while listening to a dialogue of Plato, but these facts do not affect the record of his sinister policies and ruthless acts. In these he was all too typical of his age.

Starveling goliard poets at the medieval universities and troubadours in the castles of Provence had already led the imagination far from the world-denying ideals of traditional Christianity. In the early Renaissance came Boccaccio and Chaucer to captivate their readers with alluring pictures of things seen and temporal. The tendency to secularism was later asserted with enthusiasm in Renaissance art and enhanced by the discovery and exploitation of new areas of the world which provided or promised new treasures and commodities for the insatiable appetite of Western man. The church itself became commercialized and secularized from center to extremities in an unprecedented degree, so that reformers despaired of its peaceable reform and the revival of religion had to come by way of a tragic disruption of its unity.

SECULARISM IN THE RENAISSANCE

It was on the eve of the Reformation that the secular conception of life was first effectively advocated in a systematic treatise. This is the claim to originality that attaches to Machiavelli's *The Prince* (1513). The book reflects the author's reading of ancient history and his experience of the Italian despotisms that had been erected before it was written. It is not probable that Machiavelli thought it important among his writings, nor does it furnish an adequate index to his thought as a whole. In the *Discourses*, a superior work, he expresses regret that the loss of the religious spirit, which he attributes to popes and clerics, has robbed political life of positive motives. But the religion he wants is one which the state may use for its own ends, and which unbelieving magistrates may encourage in their subjects. He also gives, in that work, some countenance to democratic elements in government, and to humane and considerate treatment of the governed—conceptions alien to *The Prince*. But it was this treatise of secondary value that historically overshadowed his other writings and, more than any before it, voiced a secular philosophy of government.

Some would say that it presents not a philosophy at all, but merely a practical guide to rulers. Machiavelli wholly obliterates the doctrine of natural law—man's God-given sense of justice, of right and wrong, on which, in older thought, all law and government were supposed to rest. He likewise excludes the authority of Scripture and Christian theology. His view of the state is alien alike to the views of Cicero, of Augustine, and of Aquinas. The notion of Augustine that princes "are happy if they rule justly, . . . if they make their power the hand-maid of the majesty of God" is entirely out of Machiavelli's thought here, as is also the ancient contrast between tyrant and king. He admires Caesar Borgia, who, by ruthlessness and treachery, had gained a fleeting power. When Erasmus responded with *The Christian Prince* (1515), the great humanist stood in the true succession of the classic-Christian tradition which had flowered in the "Mirror of Princes" literature stemming from Augustine's *City of God*.[3] "The tyrant," says Erasmus, "desires to be feared, the king to be loved," and counsels the prince: "You too must take up your cross." The prince of Machiavelli relies upon the fear rather than the love of his subjects, and in the pursuit of power shrinks from no infamy or inhumanity. It has been said in behalf of the Florentine that he was a patriot who would do evil only that good might come to his country, and that he was merely adopting a theory that corresponded to the common practice of his time. One wonders why he did not reflect that since the methods he advocated had been duly tried without bringing peace or unity to his distraught Italy, it would serve no useful purpose to advocate them now. The point I would stress, however, is that Machiavelli in this book flouted the authority of a divinely given natural law and all religious sanctions, expelled ethics from politics and conscience from government, and abandoned the people to the exploitation of their rulers. Such is the pattern of secularism in one great realm of life, the realm of politics, and the twentieth century has seen the large-scale application of the pattern.

It is sometimes said that the Renaissance was revived paganism, and that Machiavelli, with his allusions to the goddess Fortuna, was a pagan. But his paganism was a mere fashion, not that of a believer. Through a life full of lapses from the Christian virtues he remained undisturbed in his adherence to the church. But he feared not God nor regarded man. Paganism has often, it is true, exhibited the phenomena of inhumanity; but sincere paganism is not secularism, and the two should never be confused. Paganism is marked by reverence; higher paganism by reverence for an object superior to man. Demosthenes once observed that all mankind has altars dedicated to justice and mercy, but none to pitilessness or perjury. To pure

    [3] See L. K. Born, *The Education of a Christian Prince by Desiderius Erasmus*, pp. 1-125; and J. T. McNeill, *Christian Hope for World Society*, pp. 89-93.

secularism these are matters indifferent. Someone will say, and quite truly, that the appalling conflict of religious communities in contemporary India does not help my argument here. I am not prepared to make a critical evaluation of the religions embraced by these communities. Perhaps these religions lack a tradition of concern for social ethics. But I am convinced that there are elements in all three of them that have been neglected by those of their adherents who have committed atrocities. Our present interest, however, is in the phenomena of secularism in the Christian West, where also the professed religion has not always controlled the behavior of its professors.

Theocracies too, and even Christian theocracies, have striven to maintain themselves by methods of injustice and cruelty. But where there is reverence, and certainly where there is reverence for a God of justice and mercy, there remains at least a basis, a standing ground, for effective criticism of government and society that is bound to assert itself. Thus the Inquisition and Puritan intolerance in New England were alike criticized by Christians on the basis of Christian teaching. But cast off reverence, and you forfeit the means of such criticism, and of the protection of human values.

The influence of *The Prince* upon the princes was certainly considerable. It was prepared in the first place for Lorenzo de Medici the Younger, who at the time had prospects of the mastery of Italy. He, like many other princely readers, hardly needed its advice. From Charles V to Frederick the Great, from Napoleon to Mussolini and Hitler, they read it and found themselves reflected in it. It was, as Voltaire pointed out, Machiavellian strategy on Frederick's part to write a book against "Machiavel." But *The Prince* was not in favor with the people; and its author, at the close of his life, felt the bitter resentment of his own fellow citizens. The Florentines, in revolt against the very prince for whose guidance the book had been written, denounced Machiavelli and the immoralities he had advocated. The treatise has been widely condemned by liberals and generally execrated by religious leaders.

In the Renaissance men's eyes were dazzled by the temptation of "the kingdoms of the world and the glory of them." Yet the victory of secularism was far from complete. It has been shown conclusively, for instance, that many of those who brought to Europe the fruits and spoils of newly discovered lands retained through much rough behavior some element of the religious conscience.[4] Moreover, the Reformation followed the Renaissance and turned the Western mind to religious concerns. Most Western men of the sixteenth century respected religious motives and clung to some form of Christianity. Accumulated national, social, and economic forces sought support from the religious parties for their contending causes; and religion was betrayed into subordination to Hapsburg, Valois, and Tudor rulers with their secular policies. Yet in some areas a fresh testimony was made to religious ideals and to the Christian way of life set forth in the New Testament. Europeans were less secular-minded in 1600 than were their forefathers of 1500.

SEVENTEENTH-CENTURY SECULARISM

When we reach the seventeenth century, we see distinct forecasts of our modern problem of secularism. Increasing numbers of men were engaged in commerce, which began to form a network about the world and offered exciting opportunities of inflated profits and easy wealth. The knowledge of the centuries was assembled, classified, and made available as never before. With Galileo and Newton science, which had been going round in circles through most of the Christian era, entered on an uninterrupted advance, of which Francis Bacon was the popular prophet. In Thomas Hobbes philosophy was made to rest upon the notion of the collision of material bodies, and social philosophy was made to begin with the acknowledgment that man is by nature competitive and not social, except for honor or profit. To restrain human contention and anarchy Hobbes creates the Great Leviathan, a secular monster, under whose authority religion is subservient, impotent, and negligible. The "phenomenalism" which John Laird has stressed in expounding the philosophy of Hobbes—the view that "phenomenal appearances" are themselves real things and neither screens projected by real things nor symbols for them nor surfaces over them—is entirely congenial to secularism. Phenomenalists, says Laird, insist "that if only we trace phenomena with sufficient persistence we shall describe all that there is to describe, and that there is no reason to dream of anything else." [5] To the twentieth century

---

[4] Louis B. Wright, in *Religion and Empire*, offers numerous examples of "godly buccaneers" who were redeemed from mere barbarity by religion.

[5] *Hobbes*, ch. iv.

this notion is familiar to the point of dullness, but it did not fail to startle the seventeenth century. Hobbes was assailed by the leaders of religion; nevertheless by reason of his intellectual power and range he undoubtedly made a greater impression on the Western mind than Machiavelli had done. Descartes too, from a very different starting point, added something to the making of a philosophical environment for secularism. The effect of his sharp division of the universe under the categories of thought and extension, and of his mechanistic conception of the material order, was to remove a great area of life from the field of operation of spiritual forces. His own unsatisfactory effort to offset this result gave rise, indeed, to the "occasionalism" of Malebranche, in which mind and matter interact by an infinite series of divine miracles. Others religiously inclined could draw some comfort from his argument for the existence of God. But eighteenth-century materialistic rationalists, such as d' Holbach, were also his heirs. In the latter part of the seventeenth century, under the pressure of new commercial and intellectual interests, religion was moving out of the foreground of consciousness. The pursuits to which we give our time and thought tend to exclude those matters which we merely acknowledge to be important.

Let us be careful not to lose our bearings. It would be erroneous to suppose that new philosophies necessarily create new eras. Both Machiavelli and Hobbes were, like better prophets, rejected by most of their contemporaries; and it was only by a gradual infiltration that they gained large numbers of disciples. With Bacon the case seems to have been different. He was both understood and applauded from the beginning. His attack on scholastic methods and his plea for scientific inquiry coincided with the trend of his age, and his pleasing forecast of a world of gadgets and good health proved almost as fascinating to the seventeenth century as to the nineteenth. He captured the imagination of men by his conception of a coming age of beneficent science which would create the *regnum* (or *imperium*) *hominis*, "the empire of man over things." This inevitably suggests the language of Swinburne's *Hymn of Man*: "Glory to man in the Highest, for man is the master of things"—but Bacon had no thought of elevating man to the place of God. The religious coloring of Bacon's thought is deistic, though he lived before the age of deism and perhaps thought himself orthodox. He is innocent of the suggestion that the bringing in of his brave new world would involve any repudiation of the claims of religion. So also were those who in the seventeenth century shared his scientific utopianism. Milton would emphasize in education the study of nature for its evidences of the work of God. John Amos Comenius, international reformer of education and bishop of the Czech Unity of Brethren, felt no difficulty in combining the Baconian dream with a sincere piety. The same may be said of the orthodox and missionary-minded Robert Boyle, and of numerous other devout or religiously conforming scientists of the Royal Society. Newton found in science sustenance for a more than commonly reverent deism. Leibniz, who, on the Continent, came to the front as both scientist and philosopher, held firmly to a religious view of the universe and took a lively interest in church problems.

Not one of these great men was consciously irreverent or antireligious. They knew that in scientific researches they were, as Kepler had said, thinking God's thoughts after him. Yet the effect of their work was to bring a weakening of traditional Christianity by opening up a field of knowledge on which the Bible and the theologians could not be made to appear authoritative. Some of the more negative deists and later antireligionists were to employ the discoveries of science in a spirit far different from that of its great modern founders, to undermine the foundations of religion itself.

The increasing subjection of the churches to the state in all European countries produced its fruit of secularism among the clergy. The Papacy, weakened and humiliated by the Peace of Westphalia, felt the pressure of national interests and was long unable to acquire new spiritual strength. A rich French Roman Catholic literature of piety was, indeed, produced in the seventeenth century; but it spent itself without seriously challenging the Gallican system of royal control of church offices, and an allied system was introduced by Joseph II of Austria in the later eighteenth century. Thus the Roman Catholic Church lay in secular bondage in great areas of Europe where it was the dominant faith. Anglican, Lutheran, and Reformed established churches were generally in a similar position. The efforts of some of the English Puritans, and later of the Scottish seceders, to assert independence of Erastian control led, indeed, to an advance of religious liberty, but not as yet to the emancipation of established churches from state interference with its secularizing effects.

INTO THE EIGHTEENTH CENTURY

Religion, indeed, fought back not uncourageously against the progressive secularization of life. In the century and a half from William Perkins to William Law, from Johann Arndt to Ludwig von Zinzendorf, Puritans, Anglicans, and Pietists put forth a copious devotional literature, much of which reached a wide reading public. That these works of piety, and the preaching labors of the writers and others like them, met a serious response cannot be denied. Not in vain did Jeremy Taylor call men to "holy living," Richard Baxter to "heavenly-mindedness," and Philipp Jacob Spener to "mutual edification" and heartfelt piety. Yet the eighteenth century moved away from their ideals. The writings of William Law amply report the prevailing complacent secularism of early eighteenth-century England, which they are designed to combat. The age of Walpole (1720-40) had no appreciation of religious values. One of the most typical as well as one of the best drawn of Law's characters is Calidus, the businessman who is completely engrossed in business all the week and must restore his health by Sundays in the country. Religion was thus being pushed out of the time schedule. The coming of Frederick the Great in 1740 shattered the decayed remnant of the Pietists and ushered in the era of German rationalism.

Law's works were addressed mainly to the prosperous classes of England, who, on a variety of evidence, were vain, irreligious, indulgent, and socially irresponsible. Wesley took a wider sweep and undertook by deliberate choice an apostolate to the poor. He found them in sorry need of religious enlightenment and revival. His movement was astonishingly effective, and it set up chain reactions which are not yet spent. It had its counterpart in Anglican evangelicalism, with its powerful influence for social reform. But the ultimate objectives of the evangelical leaders of the eighteenth century have never been attained. It was inevitable that a man who took the world for his parish and prayed to be delivered from "half-Christians" should be the beginner rather than the finisher of a task, and it was appropriate that he should send from his deathbed to another leader the message: "Go on in the name of God." Something has been achieved since then, but the tide of secularism has rolled back upon the modern world. On the Continent, Diderot, Rousseau, Voltaire, and d' Holbach were Wesley's contemporaries; and Gibbon's English classic on the history of Rome was soon to insinuate a contempt for early Christianity like that of these French savants for its current forms. But perhaps we should look for more important clues elsewhere than among the pontiffs of the Enlightenment.

Wesley found the disease of secularism breaking out in the very camp of the saints. This is where the history of religion has many a chapter of paradox. It was Jeshurun, "the Upright," who waxed fat and kicked. "Riches swiftly increase on many Methodists, so-called," Wesley wrote in his *Journal*, July 11, 1764. "What but the mighty power of God can hinder their setting their hearts upon them? And if so, the life of God vanishes away." He saw at work in all Christianity a law of deterioration. The diligence and frugality encouraged by its teaching cannot but beget riches, and riches in turn beget pride and worldliness, which destroy Christianity. Wesley was here in touch with the ultimate problem of secularism. It may be illustrated at many points of history. We have seen that secularization was the price paid by the early church for its victory in battle with the Roman state. The Cistercian monastic movement of the twelfth century offers another example. It was entrapped into secularism by the very consequences of its devotion. With their peculiar zeal for the ascetic poverty and labor the Cistercians betook themselves to forbidding wastelands. These they quickly transformed into fruitful fields, gardens, and pastures, the products and the management of which sapped the spirit of ascetic devotion. Puritanism, from its early adherents with their awe-stricken consciences to the Yankee trader type, passed through a parallel transformation. In all of these instances there was a staunch remnant, but the spiritual deterioration was widespread. Wesley offered a good prescription for the disease in his celebrated triad of injunctions: "Gain, save and then give all you can." But along this path there are glittering temptations; in 1789, no doubt in a moment of discouragement, he thought it probable that only five hundred of the fifty thousand Methodists were fulfilling the last and chief of these precepts, and he voiced a gloomy forecast for the future state of all the rest.[6]

[6] *Works of John Wesley*, ed. by John Emory, 5th ed., II, 438.

SECULARISM COMES TO THE NEW WORLD

Meanwhile had begun the vast enterprise that is America. It is the northern continent of the New World with which we are concerned, and specifically that part of it which became the United States. Three centuries ago the still unimagined resources of this Continent had just begun to be exploited by explorers, conquerors, and colonists. The history of both Canada and the United States was for a long period mainly the history of a moving frontier, behind which a more permanent civilization slowly grew up. While the natives were being introduced to the white man's religion, which was good, and to his morals, which were evidence enough that he often laid it aside, their lands were narrowed until they became negligible fragments of the whole. Schools planted by Congregationalist Puritans and Scotch-Irish Presbyterians brought the culture of Protestant Britain to dominance over other intellectual traditions. Presbyterian sons of log colleges, Baptist farmer-preachers, and ardent saddlebag apostles of Methodism, with other types of frontier missionaries, spread the gospel about the land, combating everywhere the spirit of secularism, and sometimes in debate with one another. A century ago their differences became less harsh, and they began to feel strongly their partnership in the claiming of America for a common Christianity. The spiritual debt of later generations to these religious pioneers is incalculable. But the habits of the people were molded in large degree by the challenge of economic opportunity, of which full advantage might be taken only by concentration upon material things. The stone fences of New England farms—a vast monument to the muscle-testing labor of generations—and the railways that weave their spiral paths over the Canadian and American Rockies or make a network through the granite floor of Manhattan are alike lasting reminders of the fact that our energies have been very largely given to the mastery of our material resources. Busy with such tasks, many postponed religion until they forgot its claims. These things ought they to have done, and not to have left the other undone.

Much of the physical occupation and exploitation of America had been achieved with bare hands, simple implements, and ox power before the Industrial Revolution was far advanced. Some of us are old enough to remember a time before technological inventions had greatly affected the life of ordinary people. They have now invaded life's every nook and corner. Walter Lippmann has observed that "the invention of invention" is the mark of modern man. We have come to assume that if we need a tool or an instrument of mechanical power we can soon invent it. The first appearance of power inventions often shocked religious conservatives. Instinctively they felt the challenge of the machine to all that was thought of as stable, and particularly to traditional religion. The objectors went unregarded. America, engaged in her ardent assault upon the resources of nature, welcomed the beginnings of industrial power and became so adept in technology that she has recently surpassed Europe in achievements in this realm.

Along with this development came the growth of commerce, the mushrooming of ill-governed cities, and the acquisition of enormous wealth by a few. If we have a sense of the human comedy, we may be vastly entertained by some pages of Miriam Beard's *History of the Business Man*,[7] in which Miss Beard describes the bejewelled ladies and gilded youth of the nineteenth-century American *nouveaux riches*. The wife of an American Croesus appeared at the opera wearing a crown modeled after that of Queen Victoria and valued at $1,500,000. The "shindigs" of opulent young wastrels were wondrous to behold. There was some repentance, we are glad to learn, about 1910, at the end of the era of this crude ostentation and prodigality. The spirit of secularism was by then, it appears, expressing itself in the quest for comfort rather than in the display of "barbaric pearl and gold"; and its votaries were providing their children with education for social advantage and security. William James about 1900 found "a certain trashiness of fibre" in children too softly brought up. He affirmed that "the desire to gain wealth and the fear to lose it are our chief breeders of cowardice and propagators of corruption," and that "the prevalent fear of poverty among the educated classes is the worst moral disease from which our civilization suffers."[8] Today, despite the experience of an unforeseen era of discomfort and heroic struggle, the criticisms of James still have validity. There are firms advertising their methods of directing young men to retirement with a comfortable income into irresponsible ease at the age of fifty!

[7] Pp. 641-53.
[8] *Varieties of Religious Experience*, pp. 362, 369.

Christianity responded to "Big Business" in two ways. William Warren Sweet has pointed to the increased efficiency of organization in the churches under the influence of business methods, and of lay activity in educational and benevolent enterprises.[9] It was also the era of the social gospelers, who assailed the methods of the plutocrats and pleaded in the name of religion for economic justice and the rights of labor. A similar though less aggressive social movement ha occurred in Great Britain, particularly in the Anglican Church.[10]

SECULARISM CONTINUES THE ATTACK

The modern aspects and American phases of thought conducive to secularism offer a subject too extensive to be treated effectively here. Of the vast number of eighteenth-century immigrants to America not a few were affected by deism, a type of doctrine often vaguely embraced by those alienated from Christianity and hostile to the churches. Harvard had made a place for deistic thought, and Yale was instituted largely to combat this danger. Yet we are informed that on September 30, 1797, "the Honorable James Kent, of Puritan ancestry and Yale training," remarked with satisfaction to a like-minded friend in his club that "men of information were now almost as free from vulgar superstition or the Christian religion as they were in the time of Cicero from the pagan superstition, . . . except the literary men among the clergy." The influence of French anticlerical rationalism and naturalism came largely through the alliance of the colonies with France. Ethan Allen exclaimed in 1779, "My affections are Frenchified," and he thought Louis XVI "auspiciously influenced by Heaven." Five years later he published his *Compendious System of Natural Religion*, in which he is the disciple of Voltaire and d' Holbach. The Deistic Society of New York State, the Society of the Ancient Druids at Newburgh-on-the-Hudson, and the Theophilanthropists of Philadelphia zealously combined republicanism with deistic opposition to scriptural Christianity. The influence of Thomas Paine, one of the most aggressive of the deists of his time, hardly needs emphasis. His return to America in 1802, after a fifteen-year absence, was exultingly hailed by a deistic weekly organ: "The Chris-

---

[9] *The Story of Religions in America*, pp. 492 ff.
[10] Cf. D. O. Wagner, *The Church of England and Social Reform Since 1854.*

tians," says the writer, "already tremble for their superstition." [11]

Nineteenth-century Europe continued to produce movements that stimulated anti-Christianity in America. The Positivism of Auguste Comte was one of the most important of the secular philosophies because of its influence upon sociology and its endorsement of science. Comte was content to seek truth in phenomena, but he had a profound sense of the moral aspects of social behavior and the need of its emotional sustenance. He accordingly promulgated a "religion of humanity," which recognizes a universal Being or *Grand Fétiche* and employs rites freely adapted from those of Roman Catholicism. A French sociologist, in a book published forty years after Comte's death, observed the obvious truth that " 'humanity' does not fully satisfy the conception of causality, nor the conception of finality." This author, M. Guyau, would go further. He analyzes the trend of thinking, as he sees it, under the general theme "The Non-Religion of the Future." [12] He reports with approval Renan's personal declaration to him that "non-religion is the end toward which we are marching." [13]

Comte's influence was much greater in England than in America. But Albert Post has found that between 1825 and 1850 various forms of "infidelity" were widely diffused, though often secretly embraced. The St. Louis newspaper that expressed the sentiment "Lord, do not meddle with us; we will take care of ourselves" only mildly expressed the blasphemous opinions of a large section of the German population of that area,[14] and from many other sections the evidence of a revolt of opinion against Christianity is almost equally strong. The effect on our system of the separation of church and state, with its corollary in the exclusion of religion from the curricula of public schools, will be treated later in this book. The great relative increase in church membership from the Revolution to 1900 depended in large degree upon revivalism rather than Christian nurture, doubtless with

---

[11] I am indebted here to G. A. Koch's very informing study, *Republican Religion*, chs. i-v.

[12] This is the English title of the book *L'irréligion de l'Avenir* (Paris: Alcan, 1897); 7th ed., 1912.

[13] " 'Oui, c'est bien cela,' disait-il, 'l'irréligion est le but vers lequel nous marchons,' " p. 321. Cf. p. 314.

[14] *Popular Freethought in America, 1825-1850*, p. 198, quoting Carl E. Schneider, *The German Church on the American Frontier*, pp. 32-33.

some resulting weakness of resistance to influences hostile to Christianity.

Nearly contemporary with Comte were David Friedrich Strauss and Charles Darwin, names respectively symbolic of the new power of biblical criticism and the new biological science that linked men with the lower orders of life. The embarrassment caused in church circles by these authors and their congeners was extreme, and the blood pressure rose higher when Karl Marx's dialetic materialism came to be well known. The Victorian age was anything but a halcyon period for religion. The champions of secularism were provided with plenty of ammunition. The movement led by George J. Holyoake, to which in 1851 he gave the name "Secularism," was only one of many expressions of the secular drift. In Holyoake, as in some twentieth-century advocates of secularist theories, we find the qualities of social purpose and idealism, by which they are clearly to be distinguished from the moral and spiritual Philistines. More celebrated was the arrogant, energetic, and honest Charles Bradlaugh, "the Iconoclast," who died in 1891. He had been a disciple of Holyoake but was more extreme, and as an assailant of Christianity he kept himself before the public for many years. At the same period in the Midwestern United States Robert Ingersoll, a minister's son, employed his oratorical gifts in a remarkable apostolate of unbelief, which called into existence little groups of the religiously disgruntled whom the orthodox called "infidels." It would be futile to attempt here to follow this theme into the present century during which positivist and secularist interpretations of life have been aggressively and sometimes ably presented.

Thus Christianity has been under continuous attack by a variety of forces in modern thought. Some of the assaults have been of lasting significance, and some of only temporary effect. Many of the movements concerned have been "secular" only in degree and hardly at all by intention. Some of them have embodied a good deal of social idealism and have emphasized values which the churches ought never to have neglected, and some of them have stimulated theology to self-correction. On the other hand, whether designedly irreligious or not, they gave opportunity to the spirit of irreligion, which seized upon their untraditional arguments as a ground for discounting the practical claims of religion itself.

What of the Future?

The events of the twentieth century have brought profound dis-illusionment to those who thought that science would quickly prove man's redeemer. To some extent the secularist confidence in a utopia conceived in irreligion and born of mechanical power has been broken down. Yet secularism, like apocalyptic prognosticators when the critical dates they fix upon pass uneventfully, will set before itself new and inviting expectations. It may be at the moment rather bankrupt of living ideas, as those of Marxianism grow stale. But it is the least demanding of creeds, and for that reason the most easily popularized. Moreover the American mind has been conditioned to receive it by the historic intensity of its response to the challenge of the material world and the complacent realization of prodigious achievement in the realm of material power. Christianity has, indeed, often been startled by the daring thought of rationalist critics, ma-terialistic naturalists, and Marxian realists; but it has shown a remark-able capacity to absorb, with the lapse of time, much of the matter of their arguments, without losing its own continuity or institutional strength. In contests of thought Christianity has a way of losing battles and winning the war. But the victories of thought are not always reflected in the attitudes and actions of men. These are more subject to desire and habit. A practical and habitual secularism has been let loose which will not readily yield to persuasion. It has been fed from modern man's concentration upon the problems of his physical environment. The winning of a livelihood has suggested the accumulation of wealth, and the progressive conquest of nature has whetted the appetite for power. Besides, we who censure the secular-ist and point to the folly of his expectations have ourselves made blunders and miscalculations which invite his criticism. In the light of history we ought to bring a great humility to the consideration of this problem, along with the conviction that in this era of machine power, as in earlier ages, it is only the spiritual man who is the master of things.

Part

II

SECULARISM
IN CONTEMPORARY CULTURE

SECULARISM
AND CHRISTIAN HIGHER EDUCATION

Goodrich C. White

SECULARISM, AS A PHILOSOPHY OF LIFE OR AS A WAY OF LIFE, LEAVES God out. Secular education, in philosophy and in practice, leaves God out. Simply enough, then, Christian education, at any level, keeps God in and interprets human life, human history, and human society in terms of their relationship to God and his will and his purposes for man.

Simply enough, yes. But the problems posed for Christian education in a secular society are not simple. For the Christian college to be truly Christian in a "supporting atmosphere" of secularism, with "secularism within the church scarcely to be distinguished from that without," is asking the impossible.

The colleges and universities of the church are no longer, if they ever were, devoted solely or even primarily to the teaching of religion. Properly enough, they are serving society in many areas of intellectual and professional interest which have no essential relationship to religion. In curriculum, in organization, in procedures, in patronage, it is often difficult to distinguish them from those institutions which, with no invidious implications, are set up to serve wholly secular ends and which, in so far as religion is recognized at all, make it an incidental side issue, responsibility for which is left to agencies other than the institution itself.

Questions are suggested here into which, under the present topic, one cannot properly go. But sooner or later the church college and the church will have to face them squarely: How can the church college properly delimit its field, define its special function (in practice as well as in claim), and thus both justify and assure its survival?

RELIGION IN THE COLLEGE

But there is suggested one distinction between the institution, "church related" or not, which is professedly Christian and the institution which, under law or under the tradition of the separation of church and 'state, must refrain from any direct support of an "establishment of religion." The Christian college or university can and should concern itself institutionally and administratively with religion, with making God at least potentially a part of the developing philosophy and way of life of students. I hope that I do not need to say that I recognize the splendid leadership and the vital concern for religion of many of the administrative officers and faculty members of our "secular" institutions and the great contribution they are making, personally and individually, to the encouragement of student religious life. But the institutional difference remains, and a special responsibility is assumed by the 'institution which is avowedly Christian.

There is one other plain implication: it is by affirming God rather than by attacking secularism that the Christian college can best meet the issue; not so much by attempting to prove the fallacy and the weaknesses of secularism as by presenting constantly and effectively the better way will we "overcome evil with good."

Let me repeat what I once said:

I am firmly persuaded that the only hope of the world is to be found in a revival of religion. And I believe that the Christian college can and must have a part in this revival. But there is danger almost in the very words. The revival to come must not mean a reversion to superficial emotionalism and a resort to the techniques of sensationalism. The answer to the dangerous success of some of the divergent sects, with their appeals not only to a literalistic interpretation of the Bible but as well to superstition, to racial and religious prejudice, and to some of the baser instincts of man—the answer to and the safeguard against their threat to "high religion" is not a resort to their methods. The religion that is revived must be, at least for those who are capable of it, a religion that enriches and ennobles and dignifies the mind, that justifies all man's strivings to lift himself above the beast, and all his aspirations toward truth and beauty as well as goodness. It will be, then, a revival that demands hard thinking and intellectual courage as well as faith and conviction and devotion. In such a revival the Christian faculties of Christian colleges may be expected to play a part as they touch the minds and the lives of their students at the highest levels. Such a revival may come "not with observation," nor as a result of campaigns and programs. It can come, in part at least, as the result of the quiet, persistent striving of Christian teachers themselves to understand and to help their students understand the Christian interpretation and the Christian way of life in its richness and fullness.

And I add that for Protestant Christianity the way cannot be that of dogmatic authoritarianism.

It is of the essence of Protestant Christianity that each individual must discover for himself the meaning of the Christianity to which he gives allegiance. It is not the easier way. . . . But . . . Christian faith and philosophy cannot be, for us or for our students, simply accepted and transmitted. They must be experienced and understood in relationship to life and to the world of nature and of man in which we live. So experienced and understood, they may indeed become "the truth in which all other truths find their meaning"; both the source and ground and the final justification for all the other values that contribute to effective living and that constitute a part of the humane tradition.[1]

If the Christian college and university are to have a part in finding the answer to secularism, the church must be less suspicious and distrustful of its institutions of higher education. And the colleges and universities must be more worthy of the trust and confidence of the church. Their common task and responsibility, beset with common difficulties, is to give religion—to give God—a place in the world of today and tomorrow.

They cannot deny the findings of science. They must find a way to interpret them as revealing God's ways of working in his universe, a universe vaster and more complex than man's mind at its best in earlier days could possibly conceive it to be. This means that they must find a way to interpret God and man's relationship to him in such a way as to do no violence to man's knowledge of this new universe. And this, in turn, means a conception of God far more sublime and, once achieved, more deeply satisfying than the childish or primitive ones which all too often are held in "logic-tight" compartments by minds that are otherwise grown up, or which, once questioned and discarded, carry away with them all faith and all interest in religion.

[1] *An Adequate Program for the Christian College.* Reprint from minutes and addresses of the annual meeting of the Association of Schools and Colleges of The Methodist Church, Cleveland, Ohio, January 8, 1946.

STUDENT ATTITUDES TOWARD RELIGION

There is, of course, much indifference among our students to religion and to the church which represents it. Most of this indifference is not antagonism in any thoughtfully critical sense. It is more apt to be, rather, a reflection of the indifference which characterizes the milieu in which the student has lived and perhaps still lives off the campus. Absorption in the secular—sports and politics, getting ahead, business and professional success—characterizes the home and the community which have produced him. He may have "gone to church" conventionally, but nothing "took hold of him"; and once free to manage his own time, he simply drops church—and God and religion —out of his scheme of things.

There is too some conscious, even self-conscious rejection. There is much of questioning and of disturbance. The youth is maturing. He is thinking. He is making decisions and choices. If his religious knowledge and understanding and convictions do not also mature, religion will drop out or be rejected, or there will remain the inconsistencies of logic-tight compartments, or the conflicts will persist that disrupt and cripple. It is the thoughtful and the concerned among our students for whom these difficulties and dangers exist. It is *our* failure if we do not provide for these students the best opportunities for maturing religious insight and understanding.

There are signs of a depth of yearning and a persistence of seeking that give promise and offer opportunity. Often seeming indifference or antagonism may mask a deep and vital concern about God and man's relationship to him, about the meaning and motives of life, about the basis of right and wrong, about the survival of human personality —about the great ultimates. For these types of students—the indifferent, the antagonistic, the seeking—and others we must have, and be willing to help them find, the answers to their questioning and their seeking and their need.

And even for those who are most responsive, who are already committed, and who participate in religious "activities" with zeal and earnestness we must be concerned that they too grow in religious experience, insight, and understanding of the grounds for the faith that is in them. The person whose religion remains childish while he grows up in other ways is not safe, nor is he likely to be as useful and as helpful to others as he might otherwise be. There are many such. We find them even in our faculties—men who have not taken religion seriously enough to think about it; mature and able in their special fields but, however sincerely devoted, childish in their religious thinking.

I have said that we must have and help the students to find the answers. We must also be constantly seeking ourselves. The interpretation of religion and of religious faith in God and man in terms of our modern knowledge is not easy. Facile and superficial "reconciliations" will not suffice. The church and the church college are challenged, without wavering or lessened fidelity, to do some hard thinking.

It is not a matter of denying or minimizing the values of scientific knowledge and understanding, of technological advance, of humanistic culture—literature, art, music—or of the analysis of the problems of human living together. It is, rather, a matter of "something more." There must be supplied basic principles of interpretation in terms of Christian philosophy, which make possible the synthesis of these real though lesser values into higher and more inclusive values, which find the basis for all values and the motives of life and aspiration and striving in a deep and satisfying faith in God and in man as God's creature.

This "something more," however, cannot be thought of as simply *added on* to a body of knowledge—scientific, historical, and interpretative—which has been developed in completely secular and godless terms. It must, in some way, be infused into the whole growing structure of knowledge and understanding which the processes of education offer the developing mind of the student. To "tack on" religion and religious interpretations to facts and principles which have been presented in a context and spirit that ignores them is artificial and unconvincing and will so appear to the student. The Christian teacher does not need to be preaching and talking about God and religion all the time. But in his teaching, whatever his special field, he can, I think, appropriately and constructively find place for God and human ideals and responsibility and faith in values which transcend bare facts and empirical generalizations. The student who is concerned at all will inevitably be disturbed if he moves from the scientfiic laboratory or the history classroom to the chapel and sees no possible connection or consistency between the things under discussion in the two places. The omissions and the implications, as well as obvious and explicit denials of the values of faith and of the religious interpretations of life, need to be carefully watched. The more thoughtful student will note the omissions and catch the implications—and at least wonder.

There is place and need too for direct consideration of the problems of religion in the classroom. The courses in religion in the Christian college may be frankly and unashamedly "apologetic," in the technical sense; but the issues of Christian philosophy and of theology can and should be discussed with the same open-mindedness to question, the same sincerity, and on the same intellectual level as are the issues in any other course in any other field. The Christian college cannot content itself in the presentation of the great Christian doctrines with procedures that challenge less than the best of the intellectual interest and capacity of the best students.

The Intellectual Challenge to the Church

The difficulties are great, and it is easy to dwell on them. And the most serious difficulties are not those of programs and procedures. They root deeper. There is the simple fact that secularism, for reasons and with implications ably presented in other chapters in this book, has become "the supporting atmosphere of our culture." The task of finding "paths out of our contemporary secularism and the frustrations in which it involves the spirit of man" is a task which the Christian college or university shares with the Christian church by which it is fostered.

And there is the further fact, stated very simply, that interpreting God and human freedom and responsibility and survival in terms of our modern knowledge of the world we live in is not easy.

Rufus M. Jones, Quaker sage and saint, wrote an article entitled "What the Modern Man Can Believe" in *The Atlantic*, November, 1947. Briefly but clearly and penetratingly he describes "three 'bloodless' revolutions, revolutions in the realm of thought which have produced, for those who *know*, a completely altered world outlook." He goes on, then, with insight, with faith and deep conviction, and with tempered optimism, to discuss the implications for religion, ways to meet the difficulties, and the outlook, affirming that "there are many grounds for predicting an increase of wisdom and spiritual leadership within the churches of Christ, and there is a promise of a more creative and dynamic religion for the future."

Here is the intellectual challenge to the church and to its colleges and universities. It is a challenge that must be met if religion is to interest and hold the best minds of today and tomorrow.

It is a challenge that must be met squarely. Thoughtful and sincere young people will not for long be satisfied with evasion or compromise. Logic-tight compartments will not satisfy them. If they are really concerned, they will seek and demand consistency; else they will turn their back on the whole business of religion as outworn and outdated, and they will become, at least in practice, agnostic and secularist. Reason, surely, cannot supply all the answers. But religious faith can and must be made reasonable, so that it can undergird life and work. Otherwise education simply contributes to the production of "the fruits of secularism: mediocrity, disorganization, and superstition."

Urgent as it is that this challenge should be met, it must be said that it may be long in full accomplishment. I quote, as I did before, from Dr. Theodore Ferris, writing on "The Teaching Office of the Church":

The teaching of the church lacks power because its teachers lack confidence, and . . . they lack confidence because they are confused in their own minds. . . . No single person can hope to clarify the mind of the church. It must be accomplished by a union of the best minds applied to the toughest problems of faith and life. It took three hundred years or more to clarify the mind of the church in terms of ancient and classical thought. We need not be surprised if it takes at least that long to do it again in terms of the mysterious universe which has been described to us by the modern pioneers of thought.[2]

I add that it is probably true, though I would prefer to say it differently, that, as *Life* puts it, we Methodists are more adept at "tireless preaching, skillful organizing, enthusiastic publicity" than at "intellectual subtlety and theological precision"; that "the Methodists can be counted on more for zeal than definition." [3]

Zeal is needed. And, of course, we are thinking here, not of intel-

[2] In *Religion and Education*, Willard L. Sperry, ed.
[3] Nov. 10, 1947.

lectual subtleties and theological precision, if they are taken to relate to the minutiae of doctrine and creed and ritual, but of the hard thinking, tough thinking, of a high order that will be required if our young people are to be satisfied on the fundamentals—the real fundamentals—of religious faith: "the being and nature of God, His character and activity, the possibility and the realization of communion with Him, the bases of Christian ethics, viz., the nature of man and the objective reality of the moral standard, both social and personal, the survival of human personality and eternal life." [4]

These are the questions about which our thoughtful and disturbed young people of today are deeply concerned. Failure to give them or to help them find satisfying answers to such questions will mean their loss to the church, to religion, to God. It will mean for them commitment to secularism and its fruits in living. It may mean nihilism, moral disintegration, personal tragedy.

I see in this tremendous intellectual challenge the chief responsibility of our Christian colleges and universities in confronting the "practical atheism" of secularism. The task is one which cannot be left wholly to theologians and philosophers. It is an enterprise in which all who are in any way competent and who are committed to the Christian way should have an interest and some part. It is a long-range undertaking, demanding the best of consecrated intellect.

I have suggested that the answer to secularism must be positive. We must teach religion effectively, persistently, and unashamedly, in a way that challenges intellectual interest and assent. We cannot require it or impose it. We can *teach* it, so that God and faith and freedom and responsibility and ideals and immortality find a place in the philosophy and in the lives of our students.

I have put major emphasis on the intellectual challenge of secularism because it seems to me that this is the peculiar and special challenge to which the Christian college and university should be responsive; it is here that the special responsibility of Christian higher education lies.

This emphasis does not, of course, discount in slightest measure the need for commitment, for deepening experience, for worship, for participation. Opportunity for these the Christian college must

[4] Frederick C. Grant, *The Practice of Religion*, p. 2.

provide as a part of its educational program and as a part of its concern for the total life of its students. But the *distinctive* responsibility of the college and university is in the intellectual realm; if the Christian college fails there, it has failed in its peculiar task, and its efforts in other areas may well be left to other agencies. And, it may be added, commitment and its consequences in living become difficult or impossible for the thoughtful student who finds no place in his developing intellectual life for God and for ultimate and enduring human values.

For the immediate future we must not in our colleges and universities do less than we are now doing. We should do much more and much better. The "official" representative, or representatives, of religion on the campus should be men of intellectual and personal stature equal to or towering above the representatives of any specialized interests. Our courses in Bible and in religion should be continued, and perhaps greatly improved. In our programs of "religious activities" there should be no lessening of emphasis upon prayer and worship, upon service, or upon "wholesome recreation and social life." Our "religious emphasis" periods—we used to have "revivals"—should be continued, and perhaps improved. And so of our chapel services. But all this, however good, is not enough. The institution and its faculty cannot disclaim further responsibility, once it has provided all these things. Secularism should be guarded against, whether by implication and omission or by explicit expression, in textbook and faculty utterance. Safeguards should be set up against the cynical, the indifferent, the scorner in the faculty; this can be done and must be done without rigid requirements of credal conformity or of specified types of religious participation. And there should be faculty groups studying and thinking about religion, studying and thinking as hard as they do about the "subjects" in which they are trained as specialists or about curricular readjustments.

There must be the willingness, the opportunity, and the urge for faculty members and students to think together, to search for and to find the answers to questions about life's purpose and meaning in terms of the God revealed in Jesus the Christ. The faculty member who joins in such search need not profess to be an "expert" in religion nor to know all the answers in advance. But he should not be content merely to pass on his responsibility to the "professional religionist." For it is only as "high religion" becomes both possible and winsome to the best of our youth—guided on college and university campuses and in the larger church by devoted, humble, courageous, and thoughtful teachers, themselves seeking to grow in understanding and in depth of experience—that the challenge of secularism will be met in terms of "a more effective human medium for the spirit of God." For in such process each of us will, as individuals, "by unified and concerted practices and responses alter the spiritual quality of his own interests and obligations."

SCIENCE AS A SOURCE OF SECULARISM

Carl Wallace Miller

AMONG THE MANY FACTORS WHICH HAVE CONTRIBUTED TO THE
secularization of modern society the success of the scientific method
in adding to our useful knowledge deserves a prominent place. Few
competent scientists would maintain that these discoveries make impossible a theistic philosophy of life, but there are fewer still who
do not feel that a critical revaluation of current religious ideology
is called for. The very foundation of experimental science is the
conviction that an experiment means something; that if it is repeated
under identical conditions, the result is bound to be the same. If
carefully and consistently performed, it tells us something which is
unalterably true about the nature of our environment. The aggregate
of such experiments gives us a true, if perhaps an incomplete, picture
of nature. Religion, on the other hand, is associated in the minds
of most people with supernaturalism, the existence of something
which overpasses the bounds of natural law, and provides resources
that are not limited by facts discovered in the laboratory. The conflict between religion and science is therefore viewed by most people
as a conflict between naturalism and supernaturalism. But such a
formulation places the supporter of theism in an exceedingly difficult
position. As soon as any phenomenon is shown to exist in nature,
it at once becomes natural and is accepted by the scientist as part
of his system. Thus the supernatural is merely that which has never
been shown to exist, and the theist is called on to defend that which
is not against the champion of that which *is*. If religion is to maintain
itself successfully in the modern world, it must not be trapped into
any such interpretation of its meaning or mission.

It is generally recognized today that the crying need of human
society is the evolution of a world community in which each people
is permitted to develop its own culture and to exchange freely its own
ideas and insights, its own unique products, its own gracious customs, with all other peoples. We need one world in an ethnical,

geographical, and cultural sense. Yet the need would appear to be just as great for one world of the intellect and of the spirit. Few Americans would view with satisfaction the prospect of bludgeoning the Russian people into acceptance of our culture by use of the atomic bomb, even though that were possible. Convinced though we may be of the superiority of our own institutions, our consciences would still warn us that we might well be trampling under foot certain flowerings of the human spirit which could be used to beautify our own way of life. So it is in the area of the conflict between science and religion. Our present American culture, defective as it may be, still provides for our people the greatest measure of happiness and well-being which has been the lot of any people in human history. This well-being is the consequence of scientific progress on the one hand and of the fruits of Christian idealism on the other. The future depends on our ability to forge these two elements of our culture into one world of the mind and spirit.

It would be futile to insist that there are no real difficulties to be surmounted in this task. There are vast differences in temper between the trained scientist and the specialist in the field of religion. The source material which they use is largely different. The scientist seldom has to revert to sources which antedate the work of Galileo and Newton, whereas our philosophical and religious ideas are gleaned from the most ancient records of human culture. The scientist uses words to express ideas and is never satisfied unless they are precisely defined to yield the same connotation to all his associates. The Christian minister, on the other hand, often uses words as a poet to produce an emotional effect, while leaving the exact meaning to the manifold interpretations of his listeners. Unfortunately there are few scientists who have been thoroughly trained in religious ideology, and few clergymen who have more than a smattering of scientific knowledge. Each is bound, therefore, to misinterpret the other, and the man on the street is bound to misunderstand both. Indeed, there never was a time when it was more incumbent on people who have some understanding in both fields to make such contribution as they can toward correcting these misconceptions.

The scientist is quite generally reproached with being materialistic. If this means that he does not make free use of the concept of God in his daily undertakings, he must plead guilty. Yet most of his tasks have to do with the everyday things which he finds about him, and he is seldom concerned with their origin. A few scientists have turned their attention to the problems of cosmogony, but none of their theories have attained the goal of general scientific acceptance, and all carry us back only to a state of the universe which is just as mysterious as it is at the present day. During the eighteenth century some of the greatest pioneers in science, notably Laplace, stimulated by the extraordinary success of their scientific tools, sought eagerly for solutions to the ultimate problems of the universe. Today such an achievement by any method which we can readily visualize seems highly unlikely, and the label "materialistic," so freely applied to science, would appear irrelevant. It may well be an heirloom, inherited from the "Age of Reason," which we have not yet had the intellectual vigor to discard. Science has been highly successful in discovering and describing natural phenomena, but surprisingly unsuccessful in gaining any profound understanding of why these phenomena occur as they do. When any investigation is pursued far enough, we always arrive at the shore of the great sea of our human limitations, and we can only marvel at the infinite wisdom which is exhibited in the majestic path we have traversed.

The current goals of physical research are much more modest than the man on the street supposes. Having learned during the nineteenth century the apparently indestructible chemical elements which exist in the world about us, the physicist has learned during the early decades of the twentieth century that these elements are not after all unchangeable, that he can, with his cyclotrons and uranium piles, transmute one element into another. More than this, he has created hosts of new elements which never before existed, except perhaps in extraordinarily minute amounts. During the next half century he can be expected to delve more and more deeply into these new nuclear reactions to find ways and means for utilizing the energy and the new materials which are obtained in this fashion. But he will still have little to say about how these mysterious possibilities came to reside in the matter which makes up his material environment. The astronomer will study with better and better tools the nature and properties of the stars and their distribution through the vast universe, but he can scarcely hope to provide any so-called materialistic explanation for them. Psychologist, poet, and historian can plumb the heights and depths of the human spirit. They can study the manner in which it has borne fruit through countless ages, but they can scarcely account for its presence within the human frame or the forces which now and then cause it to erupt into new achievement. We can hardly look on science except as a technique for enabling man to tap the practical resources of his planet. It is not and can scarcely become a philosophical gateway to an understanding of their mysterious origin and ultimate purpose.

THE PLACE OF MIRACLES

The contribution of science to the secular temper of the modern world has therefore not resulted from any real conflict between its discoveries and fundamental religious concepts. It has not resulted from the outspoken hostility of many competent scientists. It has been in part a consequence of widespread ignorance of the true nature of both science and religion, but it has also been due in no small measure to the strategy of the church itself. For the church has repeatedly chosen to wage rear-guard actions in defense of positions of dubious value in the no man's land between religion and valid areas of secular thought. This it has done despite its deep realization that its true citadel lies within the hearts and spirits of mankind.

Throughout its history the church has based its appeal largely on its ability to work miracles. It has pointed reverently to the accounts of miracles performed nineteen hundred years ago. Yet it has been singularly unsuccessful in demonstrating any similar ability in the modern world; and, puzzled by such failure, it has been able only to hold out the hope for some better state beyond the grave. Meanwhile the scientist has been patiently pushing forward the frontiers of medical knowledge until today the life expectancy of an individual has been so extended as to raise serious questions regarding the adequacy of the world's food supply in another generation. The man on the street may not be too much concerned about the origin of the resources being tapped by the scientist, but he is tremendously impressed by the benefits which accrue to him from these colossal discoveries, and he cannot help making unfavorable comparisons between the claims of the church and the actual achievements of the secular-minded research worker. Is it any wonder that if miracles are to be the test of the prophet, the mantle of Elijah should have fallen on the shoulders of the scientist?

THE AUTHORITARIAN APPROACH

A second cause for the relative esteem in which science is popularly held has been the authoritarian approach of most religious bodies. In the scientific method no authority is recognized. All results are based on actual observations, and nothing which is not experimentally reproducible is accepted as a part of the scientific system. Competent scientists would seldom go so far as to maintain that all significant features of human existence are capable of being brought within this reproducible system. Two men with very similar background and training face a moral problem. One responds in one way, and the other in a diametrically opposite fashion. It seems improbable that any experimental study could predict the outcome of such a moral struggle. We are dealing with a problem which falls outside the useful sphere of the scientific method. This does not mean, however, that the scientist is not interested in such questions. He is intensely interested in them because the aggregate of human responses to such situations determines the conditions under which he must pursue his own activities. Nevertheless, the very nature of his training makes an authoritarian approach repugnant. For nearly two thousand years science remained stagnant because of the authority of Aristotle, and the modern world became possible only when the human spirit was able to rise above the taboos of Greek philosophy. For a hundred years the opinion of Newton with regard to the nature of light was so revered that progress in optics was practically at a standstill. Indeed, it is probable that few desires in the heart of man have brought him so much misfortune as his craving for some authority to relieve him of his own moral responsibility. Among primitive peoples the slightest desire of the witch doctor was respected. The highly cultured Roman observed the warnings which he found in the entrails of poultry, and only too recently the whole German nation went down to ruin as it followed spellbound the strains of its pied piper. On the other hand, the greatest sagas in human history have been written when men have come to a new awareness of their rightful dignity and have nourished within their own free spirits the seeds of creative achievement.

Nothing is more characteristic of the American temper today than its deeply rooted suspicion of authority. Government is viewed as stemming from the people themselves. Freedom of speech and religion are guaranteed by the Bill of Rights. Our educational institutions jealously guard the right of their faculties to pursue both teaching and research under conditions of maximum intellectual freedom. Indeed, even in the relation of parent to child the concept of authority is gradually giving way to that of responsibility. Yet in the realm of religion the idea of authority still retains its attractiveness for many people. The Roman Church, with its doctrine of papal infallibility, still serves as a refuge for people who feel their own inadequacy in the face of the epic confusion of modern life, and Protestant churches cling desperately to the doctrine of the infallibility of scripture. It is fair to say that the work of Protestant scholars during the nineteenth century gave much support to the "profitableness of scripture for teaching, reproof and moral discipline," to use the phraseology of the Moffatt Bible, but fell short of establishing its infallibility. Without attempting to argue this point of theology, we must admit that the very idea that ultimate authority is to be found in ecclesiastical body or ancient manuscript is utterly foreign to the thinking of an increasingly large fraction of our people.

THE CHURCH AND SCHOLARSHIP

Finally the church today is at a disadvantage because of the position it has often taken with regard to scholarship and education. Christians have too often accepted uncritically the dictum of Paul that "the wisdom of this world is foolishness with God," and have comfortably excused themselves from the labor which scholarship demands. Yet while the church has been content to murmur its ancient shibboleths, the builders of modern society have been attacking their problems with all the resources of exhaustive study and research. The most brilliant intellects in our universities are constantly being recruited for these tasks and are being trained and sharpened by years of life-sapping toil.

The church has not always been marked by the carelessness of its scholarship or the repetitious use of obscure phrases so prevalent today. During the early years of Protestantism in this country it was the center of intellectual life. Colleges and universities were founded under its auspices, and it was the eager patron of all that was good and wholesome in the cultivation of learning. Historically it was indeed the mother of the arts and sciences, but today, in the words of Professor William E. Hocking, "it would devour its own offspring." It would be futile to deny a modicum of reason for this changed attitude of the church. Incompatibilities have developed between the results of secular scholarship and traditional ecclesiastical affirmations. These incompatibilities are unlikely to be resolved, however, except by the emergence of an equally inspired scholarship within the church. As far back as the early twenties S. Parkes Cadman was asked in a radio program whether he believed the church would be most benefited by the work of a great evangelist or of a great theologian, and he declared himself whole-heartedly for the theologian. It would appear, indeed, that the need for constructive theological research is today even greater than a generation ago. It will only come about, however, if the church is able to recruit into its service young people with the highest talent, and only then if these young people can be persuaded to devote themselves tirelessly to the exploration of many virgin fields in this realm of human culture.

The task to be performed can be understood best if the totality of our knowledge is compared to a crossword puzzle. Man's problem is to fill in the great words which represent the very fullness and meaning of life on our planet. In the past there have been periods of inspired progress when mankind has grown "like corn in the night." One such was the few short years of Jesus' ministry, when the words "God," "righteousness," "love," "compassion," "altruism," and "sacrifice" flowered into new significance and set the pattern for new human relationships. Still another period of progress has taken place with the growth of our scientific industrial civilization. It is studded with such words as "electricity," "optics," "atoms," "micro-organisms," "vaccines," "anesthesia," and "surgery."

Theologians, beginning with Paul, have struggled for nineteen hundred years to fit the great words of the Christian heritage logically and properly into one corner of the crossword puzzle. Many of them lived and died without realizing that there were other continents of knowledge yet undiscovered, and believing that the only task which God had for mankind was to fit these Christian concepts neatly and constructively into human lives. Yet through all the years of theological controversy men and women were shivering in cold and drafty houses, and dying like flies from smallpox and plague, even though in God's infinite purpose there were ready at hand such boons as coal and oil and penicillin. These flowerings of the human spirit have grown like frost crystals on the windowpane, gradually appearing and developing in all their beauty and symmetry. Just as theologians have sought to fit the appropriate words of the Christian tradition into their corner of the puzzle, so scientists have sought to comprehend in all its majesty the beauty unveiled within the physical world. It has been a breath-taking experience. In my own short life I have seen the discovery of X-rays and the electron, the mysterious emergence of relativity and the quantum theory, and the first vague premonitions of the energy to be unlocked from the atom. Much has been fitted together into a single perfect pattern of cosmic grandeur, but there is no unabridged dictionary, and many words must still be discovered to fill the vacant spaces.

Even more important, perhaps, is the problem of discovering the words which will tie one corner of the pattern to the other. If in this process certain concepts which seemed to occupy key positions in the theological pattern have to be removed and replaced by longer and more abstract ones, this should not occasion too much concern. Jesus himself was accused of destroying the law when in God's providence he was merely fulfilling it.

The crucial question which the present-day church must answer is whether it shall cling to the traditional claims of transcendent authority over all other segments of human experience or whether it can arrive at a concordat with modern life and still retain its fundamental pertinence. Those who take the first position designate as materialistic any doubts as to the possibility of violating physical laws in the name of religion and designate as arrogantly humanistic any question of revealed authority by the methods of historical and literary criticism. Those who hold to the possibility of a satisfactory concordat with modern life feel that such a stand is not merely unnecessary but, if persisted in, will largely nullify the influence of the church in the years to come. They feel that the prophecy of Jesus that "greater works than these shall he do" has been abundantly fulfilled, but that the rules for performing these miracles are also written into the physical world in the form of natural law. A man who recognizes the divine origin of nature's resources, but who respects the divinely ordained laws for their utilization, should hardly be reproached with materialism.

The question of ultimate authority is more difficult to answer. The modern scholar, whether in the field of science or the social studies, distinguishes truth from error by asking two questions: Is it in accord with experience? Is it in harmony with other things which we have reason to believe are true? These are the criteria which carry weight in the modern world; and even though the individual Christian may be willing to rest his case on Holy Writ, Christianity will make its maximum contribution to society only if it is able to justfy itself by the tools of present-day scholarship.

Is it not true that you and I are Christians, not because we hold deeply to the infallibility of priest or scripture, but because our innermost spirit bears witness that the Christian way of life is the good life? We are followers of Jesus because we believe that an individual whose imagination is stirred by the teachings of Jesus is thereby saved from a life of frustration to a life of joyful service, from a social liability to a social asset. We believe this not because it is vouched for by Holy Writ, but because we have seen and experienced it. The efforts of individual sects to establish a one-to-one correspondence between the blossoming of the Christian spirit and their own unique doctrines is little short of folly, for it occurs within the cloistered confines of the Roman Church; it is found in the sophisticated atmosphere of the college classroom; and it is seen to develop within the simple heart of the South Sea Islander. Let no one suppose, however, that the pidgin English which is capable of bringing the gospel of salvation to the Polynesian is capable of stirring the heart of the twentieth-century scholar in his ivory tower, and let no one imagine that our American way of life can be preserved if we ignore the spiritual needs of the 2,500,000 young people now treading the scholar's path in our American universities. These are the people on whose shoulders the future of our American society rests. I know many of them, and can vouch for their fundamental integrity. If you and I can learn to speak to them in their own language, and pass on something of the warmth of the Christian spirit which we feel in our own hearts, I am sure that we need have no fear for the manner in which they will acquit themselves.

The Use of God's Gifts

Never in the past has it been possible to appreciate as today the extraordinary richness of God's gifts to humanity. These gifts, however, must be divided into three categories by the rules which are laid down for their utilization. First and foremost are those which an individual can have or not, according as he purposes in his heart. They are the blessings provided by the Holy Spirit as he dwells within the human breast, enriching and fructifying all of life by his beneficent presence. This it is which has kept alive the Christian way of life through all the centuries since Jesus walked and taught in the villages of ancient Galilee. The second category contains the resources of man's physical environment, which can only be tapped as he learns by toil and research the rules which govern their use. It is unnecessary to expatiate here on the long list of blessings which mankind has acquired by this procedure, extending all the way from his first crude efforts to till the soil down to his release of atomic energy. That man must eat by the sweat of his face and can improve his material comfort and well-being only by the exercise of the extraordinary powers which are part of his humanity seems to be written into the law of the universe as well as into the book of Genesis. It would be cruel indeed if priest or prophet should give him cause to believe that merely "by taking thought" these laws could be circumvented.

Finally there are those blessings which man can acquire only as he learns to work with his fellows for their common good; government "of the people, by the people, for the people" with "liberty and justice for all," public health, comfort and happiness for the aged, a high level of education, peace among nations—these and many more like them are things which not one individual but many working shoulder to shoulder can provide for man's community on earth. Are not these corporate goods of human society the business of the church as well as the health of man's inner being? Indeed, are they not the ultimate test of the fruitfulness of the Christian life? If we can believe profoundly in God's purpose for humanity, let us have faith that under God we shall yet move out into a better world.

SECULARISM IN MOTION PICTURES

Paul F. Heard

MOTION PICTURES TODAY ARE MORE THAN RECREATION. THEY ARE one of the great American arts. The motion picture especially, as pointed out in a recent issue of *Life*, has become almost a religion; millions of people flock each ·week to the great temples of the silver screen for worship, fulfillment, and release. Sometimes, through the filming of great masterpieces of literature or through the production of outstanding original stories, the screen helps to fulfill man's aesthetic and spiritual needs. At other times, however, the screen enshrines false gods, gods which are dearest to the American heart—money, glamour, and success—and climaxes these portrayals with the pitiful ritual of the happy ending, reaffirming that somehow everything will come out all right in the end.

It is inevitable that the secularism of our modern culture be reflected in the movies, since the movies reflect, as well as influence, our thought, ideals and way of life. When we criticize a movie, we must realize that in a sense we are really criticizing ourselves, for entertainment motion pictures are made for the great masses of people, to excite, enthrall, and entertain. To the tune of millions of dollars producers cannily tailor extertainment films to give the public what the public genuinely wants, to please the senses, stir the heart. And judging from the apparent financial success of certain types of entertainment, such as *Duel in the Sun, The Outlaw, Forever Amber,* and *The Postman Always Rings Twice,* the producers of such films must be right. Many of us do want to glorify sex as a national ideal. We do judge success in terms of money, power, and fame. Our standards of living, our cars, bathtubs, and beautiful clothes *are* the things which Americans hold dear. We, the meek, who might inherit the earth, find on the screen vicarious release from the twisted frustrations of our lives. We thrill at the daring of illicit love, a carefree drunken ride on a country road at night, the machinations of underworld kings who triumphantly violate the laws of a world we have found ignoble, frustrating, and dull. We disapprove, oh, yes, and insist that the villain be punished in the end, yet we flock again and again to the movies to enjoy disapprovingly the kind of life we want and dare not have.

And where is the church in all this? Does the church offer a more positive and inspiring answer to the dilemma of life than these false gods of the entertainment screen? Does it lift a sharp and incisive voice which cuts through the confusion and groping pettiness of our lives?

Let the church but lift its voice to criticize a motion picture and people flock to the theater by the millions, thus guaranteeing for the film huge financial returns.

Why is this true? One reason, perhaps, is that many films deal with the hopes and aspirations of our secret hearts. While paying lip service to our pretensions, they actually cut through to appeal to our half-recognized needs and drives. Thus the movies appeal to people where they live, while much religion, in spite of the fact that it has the answer to our deepest needs, is sometimes presented in such a way as to appeal on a far more superficial plane to our pretensions rather than to the heart and soul, thus aiding in the process of self-deception whereby we profess one thing and do another.

It is this ability of the motion picture to reach people where they live which constitutes its greatest danger and, at the same time, makes it potentially a powerful force for advancing the Christian point of view and inculcating Christian attitudes throughout the world. The skill of direction, photography, and acting, the genius of editing, the subtle but powerful emotional effect of a musical score matched to action—all these have been developed, perfected, and coordinated by the great film makers of our time. The motion picture has attained a high standard of technical and artistic excellence. Many films produced are wholesome entertainment; others treat great themes with penetration and insight.

Yet still other films reflect and advance the secularism of our time, ranging from problem movies, which solve everything on the human plane, to the movies which deify and enshrine the aspects of our culture to which our allegiance is really given. Thus far has the motion picture tended to standardize and pepetuate the myths and rituals of our pagan world. Even films on specific religious themes, such as *Going My Way* and *The Bells of St. Mary's,* while excellent as far as they go, have not dramatized the dynamics of real religion and its relation to specific problems of our lives, but rather have made religion appealing by identifying it with humanitarian ideas of service.

And yet there is an increasing recognition among the public at large of a need for real religion. There is an urge and a spiritual searching today stronger than ever before, a suspicion in the public mind that perhaps religion does offer the answer to the basic questions of our time. Movie makers are discovering with wonder and amazement that God has a strong box-office appeal.

How Can the Movies Help?

The motion picture can be one of the most powerful means of bridging the gap between the secular and the sacred. How can Protestant Christianity best make use of this powerful medium of communication? Here are three ways:

1. Protestant churches must produce their own nontheatrical motion pictures for distribution to churches, clubs, schools, and secular groups.
2. The churches should adopt a positive and constructive program for interpreting the Protestant point of view to producers of entertainment films.
3. Money must be allocated, thousands of dollars—even millions— to enable the church to achieve these ends.

In carrying out the phases of the above program there are a number of basic questions regarding portrayals of life on both the theatrical and the nontheatrical screen about which the church must clarify its point of view. First of all, what should be the attitude of the church to the portrayal on the screen of problems of evil and sin?

Conflict is an essential ingredient of drama. In the elementary phases of dramatic writing the conflict has very often been between the forces of "good" and the forces of "evil," these forces embodied in persons. Thus arose the familiar types of the hero, the villain, and the heroine. Nearly always, of course, the villain was foiled at the end, and the heroine gathered comfortingly in the hero's arms. For if the hero did not shoot the villain, there was a time when the shot might well come from the audience instead, and many an early screen was punctured by bullet holes which testified to the stout virtue of the audience of that day.

This type of thing characterized early plays in the United States, and the general formula of hero, villain, heroine, and the happy ending has persisted in the movies from their beginning. Yet while the heroes were generally endowed with virility and skill in scaling garden walls, the heroines for whom they performed these manly feats became increasingly colorless, conventional, and dull, and hardly seemed worth the effort. Then followed the glittering era of the "bad" woman of the screen. To counteract the colorless qualities of the heroine, women became the villains and, whether demure or bold, used provocative glance and sinuous curve to lie, murder, and seduce their way through eight reels of melodrama, or to influence the otherwise manly and virtuous males, who succumbed momentarily to their spell to throw virtue to the winds and, for their sakes, live lives of wickedness and sin.

The villain too underwent a strange metamorphosis. He trimmed his mustaches, became more sleek, cultured, more engaging, and often fooled the innocent maiden with his manner and charm. In certain films, at least, one could not help believe that the heroine probably preferred him after all; and, whether or not the villains and their victim came to a bad end at the last, they obviously enjoyed themselves so much during the course of their evil-doings that their punishment seemed last-minute and perfunctory, something which might perhaps have been avoided with more care.

This, of course, is an extremely superficial treatment of the problem of evil; and, to a mature adult of today, these early portrayals are recognized for the nonsense which they are. Yet today this treatment still persists on our modern entertainment screen. The old formula reappears, clothed in a more credible story and sometimes stunning film techniques. Crime and gangster films have portrayed men who violate the laws of God and who are ultimately punished in the end, but the portrayals have been such as to glorify and glamourize these characters in the process. The fact that they came to an evil end is lost on the audience in comparison with the daring and gay bravado of their acts, and much of the audience may have been unconsciously rooting for them all the time. Women have been portrayed on the screen who perform incredibly immoral acts with little disturbance to either their coiffures or consciences; often too they come to a bad end, but it is the laws of man, not God, which provide their retribution.

What Attitude Should the Church Take?

The answer of the church, it seems to me, should not be to encourage attendance at such films by a publicity campaign against them. The church must rather interpret Christianity to the creative people of the screen so that they will give their product greater depth and reality, and the Christian point of view.

A church group once said: "This film contains murder, drunkenness, rape, and incest and therefore is not a fit film for church people to see." While this film may have been a deliberate concoction of these elements designed to appeal to public taste, is this a valid statement to make? Should the church encourage our people to hide their heads in the sand and fail to face the hard realities of life? People sometimes criticize the church as having a dishonest and stultifying attitude toward freedom of expression in the arts. Many feel that the church point of view is primarily propaganda for a superficial Pollyanna interpretation of life which simply is not true. Often we are called "do-gooders," and it is said that the only kind of films or literature we like are stories about dogs, or stories which picture life with a sticky sweetness as being simply wonderful in this best of all possible worlds.

While encouraging the portrayal on the screen of the potential beauty and wonder of life lived according to God's plan, we must also encourage portrayals of the pettiness, meanness, tragedy, and sinfulness of man. We must help uproot the naïve idea prevalent from time to time on the American screen that people are all "good" or all "bad." We must encourage portrayals of characters who are well-rounded and real, both sinful and, at the same time, potentially sons of God. The portrayals of conflict between "good" people and "bad" people must be replaced by portrayals of the more profound conflicts within people themselves, their struggles with themselves and their environment and with other people like themselves, who are equally complicated and struggling, to attain fulfillment and salvation. We must portray sinful and yet wonderful man with humanity, humor, sympathy, and compassion, yet with Christ's concern for the value of human life and for the dignity which the individual possesses through his relationship with God.

Of course we should have portrayals of sin on the screen. But we should replace the glorified bad women, shopworn goddesses that they are, with portrayals of real women who are at the same time both sinners and saints. Portrayals of characters who violate God's laws should be handled with an understanding of psychology and of the social scene which reveals the psychological and social factors involved. We should delineate characters on the screen so that we will understand why people do the things they do. But the whole answer should not be psychological and social, thus eliminating moral responsibility of the individual for his acts. Punishment for sin should not be merely punishment by man for the violation of his laws. Punishment should be shown as operating on the very spirit of the sinner himself. Sinners on the screen—were they real people portrayed with Christian insight—might well have suffered punishment long before the law overtook them, whether they recognized it or not, in the depths of their innermost souls. Even if the sinner himself never repents or even recognizes or acknowledges his sin, the audience should be given a perspective on his character, a flash of insight into the dark labyrinth down which the sinner has gone.

A corollary to the problem of the portrayal of evil on the screen is the problem of the portrayal of virtue and morality so that people who act on moral principles will seem interesting and attractive. The screen has concentrated on "bad" people instead of "good" ones because of the tendency to regard many so-called "good" people as colorless or mediocre.

We should have screen portrayals of the complacency and spiritual stagnation of the so-called "good" people who confuse conventionalities with morality and mediocrity with virtue. At the same time we should have more films like *Our Vines Have Tender Grapes*, which show the drama of spiritual growth, the adventure of a life of service. We hear a great deal today of the portrayal of the average man, the little man whom life has treated shabbily, and the degeneration of his character in the process. We should have a drama of the little man who refused to treat the world shabbily in return and, with the help of God, grows and becomes big.

We must develop writers and other creative people who have

had a personal experience of God as a reality in human life, who do not share the dualism between the secular and sacred prevalent in our world today, and whose conviction will motivate and pervade their creative work. In his portrayals of people on the radio and on the screen, with all their heartaches, struggles, and joys, the writer need not always mention God but should take into account the fact that God is at work in human life. His portrayals should reflect a deep conviction of the sacrilege of sin and the sacrament of joy.

There are films which do this, at least in part; and these films should be supported and encouraged. Since the screen is one of the greatest media for attitude formation and motivation in the world today, it is the definite responsibility on the part of church people to attend good films. It is a sad commentary of our awareness in this regard that such a film as *It's a Wonderful Life*, which might well have deserved the wide support of church people, lost money at the box office for many months.

Another point at which the church encounters secularism on the screen is in the treatment of social and psychological problems. Many artistic, adult films deal intelligently with such problems yet reflect the secularism of our culture in that they state or imply answers to such problems which do not recognize the part of religion in their solution. Examples of this are such excellent films as *Crossfire* and *Gentleman's Agreement*, both of which boldly recognize the problem of prejudice, which has not been faced before with such candor on our entertainment screen. Yet these films do imply that merely understanding the problem is all that is required, that it in itself provides the dynamic for solution. Sometimes this point of view takes on an almost evangelistic fervor, and thus psychological and social humanitarianism is given an almost religious status.

Another example of this is the group of feature films on psychiatric themes which have appeared, including such films as *Spellbound* and *The Seventh Veil*. It is not in my province to judge the accuracy and effectiveness of these films from the psychiatric viewpoint. Entertainment-wise many of them have been fascinating and engrossing. Too often, however, such films have reflected the fallacy of some elements of the psychiatric profession itself, that knowing *how* mental illness arises also explains *why*. Some of these films take the form of psychological detective stories which trace the roots of a patient's malady back through a chain of contributing circumstances to an event or events in childhood. While these stories are often excellent dramatically and have a high degree of suspense, in the end the results of this tense and exciting search for the wellsprings of character somehow seem trivial and insignificant. One cannot believe that the analysis of the process whereby mental maladjustments occurred, however valuable and engrossing, is the full explanation of the difficulty and is in itself the cure. Yet some of these films imply that understanding alone is the final solution of the mystery of life.

There has been growing collaboration in recent years between religion and psychiatry in the treatment of mental illness and the promotion of mental health. Yet there are basic issues on which religion and psychiatry have not yet clearly met—the moral responsibility of the individual in mental illness; the difference between a sense of guilt, generally exorcised by psychiatrists with the fervor of a witch doctor expelling evil spirits, and the sense of sin which the Christian believes is essential to the godly life.

Screen portrayals which give us added insight into life should coordinate the thinking of religion and psychiatry on human problems, and should recognize that while psychiatric knowledge may greatly speed the solution of these problems, the ultimate solution must take place on a spiritual plane. Entertainment films on psychiatric themes need not necessarily have specific religious content, yet they should clarify psychological concepts in the light of religious truths. Conversely, portrayals of religion on the screen should clarify religious concepts in the light of discoveries of psychiatry and psychology regarding the human mind and soul. Thus religion and psychiatry may aid and strengthen each other, and both add to our knowledge and spiritual insight into the deepest problems of life.

While it may be some time before this co-ordinated point of view is reflected on the entertainment screen, immediate steps are being taken by the Protestant Film Commission to produce seven films on mental health, dramatic, human-interest stories which will embody the principle outlined above. This, we hope, will be an important aid in breaking down the barrier between the secular and the sacred in this important field.

The Treatment of Materialism

Another great secular philosophy with which Christianity is faced in this modern age is that of materialism, and this too is reflected on our motion-picture screen. Of all varieties of secularism which Christianity faces, this is perhaps the most pervading and most dangerous. This philosophy holds that our physical well-being, our standard of living, our possessions and material wealth are the important realities of life, from which all other things derive their value and worth. This philosophy draws devotees from all walks of life. It is practiced by those who exploit others for more power and wealth and who, while giving lip service to the things of the spirit, secretly regard spiritual riches as a useful compensation for those less fortunate. It is also practiced by those who hold the naïve belief that once the physical needs of man are met, his soul will somehow automatically be saved. It is undoubtedly this philosophy, taking the form of a kind of romantic hedonism, which accounts for our modern glorification of sex, not only on the American screen, but in literature, plays, advertising, and billboards—the philosophy which has also made bathtubs, plumbing, and nylon hose potent symbols of American life. It is this philosophy which, taking the form of communism or fascism, may stir the underprivileged peoples of the world to a religious fervor which somehow Christian democracy seems unable to arouse. It is terribly symptomatic of the spiritual sickness of our time that many servicemen of World War II, products of the American democratic way of life, were ignorant of the basic Christian concepts behind that way of life, and identified it with material advantages which were its products and not its essence, and were unaware of the place of God, the Bible, and the church in the development of the freedoms for which they fought.

There is need for the screen to dramatize vividly and unforgettably the religious basis of these freedoms and the contributions of Christianity and the organized church to their development. Man's right to freedom must be portrayed as arising from man's relationship to God; our national heritage must be portrayed as having its roots in the spiritual heritage of man. Here again is a field in which Protestant Christianity, through the production of its own films, may have a profound influence on the culture and thinking of our time.

While Christianity can and must encourage deeper characterization on the screen and more powerful treatment of social, psychological, and political themes, it can never effectively contest secularism through the screen unless it uses this powerful medium to portray the basic tenets of the Christian faith and their application to the problems of modern life.

The theatrical and nontheatrical screen offer an unprecedented opportunity for the church to interpret itself and its message to the great masses of our people. The deep-felt need for this use of the screen is demonstrated by the tremendous public interest in such films as *The Song of Bernadette, The Bells of St. Mary's,* and *Going My Way*. Producers of entertainment films are ready to meet this need again with more entertainment films on religious themes; the nontheatrical screen offers a potential market of nearly 200,000 churches for attitude-forming films on religious themes which the churches themselves produce.

In order to interpret itself to the hearts of the people in a world threatened by atomic war and annihilation, the church must turn to itself, clarify its own concepts, and then express itself in a new and vital way. It must demonstrate, with something of the inspiration and skill of the Master, the application of the Christian faith to the problems of today.

PROBLEMS OF THE RELIGIOUS FILM

What are some of the problems involved in the portrayal of the basic concepts of religion and the work of the organized church on the motion-picture screen?

The first basic problem in the making of religious films arises from the fact that God and faith and other religious concepts are spiritual and invisible, profound concepts which we may experience but perhaps never fully fully understand. The motion-picture camera must have concrete, specific, visible objects and actions to photograph. How can we photograph the invisible and record the workings of the unseen?

The motion picture can show God only as he works through people and becomes manifest in human life. Thus, in addition to the dramatization of the great stories of the Bible, we must dramatize modern stories which show God at work in the world today. And these stories must be convincing, real, and true. Our writers must have sufficient skill and insight to portray human emotions and actions in terms of their spiritual origins and implications. Portrayals of sin must be handled in such a way that when we see characters performing sinful acts we realize with renewed vividness that here is a violation of God's law, not because the dialogue or a Greek chorus tells us so, but because we see in dramatic terms on the screen the effect on the characters themselves. We must have characterization and dramatic writing which will provide us with an insight into the divine character of man and which will enable us to see both the depths of his sin and the possibility for his redemption.

We cannot be obvious, preachy, or abstract when we are attempting to embody in terms of dramatic stories deep religious truths. We must create characters who are real people, understand the depths of their motivation, and weave stories in which, even though the characters themselves may not discover it, the audience may glimpse the ultimate meaning of life, not explained to them in abstract terms but inherent in the very fabric of the story. This was the technique used by Christ himself, and we must strive to emulate the Master in this regard. Christ appealed to people in simple, graphic terms. He told stories and often left people to draw their own conclusions. He used the imagery of the farm, the street, the market place. If we are adequately to interpret Christianity to the world today, we must also use these techniques. We must present the Christian message in simple, direct, compelling human terms.

An important part of religious film production is the portrayal of the actual religious experience of characters who on the screen come into a new and real relationship with God as revealed through Christ. In the film *Going My Way* we see a cleric performing acts of humanitarian social service, but we are never shown the depths of his character, or given more than a glimpse of the religious motivation for his acts, or see him pass on this motivation to others. But in future portrayals of religion we must show the gradual, slow process of spiritual growth which has no sudden climax but which flows triumphantly into the more abundant life; we must also show the wonders of conversion, which is sudden and dramatic. Yet sudden conversion is not credible on the screen unless we also portray the steps which gave it rise—the slow realization of the preciousness and value of a life given to God and, in contrast, the revulsion, the pervading sense of sin at a life petty, ignoble, and half-lived; the struggle within the soul, growing more and more violent and finally breaking in one great, blinding flash of insight and commitment which relaxes and transforms a life.

In our portrayals of Protestant ministers on the screen, the characterizations should not be stereotyped or stilted, but real, down-to-earth, and human. The personality of the minister should be portrayed as warm and appealing, yet having qualities of the divine, for in him we must see the spirit of Christ at work in the lives of men. Protestant congregations should not be caricatured, or members of the congregation stereotyped as "good" or "bad." Rather these people should be portrayed as human beings—sinners who are also saints, average people who are helped to become great, strong people who weaken, weak people who become strong. The conflict should not be between minister and congregation but should take place in the hearts of men, in those of both the minister and his congregation, as they struggle and fail and struggle again to realize their fullest potentialities under God for themselves and for the world.

The medium of the motion picture has inevitably played an important part in promoting and perpetuating secularism in our modern world. At the same time it has been intelligently and skillfully used to promote human welfare and education. This medium must now be adapted and used for Christian ends. The motion picture, both on the theatrical and the nontheatrical screen, offers one of the greatest opportunities which Protestant Christianity has had to communicate the Christian message to the masses of our people in terms that they can grasp and understand.

We must adapt to the screen the great dramas of the Bible itself, for the Bible does not state its truths in abstract terms alone, but in terms of story, poem, and song. Yet in order to relate adequately Christianity to modern life, we must also have a great literature of today. To reach the great masses of our people this literature must be dramatized on the motion-picture screen. If done with skill and reverence, such portrayal will offer to our time both a judgment and a hope.

SECULARISM IN THE CHURCH

George N. Shuster

Here, we are Catholics who don't cheat; Protestants who don't cheat; Jews who don't cheat; freethinkers who don't cheat. That is why we are so few Catholics; so few Protestants; so few Jews; so few freethinkers. All in all, so few of us. And against us we have the Catholics who cheat; the Protestants who cheat; the Jews who cheat; the freethinkers who cheat. And that makes a lot of people.—CHARLES PEGUY

Is THE CHURCH THE ANTITHESIS OF SECULARISM, AT LEAST IN ITS OWN domain? Before answering let us be certain that we understand the question. Obviously not every way in which the concern of the Christian for this world, for what is properly Caesar's, finds expression has been either illogical or wanton. For example, the church was sorely troubled by the brutal pageants staged in Roman arenas. It was anxious lest the suffering borne by those who were persecuted should corrode and embitter even faithful souls. That it should find every man a potential Christian and therefore a brother was as self-evident as was the correlative decision to be that brother's keeper.

Similarly, Reinhold Niebuhr seems to me to have commented with admirable judiciousness on the fact that religious faith is not antithetical to the nature of man. To maintain, as some have, that life according to the Beatitudes is sheer miracle and possible only to those who raise themselves to a new, transcendent order of being, is to forget that the supernatural has always been understood, in central Christian thought, as being not a distortion but the fulfillment of the natural order. The Kingdom is the property of those who are like little children. The faithful may render valor unselfish, and make of charity a gift on which no interest will ever be compounded. Nevertheless valor is always valor, and charity is forever itself.

Perhaps we can find a line of demarcation by analogy. You may recall von Hügel's comparison between man's relationship to God and a faithful dog's interest in his master. There are times when the human mind is not on the alert, or when there is confident frolicking done in the assurance that love is tireless and will abide. No doubt the church, which is of men, also knows such hours of relaxation. Then it is good-humored and indulgent. It may recall the pleasant humors of Horace, or suffer a gargoyle to take its place on a cathedral column. It may talk about the crops or pleasant weather. There will be laughter then, or the mystery of youth, or the wit which old men have harvested during their lives.

But those who look about them in this tragic time realize only too well that this is not what we mean by secularism in the church. There has been dry rot in the very beams of the temple. Almost all the tyrants who have stripped away freedom and peace were reared in the Christian faith. Some studied in theological schools. Others were acolytes as boys, or carried their Bibles with them of Sundays. When one remembers that Goebbels and Göring are reputed to have been pious little lads, enough has been said. It is probably correct to surmise that in virtually none of these cases was there what we should term immediate and conscious apostasy. Indeed, only the worst of the apostles of nihilism probably even saw clearly that religion was a mooring from which they had cut themselves adrift. There was, alas, so much consonance between the life men led inside the church and the existence they fostered outside that one could drift from faith to its opposite without so much as sensing the fateful transition.

Secularism has been defined as the spirit of power masked as conformity. It is the stance of mind assumed by those who decide that they can have what they desire without departing from any "sensible" code of morals; that, as a matter of fact, it is possible subtly to revamp standards of conduct without losing the right to a Christian coat of varnish. You can assert, for example, that God certainly wants men to love their country; and then you can go on to ignore the manner in which he has decreed that such love should take shape, and end by attributing to the aggressive state any right and power it may claim. Or you may hold that the "essence of religion" is to be honest and courteous, which means being sportsmanlike on the golf course one substitutes for worship every Sunday morning. To take a final example, you may feel that love between the sexes is valid only when the element of physical rapture in it is intense, and so you may end up with seven husbands or seven wives, each presumably a trifle more rapturous than the others. Therewith, without ceasing to be reasonable or even decorous, you have substituted for the Christian faith everything which is the opposite of that faith.

I should like to make two commentaries on what has been said. First, the phenomenon just described is not to be attributed of necessity to a failure of the church or its clergy. The gospel has its weak and worldly ministers, of course. It has always had them. But it seems to me, on the basis of such experience as I have been able to muster, that the clergy of no age has been more devoted or saintly than is the ministry of our time. When have more of them braved the wrath of tyranny? German Catholics and Lutherans may not always have proved as courageous or intelligent as one could desire. Yet when one compares their record with that of their forebears in the era of the French Revolution, or even of the Roman persecutions, the result is a kind of awestruck reverence for men one has known in the flesh. Or has there ever been an era when Christian scholarship has been more tirelessly objective than is the scholarship of men like Kenneth Latourette or Père Garragou-Lagrange? And when in England, for example, have Roman Catholicism and Anglicanism been so well led as they were during the last war by Hinsley and Temple? I am moved daily by the Christlike sincerity of men serving every Christian communion. Many of them are so good—yes, so holy and humble—that one could take off one's shoes in their presence.

Secondly, while the impact of science on the modern mind is great, it cannot by any manner of means be said to have accomplished what is attributed to it. Anyone who has even fleetingly lived close to the secret trouble of our time, which is man's inability to quell the riot in his own person, knows that "science" is no talisman with which to conjure up peace. Of course, I am not thinking of this peace as an opiate. It is merely that order of being in which the simplest things make sense, in which the fact that two times two are four is logical, or that putting one's hand trustingly in another's hand is communion and not merely contact, seems commonplace. Up and down the land there are thousands of psychiatrists aiding men and women in their quest for the peace, who repeat Cabot's phrase of "love, play, work, and worship." Has any one of them in his right mind ever suggested the worship of science? Naturally there are all sorts of philosophers and psychologists and educators who wish they would. The psychiatrists, however, know better. They see, to be frank, that suicide is more attractive than "science."

When we speak of "science" in this connection, we are not thinking at all of the epochal discoveries of so many able and industrious delvers. We are conscious only of the sickening doubt which has eaten away for so many the rationale of religious confidence. It isn't that "science" has gotten into the central place of the human heart, which is reserved for holy things. We must understand, rather, that the effect of several centuries of a humanism which subjected the documents and the creed of Christendom to hostile, critical scrutiny finally was made manifest when science appeared to indicate that nature sanctioned a kind of life which men for whom religion was a constraint inwardly desired to lead. The query became this: "If I subject the urges which I wish to follow to the yoke of Christian morals, will I not run the risk of never having what it would be interesting or pleasant to have?" Let us take a concrete illustration. Some said: "If I can enjoy sexual promiscuity without the risk of syphilis, why should not matters be so arranged that I can enjoy it also without running the risk of divine wrath?"

All this is as old as the skeptics of the Middle Ages. It is to be found in Poggio and Montaigne, who certainly knew nothing of the natural sciences. Pascal wrestled with the problem. There were English gentry in the seventeenth century who worked out schemes of accommodation without having, in all probability, so much as heard about a laboratory experiment. We must, in order to comprehend, repeat that there is a fateful drift in human nature towards gratification of the libidos. That is why totalitarianism is initially so attractive. Such a system makes it possible to shift all responsibilty to the state, to get rid of the necessity for squaring with one's conscience a thousand complex acts. To be sure, the totalitarian state then turns round and levies a fearful heavy fine. Yet people do not think of the fine at the outset. They feel a sense of exhilarating relief.

Two Aspects of Secularism

These two comments having been made, we can go on to draw the obvious conclusion. Secularism is, on the one hand, an act of retreat from the clerical leader in whom the form of Christian living is manifest, and, on the other hand, a giving in to doubt that moral and intellectual caveats are as formidable as they have been made out to be. And yet! The secularist does not wish to withdraw from religion. He is not a fiery atheist or the latest variety of neo-Hegelian. What he seeks is a formula according to which two opposing ways of life can be blended. His octave of religious values is in a sense complete, ranging all the way from the ecclesiastical music he occasionally listens to with a kind of wistful pleasure to the "good effect" which the Sunday school has on his children. He knows that night clubs and whoopee have their deleterious effects, at least upon the young. And for himself he covets a measure of respectability, which in many communities only church membership can confer. And maybe deep down in his heart he wants to die with some kind of insurance policy in his hand.

Our secularist has already sucked the substance out of a large portion of Christendom. He is not a sinner—as, God knows, all men are—who succumbs to temptation and then covers his face with his contrite hands. For he has managed to take all the thorns out of sin in advance. This is something which people can't really help, which is natural, which everybody does. He can be cruel with the comfortable feeling that a lot of folks have been cruel previously. He can gouge his neighbor or steal from the public treasury, secure in the knowledge that as a shyster or a grafter he has a long and famous pedigree. When he lies, he is aware of how seldom the truth is told nowadays. And therewith he makes the profession of the Christian faith an act of obedience to the "world." On every Christmas Eve he feels sentimental, and after every football game he is drunk. What more could one ask of a man?

I shall go on to say that the temptation to secularism is even more subtle and dangerous than all this. It may come disguised in forms which are sometimes agreeable even to an otherwise incorruptible church. Let us take as an illustration a familiar gospel story. The Roman centurion, having heard of the miracles performed by Jesus, requests help. Not only is this granted, but the Saviour bestows special praise. When it is borne in mind that probably no one was as cordially detested by Jews as a Roman official, the extraordinary significance of this incident becomes apparent. We shall not liken the centurion to a Negro, welcome in so many American churches only if no white man happens to be present. Let us suppose, rather, that the centurion was a German officer, stationed at a neutral port when a representative of the church in America happened to pass by. Is it not reported that ministers of the Christian gospel did not assist such Germans in their last agony, either out of fear of what might be said or actually out of hatred?

May one not also cite the lure of ecclesiastical imperialism, manifest in so many forms? I shall refer only to one which we like to think of as modern and which is possibly a consequence of the popularity of secularism. Men seem to applaud those forces which flatter their illusions of eternal youth and their assumption of intelligence. Seventy-odd thousand of them spend a day's wages going to a single football game, and ten million of them purchase magazines filled for the most part with cartoons. How shall the church, appealing to man's secret sense of guilt and to his desire for regeneration, compete with these attractions? If the answer is that the church must put on a dab of secularistic cosmetics, a fateful decision has been made. In the first place, no competition is possible. In this domain the resources of secularism are so incomparably greater that ecclesiastical borrowing merely reminds the spectator of an old maid in a spectacular bathing costume. And in the second place, the imitation corrodes. Men no longer see that the church is august and eternal, but find her immersed awkwardly in the flood of time.

Thus the seeming omnipotence of the secularist impulse has not only hollowed out the church as a congregation but has also even corrupted it as the *sponsa Christi*, the Bride of Christ. Sometimes the triumph seems so complete that one is sorely tried to concede that the battle has been lost. Are not ecclesiastical procedures outmoded? Is there any hope of being able to compete with the streamlined certainty of the children of time? Who has not been appalled by the naïveté of the faithful, the immaturity of their dialectic and the provincialism of their outlook upon life? How many of them really believe that it is well to suffer persecution for justice's sake, or that the meek shall inherit the land? To how many do the mansions of the blessed seem a worthy substitute for hotel suites along Miami Beach? The church is not dynamic in terms of the social and economic order, yes. But that would hardly matter if it were dynamic in the realms of religion and intelligence.

How Shall We Combat Secularism?

If we now ask ourselves whether, these things being what they are, there is anything to be done about them, we shall first of all have to avoid every temptation to be unctuously optimistic. Religion is, for most people, hard. It has always been so; and human nature continuing to be what it is, large masses of men have persisted in their fidelity only when the climate of mores has demanded it. Missionary history is replete with illustrations of the fickleness of converts, and the story of humanity as a whole is as much a chronicle of defection from ideals as of service to ideals. It is only after this has been understood, as Dibelius, for example, has grasped it in his studies of German Christianity, that one can begin to think realistically of the sociological structure of the church. We may, of course, take into account the purposeful gaiety which often lures people into a Christian communion, or the art of using the wiles of the worldly as subterfuges. But in the end all these do not matter greatly. It is the spiritual athleticism of religion which alone truly counts.

The most difficult and often the most harrassing enterprise of the Christian is sanctity. By sanctity I mean the total elimination of worldliness from the human breast, the conquest not of one's own self merely, but of other selves in order that the divine will be done. We do not hesitate to train men for scholarly endeavor or for military service through long and arduous discipline. How, then, can we expect religion to permeate human society unless we rear men and women strenuously for the spiritual life? They are leaders in this combat, and their reward is God's to give. It is because the Catholic Church has maintained the flame of monasticism throughout the ages that it has survived crises to which any other institution would have succumbed. There were always strong and resolute souls whom no lure could divert. And it is likewise apparent that when Protestant creeds have maintained the discipline of holiness their influence upon large numbers of men has been great. Whether it be Jeremy Taylor or Wesley or Bodelschwingh, the example was always far more effective than the voice. Yet there was both example and voice.

I have said that there exists in our time a community of spirits to which the quest for holiness is the supremely important adventure. Their conduct contrasts no more strangely with that of their environment than did the urgent asceticism of Paul. What I believe is needed are words in which there is to be found the luminous poetry of the Pauline tradition—words with a modern ring, close to the poor of spirit, to all those who are heavily burdened with the half-recognized guilt which rests upon their hearts, who do not quite know that the reason their inner world has collapsed is that its disorder is a negation of divinely constituted order. There can be no objection to concern with the poor in this world's goods. But our tragedy is that the more corrosive poverty of the soul has so little medicine for its malady in this our day.

No wonder that when the disorder assumes mastodontic social proportions, and greed coupled with dark lusts runs riot over continents, even the most emancipated modern spirits should begin to query whether it might after all not be true that Satan exists and is mighty. But if this query presents itself when we behold the "passion and the pride" of man arrayed in battle dress, must it not also come to mind when we see them at work, more seductively, in the individual soul? The most tragic of human failures is not the deed, the transgression, the sin. It is the error of not knowing, the absence of realization which the Saviour deplored in tears as he looked upon Jerusalem. It is, in the natural order, the failure of the mountain village doctor to know about penicillin, or the obtuseness of parents regarding what is their child's really vital problem. But in the order of daily living it is the failure to understand what the purpose of human existence is, and how this purpose may be attained. We read that quacks have built up in the United States an industry earning over a hundred million dollars annually by giving meaningless advice to people who feel in need of psychiatric treatment. Hundreds of thousands, distressed and shaken, grope about trying to find what is wrong with them, only to be fleeced by disreputable scoundrels.

But why do not these victims of anxiety come to the church? It is true that confession as administered in the Catholic Church is looked upon by millions as a healing sacrament, and that many a Protestant pastor has tried to fit himself to be a physician of souls. I have the greatest respect for confession, but I wonder if even it has not grown too perfunctory and rapid to be everything it ought to be, whether the distraught individual feels impelled not merely to list and recite his sins, salutary though that practice is, but also to talk openly and frankly about his secret trouble and what might be done

to alleviate it. Does not the clergyman's reputation for moral behavior often prove to be a barrier which the penitent cannot bring
himself to cross? Does he feel that the confessor is like Francis of
Assisi, who kissed even the leper?

In the *Paideia*, Werner Jaeger has a remarkable chapter dealing
with the parallel between the Greek conception of medical prevention in the physical sense and the Greek theory of the warding off
of intellectual disease. And, ideally speaking, all spiritual counseling
seeks to outline a regimen comparable to diet for the body. There
is also such a thing as spiritual surgery: "If thine eye offend thee,
pluck it out." But before there can be a cure, there must be a competent diagnosis. To develop a science of spiritual diagnosis for our
distraught time is the great opportunity of the church. With this
it can combat secularism, because it is the widespread need of diag-
nostic which heralds the breakdown of secularism.

This pastoral service, performed in the spirit of Christ, provides
a setting for the healing and luminous poetry of which I have spoken.
When millions of Americans discover that the church can minister
to souls, and that it will do so gladly and gratuitously, out of reverent affiliation with the boundless charity of Christ, they will strive
to put secularism out of their hearts. For they will have seen holiness
in action. Just as the good psychiatrist is a doctor who has first removed from his own mind every taint of neurotic illness, so also
is the excellent pastor one who has shriven his soul of all evil. And let us
remember that forbidding austerity is an evil too. Perhaps the most
genial, kindly, humorous man I know is a priest who has been hope-
lessly bedridden with arthritis of the spine for twenty years. There
is no one who understands better the pranks of boys or the foibles
of adults. Suffering has made him a saint he might otherwise never
have been, though he would chuckle if anyone called him a saint.
His smile has in it the cleansing water of which the psalmist speaks.
I think the pastor who scowls when the sinner comes to be washed
of his human filth is as useless as the physician who loses his temper
when a patient arrives with a set of clogged up sinuses.

What Can the Layman Do to Help?

So far I have written only of the clergy, and some of them who
read this will no doubt feel that I have been a bit presumptuous in

commenting on their estate. What I have hoped to do is to indicate that there is no use talking of the church apart from its clergy, and that all forms of anticlericalism are ridiculous and corrosive. We laymen often criticize our priests and ministers. It is our privilege to do so, and indeed it may even be our duty. But when we are honest critics, we are also grateful observers. Yet there undoubtedly is a great lay opportunity in the confrontation of religion and secularism. I shall not discuss it here in terms which would take me outside the church itself.

It seems to me that the layman can help most by rededicating himself to religious practice. From his point of view that practice is primarily prayer. He must join in the corporate liturgy of his church, knowing that a good sermon is itself a prayer. Incidentally let him hope that recognition of this fact will spread. A sermon is not a lecture, when it is any good at all. It is a period of open meditation on some of those words and ways of the spiritual life which have their origin in God. Notice Newman or Launcelot Andrewes or Philip Neri. I can assure you that laymen are profoundly grateful when they hear such a discourse. They *aren't* always when the pastor elects to discuss international affairs or economics, since they may think they could do this better themselves. But the layman must also seek to carry prayer out of the church into his daily life. If the American family would, when it is still Christian, reinstitute the saying of grace at meals, it would do itself more good than can easily be realized. It is harder nowadays to revive the ancient practice of evening family prayer because retiring is not undertaken in unison by an age that doesn't go to bed with the chickens. Yet, if on some evening at least, there could be a moment during which a psalm was read or the Lord's Prayer recited, there would be an echo of goodness throughout the night.

In short, I do not believe we can ward off the encroachments of secularism by issuing pronouncements or getting out a book. Educators talk a great deal nowadays about "personalizing" relations with students. That is, we seek to test each student, to have a chat with him about his plans and his difficulties, and to offer a helping hand when he has a hard decision to make. We don't want to throw information at him without knowing whether it is of a kind that will do him any good or whether his reception is what it ought to be.

It is my profound conviction that the Christian faith can be preached to modern Americans only if religious education is also personalized. There is no one to order conformity. Only the laborious but fruitful labor of individual conversion can turn the tide of history.

One cannot, however, conclude without remembrance of the grace of God which is given to us in hours of joy and tribulation, of light and fearful gloom. This is not a bright hour in history. But it may be, if we are strong, a period before dawn. Perhaps the birds will sing as the light rises in the east. Looking back through history, the Christian is aware of the sense of dedication with which those who have gone before went out to meet their tasks. And I think that, when he seeks to peer into the future, he understands as well that the radiance of faith to be professed will be abiding. In the present, however, we need above all charity, finding expression in individual lives, of course, but extending above all to the relations between the disparate branches of the church, so that at least there may be a feeling of common dependence and common glory. By achieving this the Christian would give the secularist a necessary and moving illustration of brotherhood.

Part

III

SECULARISM
IN POLITICAL LIFE

SECULAR CONCEPTS IN POLITICS

James E. Ward

WOODROW WILSON ONCE STARTLED A FOURTH OF JULY AUDIENCE AT
Independence Hall, Philadelphia, by remarking that the Declaration
of Independence was not a Fourth of July oration. On the contrary,
it was a document preliminary to war, "a vital piece of practical business, not a piece of rhetoric." Wilson went on to say that

> if you will pass beyond those preliminary passages which we are ac-
> customed to quote about the rights of man and read into the heart of
> the document you will see that it is very express and detailed, that it con-
> sists of a series of definite specifications concerning actual public business
> of the day. Not the business of our day, for the matter with which it
> deals is past, but the business of the first revolution by which the Nation
> was set up, the business of 1776.

Wilson continued with the observation that liberty does not consist "in declarations of the rights of man," but "in the translation
of those declarations into definite action. The thing to do, he declared, is to reduce the Declaration of Independence "to what the
lawyers call a bill of particulars. It contains a bill of particulars, but
the bill of particulars of 1776. If we would keep it alive, we must fill
it with a bill of particulars of the year 1914."

The point that Wilson made is applicable in every realm. When
the fact and problem of secularism as applied to politics and political
life is viewed historically, we find that the "bill of particulars" has
changed as compared to the present.

Two Historical Perspectives of Secularism

Two historical perspectives might be taken—one from the standpoint of the Christian West and the other from that of world history.
The second is preferable, at all events as a point of departure, because secularism has affected the relationship of individual to state
quite as formidably in the non-Christian East as in our own hemis-

phere. From this point of view, the fact of a culture, the conduct of a government and of civilization, the orientation of which is purely secular, is seen to be something new and unique. Everywhere else in the history of the world we see the culture and institutions of the state closely bound to religion.

This is true not only in the ancient Mediterranean culture, in old Rome before Augustus, in Greece before Pericles, in the old civilizations of Babylonia, Assyria, and Egypt, but equally as correct in old China, Japan, Mexico, and Peru—and even in the world of the so-called primitive peoples. All these present the same spectacle: everywhere religion is there unmistakably as the factor which dominates the culture, including whatever kind of political union which they may have possessed. It was religion which held them together socially, economically, and as a political unit.

This is not to say that there was not some form of religious decadence emerging at times. There was a continued process of emancipation of culture from certain religious restraints. However, the revolt never succeeded. As the social, economic, and political forms changed, what really happened was the replacing of one religious supremacy by another. One's concept of politics was still bound up in his concept of religion.

Perhaps the Roman Empire alone forms a certain parallel to present-day phenomena. The Romans' conception of the part the state played in their lives is closely akin to some modern conceptions, but closer scrutiny reveals the parallel to be somewhat remote, for in the Empire it was only a small segment of the people, the educated, who cast off religion. It was not the mass of the people, or even the majority of those which sustained the state and culture.

In early America too the philosophy of government and hope for democracy was closely related to religion. This was true because in the European background out of which our earliest ideas of the state and political affairs emerged the functions of the state were somewhat religious in character.

Perhaps no better proof of this fact can be found than that revealed in a study of the writings and philosophy of Thomas Jefferson, the one who, more than any other, shaped the course of American life and, more particularly, the path of political affairs.

Jefferson, a man often incorrectly called irreligious, assembled ideas on society and on government not out of any academic interest in abstract principles, but in the hope of finding something useful here on earth. In his study it was in the record of Anglo-Saxon life before feudalism that he found ideas and institutions most to his liking. He discovered that the Anglo-Saxons of those early days lived under customs and unwritten laws based upon the natural rights of man. The individual was permitted to develop freely, normally, and happily.

It is a long step from the philosophy of monarch-representing-God-on-earth to the ballot, from the doctrine "Divine Rights of Kings" to the century of the common man, but Jefferson induced a new nation to take it.

However, Jefferson was impressed by the fact that this Anglo-Saxon freedom in England deteriorated when unwritten law became written law, and when conquerors and kings came forth to all but annihilate the rights of the individual.

Would this be the course of events in America? It would, Jefferson felt, unless Americans took specific measures to prevent it. Jefferson therefore sought to fit the ideas of the past more precisely to American conditions.

In a letter discovered only a few years ago by the biographer Gilbert Chinard, Jefferson set forth his "ideas of natural and civil rights and the distinction between them." He began by asking his friend to imagine a country inhabited by twenty individuals, each a stranger to every other. Each person would be sovereign in his own natural right, and his will would be law. However, his power, Jefferson pointed out, would in many cases be inadequate to his right. Each of the twenty would therefore be in some danger, not only from each other, but from the other nineteen.

Being rational human beings, they would seek some way to exchange that quantity of danger into so much protection, so that each individual should possess the strength of twenty. The way would be found, Jefferson decided, when they learned to distinguish between

those rights they could individually exercise fully and perfectly and those they could not. Of the first kind are the rights of thinking, speaking, forming and giving opinions, and perhaps all those which can be fully exercised by the individual without the aid of exterior assistance—or in other words, rights of personal competency. Of the second kind are those of personal protection, of acquiring and possessing property, in the exercise of which the individual natural power is less than the natural right.

Very likely this is the key, as Chinard suggests, to the whole system of government evolved by Jefferson. It is pecularily Jeffersonian and American. The conflict between society and the individual is removed, for both are sovereign in their respective domains.

Thus our early concept of political affairs was one of checks and balances and of compromise, or, as Jefferson put it when discussing another matter in a letter to his friend George Mason: "In general, I think it necessary to give as well as take in a government like ours."

In the Constitution of the United States, in that remarkable group of papers known as *The Federalist*, and in the Declaration of Independence is found the fact that our early forefathers were essentially animated by the desire to free the individual from the control of the state. The church too was separated from the state, but it was the church which gave a hue to the basic conceptions of the day.

SECULARISM IN THE GOVERNMENT

More recent American history has witnessed a change of emphasis. The modern citizen has, for the most part, found a new focal center of emotional attachment; and to some it seems as vain to decry the fact as to raise the voice over woman's fashions. Secularism has crept in and seems to be at home.

Emphasis in government has shifted from the sacred to the secular, and as a result there has come a disposition on the part of many to lose respect for government. This is a normal tendency when government becomes a human affair rather than a system of God's making.

Politics and political life are free. Religious belief is no longer circumventing it. This conception is part of the environment of a world with its demonstration of man's power and capability of organization and technical achievement and know-how, relying on science to strengthen the growing belief that man, with his creative energy, is the center of the universe. Some even go so far as to acclaim that a religious outlook of political affairs is hostile to progress and to a strong social and political life.

Walter Lippmann describes with exceeding clarity the stress of the transfer from the old order to the new in his *Preface to Morals*. He writes of modern man who has achieved remarkable freedom from religious and moral taboos, but who, in so doing, lost his faith, not only in traditions, but in his objectives.

Here we have secularism at its best—or worst. There has been a separation of the departments of life from the center to which they belong, so that they become kingdoms in their own right. Business will be business; art will exist for art's sake; education will solve the mystery of human life in its own strength; politics and political life are ends in themselves. Religion too is a department of life with its own petty interests.

This fission of life into parts has resulted in a world of confusion, where the higher values are starved out and disillusionment reigns with moral lassitude. Man lacks landmarks by which to guide his conscience and fears losing his way.

In our politics we "render therefore unto Caesar the things which be Caesar's, and unto God the things which be God's." The only trouble is that Caesar's domain is so large and the things of God are so few and insignificant in comparison. One need only examine the approach Congress or a state legislature takes to a problem to find out that that which is often done is based on desire for power rather than the desire of service.

Modern Man's Dependence on the State

In the latter half of the nineteenth century and to the present day the individual, having emancipated himself from the state and having subjected the state to his will, has furthermore demanded of the state that it serve his material needs. Thereby he has complicated the machinery of the state to such a degree that he has again fallen under subjection to it and has been threatened with losing control over it.

The modern individual in the democratic state is in the position of a pampered old bachelor who has a faithful cook. He has entrusted to this servant the task of looking after him in every respect. The cook has dutifully obeyed his commands, but the master has thereby fallen completely under the ascendancy of the servant because she has become indispensable to his welfare. This is an extension of the function of the state whose paternalism tends strongly to change the psychology of individual self-reliance into a psychology of reliance upon the collective community.

This has been particularly true of our time. The philosophy of the United States during the 1930's and so far in the 1940's is characterized neither by individualism nor by democracy as they were understood in former times. The individual demanding that the state provide him with every security has jeopardized his possession of that freedom for which his ancestors fought and bled.

And why this sudden dependence upon the state? The reason lies in the aloneness of the individual. He stands on his own basis, as no Greek ever did. Man always feels himself to be bound in two respects: bound to higher powers and bound to society. The idea of an individual who stands on his own basis, an individual who is grounded in the autonomy of his own reason, is entirely foreign to the man of antiquity who conceived of the life of the individual as bound up with the life of his people, with the life of the past and with the cosmos.

DeSales, in his book entitled *The Making of Tomorrow*, asserts: "The spiritual values of the Western World, such as . . . were proposed by the philosophers of the eighteenth century and the economists of the nineteenth, are temporarily bankrupt or have become unintelligible." We could go even further and add that the spiritual values brought down through the centuries by Christianity itself seem to be in temporary eclipse.

National unity has been substituted as the supreme value in some places. Establishment of this national unity necessarily tends to emphasize the power of the state over the individual because it is only when the state has emancipated itself, both from foreign influence and from internal inhibitions, that the individual can think of emancipating himself from the state.

Nationalism is a doctrine which places the national state above all other units in the scale of political values. It places the national state above the international community, whose claim to regulation it resents as an imposition.

"Blind irrational nationalism," says DeSales, "can grow out of the decadence of all reason and all spiritual values." There is no doubt that nationalism is one of the world's greatest ills. It is one of the few things about which men think similarly. It is always latent in society, never absent. Even in its most quiescent stage in our own country, for instance, feeling runs high when a Jehovah's Witness refuses to salute our flag, the symbol of our nation and our nationalism.

Men are inclined to put a nationalist spirit into the void "left by the inability of religion, philosophy, or the faith in science to satisfy certain aspirations." This has happened everywhere in the world; and because there are numerous nations on this troubled earth, this sameness of mind is a dividing force so dangerous as seriously to threaten our civilization. The decay of spiritual values and the loss of faith in rational concepts leave men in a state of infantile fear which cries out instinctively for authority.

Each modern nation has its own form of nationalism, a pattern somewhat unique unto itself. With nationalism necessarily comes the processes of secularization. In nineteenth-century Germany both the bourgeois intellectuals and the proletarian radicals were inclined to hostility rather than indifference toward religion and the church. Both conducted campaigns to persuade people to leave the church. As a consequence, life in Germany became consciously irreligious. Later, with the advent of Hitler, this secularism was in turn broken by a new religion of tribalism. Nazism was a controversy between a primitive religion and Christianity.

To the Nazi the world was nature and yet also superman. The Nazi was a Socialist, but at the same time a thoroughly uninhibited individualist. He defined liberty solely as power, security only as protection, outrage merely as misfortune.

In Russia there has been a substitution of communism for Christianity. According to the philosophy of all the collectivists—Communists, Socialists, Nazis, Fascists, and new liberals—the government, which is the sovereign will of man acting as a mass, grants such powers and liberty as it sees fit.

The totalitarian synthesis thus takes away from the people their endowment of personal dignity and autonomy without offering in exchange a natural order which functions to their advantage. A human being might well surrender some treasure of liberty for the sake of security without finding the bargain unfair. Some might even argue that all freedom could be exchanged for security, but to be robbed of liberty and still be left wholly insecure is an outrage.

The American Scene

In the United States the attitude is one of indifference or contempt rather than hostility. This country's form of government was originally based on the town meeting idea, where every individual had the ability to stand up and make his needs and desires known to someone in authority. As our society grew in numbers and became more complex, this was no longer feasible so we resorted more and more to representative democracy. This, however, has degenerated, in too many instances, to the rule of a pressure group. Many individuals and short-sighted minority groups maintain high-powered organizations in Washington and the state capitals in order to see that they get monopolistic powers which will benefit them, and usually them alone.

The striving of a multitude of minority groups for governmental powers to be used irresponsibly and greedily, while the majority of our citizenship look on with apathy and indifference, is perhaps the most acute political problem in America today. It is secularism in a glaring form. The privilege of possessing governmental powers must imply an obligation to the group which grants them, or it will result in the group's destruction.

This is not to decry the right of the lobby to exist any more than it is to say the the citizen should not petition his government. Lobbies are dangerous only so long as the people are unaware of their existence and their purpose.

The question naturally arises: What are we, those of us who are not indifferent, going to do about this whole problem? Do we still believe in representative democracy? Do we want to preserve it? Despite its shortcomings, do we or do we not consider it superior to collectivism? Are we willing to trade our liberty for security, our spiritual freedom for bread? If not, what can we do to stem the tide of secular philosophy which tends to engulf us? Are we going to let things drift as they have drifted for many years gone by? Or are we going to realize and accept our personal responsibilities as American citizens? No one of us can do much, but we need to remember what Spencer said: "How infinitesimal is the importance of anything I can do, but how infinitely important it is that I should do it."

Justice Louis Brandeis pointed out that our American political system "demands continual sacrifice by the individual and more exigent obedience to the moral law than any other form of government." So the final requirement today for Christian citizenship is self-sacrificing patriotism—the rededication of every one of us to the ideals of the American republic.

However, before any change can take place in our political life, a change must take place in the ethical attitudes of individuals. The average church member will have to be guided by motives other than self-interest. The laws of love, human brotherhood, and social responsibility must come again to the forefront of his consciousness. The end of political action is not power. Religion cannot be divorced from political life. If we exempt politics from judgment upon the basis of Christian principles, so we must exempt all other phases of social life. But this cannot be done. Everything that is involved in the relations of men to one another should be Christ-centered. The teachings of Christ apply to all of life, or they are not applicable at all.

SECULARISM IN DIPLOMACY

Pitman B. Potter

THE INVITATION TO DISCUSS THE EXTENT TO WHICH DIPLOMACY IS carried on in our day upon a secular rather than upon a religious plane comes both as a distinct opportunity and also as something of a challenge. It is an opportunity to consider an aspect of the conduct of diplomacy to which ordinarily very little attention is given and which may quite possibly reveal features of the situation fully as important as those ordinarily discussed, such as personnel, procedure, publicity, and so on. At the same time the challenge to diplomacy, or to those engaged in it, is potentially very sharp. In so far as diplomacy has become secularized, why has this occurred? Is it not a very dubious change? And what can be done about it?

One explanation must be made before proceeding further. By the term "diplomacy" it is certain that most students of international relations understand, and rightly, the sending and receiving of diplomatic representatives and the activities of these representatives, including the negotiation and signing of treaties. But it should be pointed out that international relations are conducted today by several other methods in addition. The system of consular representation, or rather of consular administration, which is at least as old as, if not older than, diplomatic representation, with which, in addition, it is closely associated, must not be overlooked or denied its special share of attention, for it accounts for a large proportion of international or intergovernmental action. The institution of international conference, which grows out of diplomacy but reaches a much higher plane and ultimately attains to the formulation and adoption of international statutes and constitutions, is taking over more and more of the work which formerly was handled by the diplomats. International administrative agencies—such as river commissions, sanitary councils, postal bureaus, and the like—entrusted with the application of international conventions on all kinds of subjects, are taking over a good deal of the work previously performed by consuls. International courts are increasing in number and in jurisdiction, and this development is very likely to continue and become more rather than less significant. Finally, all such institutions are being gathered together in general systems, such as the League of Nations, or now the United Nations, the Pan-America Union or Union of American States, and other federal systems. There is even talk today of setting up a world government on the model of the United States or the Swiss Confederation, if not something still more highly unified. Obviously our problem is not merely that of secularism in diplomacy but of secularism in the conduct, supervision, and control of international affairs by all of the methods now employed for that purpose. As will soon appear, the answers to our questions will vary somewhat in proportion as we examine the situation in respect to the older and simpler methods of diplomacy or the newer and more advanced methods of international government.

A word may be said by way of definition on the other half of our problem. By secularism is here meant irreligion in general or, more specifically, action, or thought and action, with reference to life here and now on this earth and according to profane standards, rather than with reference to future life in another world and according to the will of God. As Dr. Loemker has so well brought out, secularism becomes a general point of view or philosophy or even a total atmosphere; but in so far as it can be sharply formulated, it seems to consist of the elements just indicated. And I hope that you will not misunderstand me if I say that for the moment I am not assuming that secularism is either good or bad, but just trying to define it clearly. It might turn out that secularism would be much more harmful in certain departments of international relations than in others, but this is a part of our main problem and must be left for later consideration.

I feel that it is also necessary to insist at this point that we cannot safely equate secularism with absence of the Christian faith or religion with Christianity, and much less with Protestantism, in spite of our own allegiances. The crucial importance of this distinction in connection with the problem which we are considering is obvious. It would be one thing to assess the value and practicability of conducting international relations according to Protestant Christian standards and quite another if we bear in mind other religious codes also. And I seriously doubt whether many of us would regard the devout Catholic or Mohammedan as irreligious or secular in any sense of that term, general or technical. Again, no moral judgment is intended for the moment but merely a preliminary statement of premises; we shall return to this question later.

Changes in Diplomacy and Conference

Reference was made earlier to a change which has come over the conduct of diplomacy—in the strict sense of that term, to return to our first question—in modern times. There is no question about the facts of the case. The staff of diplomacy formerly included a larger proportion of clerical personalities than it does today—apart entirely from the diplomacy of Rome, Byzantium, and other ecclesiastical institutions—and even where this was not the case, the diplomat was invested with a sacred character and surrounded with an aura of religious protection. Faint traces of this treatment even adhered to the consul in antiquity and in medieval times. Finally, treaty making was almost a religious ceremony until early modern times, and the blessing of the Deity was commonly invoked at the beginning of treaty texts. All this has greatly changed today. The ambassador is still held to be entitled to exceptional respect and protection—at least by most countries—but this is traced not to transcendental sources, nor even, recently, to principles of national sovereignty; rather it is based on the mere practical necessities of the situation. As for the lowly consul, although he is a very useful fellow, if not as fully appreciated as he should be, he lacks today all traces of the supernatural and sometimes all dignity and glamour. And the practice of invoking the Deity in treaty agreements has all but disappeared; it is related that the absence of any such reference in the Covenant of the League of Nations or the Treaty of Versailles called forth unfavorable comment in the United States Senate in 1919.

There appears to be little doubt that the diplomat and the treaty agreement have lost a certain amount of standing, dignity, and force as a result of the change just reviewed. Even if one approved such a change on other grounds, or saw little prospect of reverting to the older practice, there can be no denying that the change has detracted from the respect paid to diplomats and to treaty agreements. The change is probably but a phase of a general alteration of manners and morals, but its incidence is particularly noticeable here. It has undoubtedly been re-enforced by a certain amount of disillusionment concerning diplomacy and treaty making in general, to which it has, in turn, contributed.

The international conference likewise was once an institution to which a considerable amount of religious feeling attached, in part as a result of its personnel and its connection with diplomacy, and in part because it seemed in its very nature an institution of serious and solemn import. During the Middle Ages a number of church councils had, indeed, the effect of setting the style for the international conference in time of peace, and this situation persisted down to the Peace of Westphalia, three hundred years ago. Indeed, traces of this sort of thing survived well down into the present century, at least in Europe and America. By way of qualification it should probably be said that the international conference tended, because of its size and complexity and somewhat advanced or elevated status, to lose some of the religious element present in primitive diplomacy, and that the more highly developed the conference, the more secular it became.

An extensive change has, in other words, come over the scene today. The personnel of international conferences now consists predominently of laymen or—even further to the left—of technicians. The style and procedure of international conference have departed even further from those of diplomacy. Conferences are not, as once was the case, organized and held on isolated occasions, which made special preparation, and even a special justification, rather necessary. They are held largely in series, as more or less subordinate aspects of larger institutions, almost as a matter of routine, and with far less of the glamour and exceptional dignity and force of other days. As a result, international conference has, like diplomacy, lost a good deal of its moral impressiveness and doubtless some of its moral force.

Changes in International Administration

International administration is still further removed from sacred ground. Like the consul, the international administrator deals with wave lengths, metric units, vaccines and serums, exchange points, and the buoyage and lighting of coasts. These activities have originated since the religious attitude in the conduct of interstate affairs suffered eclipse, partial if not complete. Once upon a time the gods of the boundary line played some part in the delimitation of frontiers, but that was a very restricted section of international administration, and even this phenomenon has now virtually disappeared. Both religious and ecclesiastical questions are conspicuous by their absence in activities of international administration today and for rather obvious and compelling reasons. The vast increase of technical problems coming forward and demanding treatment in this field—economic and financial problems, problems of communication and transport, problems of sanitation and public health, scientific problems of all kinds—would alone suffice to explain this shift of ground. International administration appears to most students of world affairs to be the high point in international organization, the most promising type of international activity, both the most serviceable and the most effective form of organized international co-operation. It is, for example, the department, or the sector, where the culmination of international control is encountered, namely, international sanctions or enforcement. It constitutes, on the other hand, the low point or the low sector in the conduct of international relations as far as secularization is concerned. No contrast could be stronger than that encountered at this stretch of the line.

When we turn to international arbitration and adjudication, we move back a slight degree in the direction of diplomacy and sacred principles. Arbitration dates back to the dawn of international relations. It is logically a phase of international administration, but, for reasons which we cannot stop to examine here, it partakes largely of diplomacy. The arbitrator and judge, indeed, goes definitely beyond the diplomat and quite clearly approaches the priest or deity in the role which he is called upon to perform, and this has been rather frankly recognized in the past. In modern times, however, even this has changed. International law, the chief concern of the arbitrator and judge in international litigation, was once regarded as largely "the law of nature and of nature's God," or at least as derived therefrom. During the past three centuries, however, the tendency to rest international law upon international practice and agreement, upon so-called "positive" foundations, has grown to such strength and proportions that the element of natural law or divine law has almost disappeared. Today the grounds upon which the International Court of Justice of the United Nations is instructed to base its decisions contain only secular elements. More and more international law and adjudication resemble the pedestrian and prosaic procedures of the county court.

When we come at last to those very general systems into which the individual international institutions of special character that we have been reviewing are gathered, such as the United Nations, the religious note is all the more conspicuously absent. It is, in fact, in connection with the individual and original institutions of international action that the deeper emotional and religious motivations and expressions emerge rather than in the more or less synthetic and certainly more derivative and general institutions, which arise at a level much farther from the roots of human life, individual or social. Finally there exists a still further reason why secularism provides an easy escape from difficulties on this level, a reason connected with the fact that such systems are general, not only with respect to the types of institutions involved and subject matters treated but in membership as well; of this more later.

CAUSES AND EFFECTS OF SECULARISM

Now, if you will permit me, I will indulge in a personal confession. I have long been aware of the increasingly secular character of international organization and procedure as just reviewed, although I have never spelled it out in as complete detail as this until now. I have also regarded this secularization as a good thing, although I was not unaware of the loss of prestige and influence on the part of various international institutions as portrayed above. My attitude was derived in part from a very general preference for reason as over against emotion as a basis of human living, and also from a feeling that the conduct of international affairs would be improved by being simplified and kept upon a plane of practical utility. I do not believe that these preferences seriously interfere with my perception of the actual state of affairs. I shall be interested to see what happens to them as I proceed to consider further why the secularization in question has taken place, its beneficial or harmful character, and what is to be done about it.

It seems quite clear that the reduction and near elimination of the religious element from the conduct of international relations resulted from the rather general secularization of individual and social life during the latter part of the nineteenth and the early part of the twentieth century rather than from any causes peculiar to the international sphere. A similar effect has been noted in national and local government, in education, and elsewhere. There had, moreover, been felt or heard no particular objection to this element in diplomacy and treaty making on the part of those affected by it previously. The alteration of the machinery and procedure for the conduct of international affairs (development of conference and administrative agencies and kindred institutions) provided a peculiarly concordant background, as has been seen; but the real causal factors operating in the situation lay deeper. Diplomacy merely suffered from a general secularizing process which was being felt at the same time in almost all walks of human life. In this respect it hardly seems necessary to differentiate among the various forms of international institutions examined.

Perhaps we should push this analysis a little further. Is it not true that the splitting up of the churches into many sects intensified the danger of secularism in the conduct of public affairs? It was obviously impossible to split up the public interest and government in the same manner, and the only remedy was to transfer this action to a secular plane. The fact that some of the sects were, in their very origin and nature, intensely religious or pietistic also redoubled the difficulty of retaining a connection between them and the conduct of public business. Finally, in so far as certain sects developed pacifistic views, and became highly critical of international relations, the effect was enhanced still further. All this is said for the moment merely by way of explanation, not in order to imply any judgments or conclusions.

Room for differences of opinion is obviously available on the issue of whether secularization has helped or harmed the conduct of international relations, and if so how much. If one believes that any secularization is harmful, he will tend to see harmful effects of that process in the international field. If he believes secularization to be beneficial, he will tend to discover improvements as a result. Both of these general attitudes or prejudices are rather unreliable as guides to sound conclusions at this point. The loss of prestige and influence on the part of diplomacy and treaty making already noted will confirm the former. On the contrary, it may be hard to detect any improvements in diplomacy which could be chalked up on the credit side unless it is that men are now compelled to judge the value of international institutions and procedures more rationally and objectively than when they were part of a ceremonial, although this is a gain as far as it goes. The major improvemets in international organization in recent decades may have contributed to furthering the process of secularization, but they did not result therefrom.

I should like to go as far as I can in conceding a loss in international relations as a result of secularization. Undoubtedly there has been a considerable loss of inspiration and of sanction—in the ancient meaning of that term—for international transactions as a result of their increasing secularization, leading to the impairment of influence already mentioned. I recall a reference in some of my reading as a college student a good many years ago to "the appalling dullness of unreligious people," as I remember the phrase. Well, international relations and diplomacy have tended to become pretty dull at times, when not lighted by the flames of possible or actual war. At the same time we should avoid exaggerating the extent to which diplomacy was, even in the time of the Holy Roman Empire or the College of Fetiales, truly inspired or controlled by religion. Too often the sacred note was invoked to cover most evil political machinations indeed. It is extremely difficult to assess the precise extent to which diplomacy has lost ground as a result of secularization, especially when such great improvements have been made in that activity in other ways.

One line of thought might be mentioned here in order to complete our statement of the problem, and then left after brief treatment in view of its inconclusive character. Is it to be asserted that no department or type of human activity—such as bridgebuilding or discharging one's debts—can properly or wisely or safely be left to rest on a secular plane? Or may some activity be allowed so to rest if it does not relate to the more ultimate or mystical aspects of human life? If such exception can be made, perhaps some aspects of the conduct of international relations might fall within that group, although it is perfectly certain that diplomacy and international co-operation do deal with deeply significant human issues. Perhaps it might be suggested—with all respect—that if anybody in the world needs to pray and pray hard today, it is precisely the diplomat and the international official!

A great deal of difference in our conclusions will be made, of course, by the rigidity or flexibility of our definition of secularism, referred to at the very outset. If we require reference to an afterlife in another world and divine guidance in order to avert the charge of secularism, it is going to be difficult for those in charge of international affairs to comply. Certainly international relations are conducted with the improvement of living conditions here and now, on this earth and in our lifetime, as the goal; and it is difficult to see how this could be otherwise. Similarly, it is difficult to see how, given the nature or the subject matter of international relations, it would be possible for diplomats and international administrators to regard the divine will or any other transcendental standard as their guide except in a very general manner. On the other hand, if by religion or the religious attitude we mean serious, sincere, and constant concern for the welfare of humanity, spiritual as well as physical, and a loyalty to the highest ideals which men have formed concerning their relations one to another and their place in the universe, then the prospect alters immediately and profoundly. Indeed it is not too much to say that in the past century—since the Crimean War, the American Civil War, and the decade 1855-65, in general—a noticeable change has come over the conduct of international relations. In spite of Bismarckian *Realpolitik*, continued British imperialism, dollar diplomacy, atavistic Italian and German and Japanese brutality, and Marxian proletarianism the vicious cynicism of the eighteenth and early nineteenth centuries has given way to a much more socially conscious and conscientious attitude. If, to avoid the charge of secularism in the conduct of international affairs, you demand otherworldliness and the adoption of a close and literal adherence to the word of God, you won't get it, and then you will have to admit that this is one area where secularism is unavoidable and must be tolerated. If a deep concern for the welfare of men's souls and bodies, according to the highest inspiration and enlightenment available from the most devoted and religious leaders of humanity is sufficient, then there is no need to despair.

One other somewhat formal aspect of the situation, and yet one which has a serious bearing upon the essential core of our problem, should be mentioned. Reference was made earlier to the criticism of the League of Nations Covenant on the ground that it contained no reference to the Deity. The same thing might incidentally be said concerning the Charter of the United Nations. The inevitable rejoinder must be, however: "To what deity would it be possible to address an invocation in such circumstances, given the diversity of creeds followed by the member nations?" It seems rather pitiful that, in avoiding favoritism among the gods, we should end up by having no God at all. I well remember how shocked I was when I went from the mild religion of Harvard to the absence of any religion at all in the state universities of the Middle West, the product of the effort to be nonsectarian! But the fact is that if we wish to avoid secularism in international affairs, we shall have to be willing to transcend not only the boundaries among denominations and sects in the Christian Church but also the boundaries between Christians and Jews, Christians and Mohammedans, Christians and Buddhists, and other religious faiths. If we do this, we can hope for sympathy from many quarters in the matter which we have at heart.

In sum, it is quite accurate to assert that there has been a strong swing in the direction of secularism in the conduct of international affairs in the past century, for special reasons peculiar to that field, but more because of general social trends outside. But the present situation is far from hopeless. Trends in the direction of unity among the churches are undoubtedly having a beneficial effect in this connection. If a moderate attitude is taken in what is demanded of the diplomat and international administrator, results may be had far above the level of behavior a century and a half ago. Nowhere today do men engaged in international affairs feel free to boast of their indifference to the deeper principles of the human spirit as they did only eighty years ago or less. It probably is definitely too much to ask for the conduct of international affairs with a specific reference to another life in another world. It is distinctly not too much to ask our representatives and public officials to seek and to serve the spiritual as well as the material needs of men in their activities, and not merely the political expediences which today too often serve as their guide.

SECULARISM
IN THE INTERNATIONAL NEIGHBORHOOD

Sherwood Eddy

THE WORLD TODAY IS AN OVERCROWDED INTERNATIONAL NEIGHBORHOOD —but there is no brotherhood. It is like a congested slum in one of our great cosmopolitan cities. The impoverished masses speak many languages, as tenement is piled upon tenement, but they share little of the wealth, the culture, the education, the patriotism, or privileges of one citizenship or of one brotherhood. Through our own fault they are largely unassimilated "foreigners" from sixty-odd nations, none of whom is our brother. Instead of "*one* world," so long envisaged under the ideal of Christian brotherhood and a great century of foreign missions, we have, in fact, two worlds, based on two ideologies that are at swords' points, in the condition of what Walter Lippmann calls a "cold war." There are many who fear that this cold war may develop into a shooting World War III.

Christians must recognize clearly that if World War III should come, it would not be just "another war." We ended World War II with an atomic bomb that could blow up one city like Hiroshima, kill a hundred thousand people, and devastate twenty square miles. But if—God forbid—World War III should come, we would begin with a bigger and better bomb that would devastate four hundred square miles, blow up a state like Maryland, and kill—immediately or by a lingering death—an unknown multitude of people.

Vishinsky was right at one point: we *have* warmongers in the United States. There are men in our country who consider themselves patriots, who honestly believe in a preventive war against Russia. They know that we could destroy a score of the cities, industrial areas, dams, and power centers of western Russia in a few weeks, and they think that this would end the war before it began. But the Soviet Union, with the largest land armies in the world, already in force in Berlin, in Vienna, and in many strategic cities in Europe, within a week of the dropping of our first bomb—or long before it, if they saw it coming—

would be in Paris, in Rome, and in all the strategic capitals of Europe. We could not bomb and destroy a million French men, women, and children, or a million citizens in Rome, because of the presence of a small Russian army. We should then be in for another Thirty Years' War which no one could win. Then all continental Europe, perforce, would go Communist. Just as no man dared lift a hand against Hitler when he dominated his sixteen slave states, no man could effectively lift a hand against Stalin. Harold Laski told me that if Britain were in this war, civilization as we know it would perish in the British Isles. He told me that he flew for a thousand miles over Russia in the path of devastation left by the armies of Hitler, that he saw standing hardly a house or factory, a village or town. Eighteen million were dead, soldiers and civilians, and twenty million wounded or crippled in Russia.

Surely if we are Christians—and there are seven hundred million who profess to be such in our wartorn world—we must find some solution other than atomic war, which can now wreck wide areas on our planet. Or by the creative and constructive release of atomic energy we can build a new and better world. But to build a better world there is no other way than God's way, the Christian way. The world must not be an overcrowded and impoverished slum neighborhood—a babel of many languages and ideologies—but *one brotherhood.* And that is the responsibility of the Christian Church. For us it is a matter of life or death, of victory or defeat, of the highest glory of God, with peace on earth among men of good will. Or it will be our final shame and inexcusable failure in a world devastated by atomic war.

A LOOK AT THE WORLD

I will now endeavor to write of this overcrowded neighborhood among thirty nations where my traveling work has taken me for the last fifty years. We shall glance rapidly over a world that is even now lining up on one of the two sides of this cold war, or at small nations striving desperately to maintain their neutrality before an all-engulfing war of wide destruction. A little more than fifty years ago I went to India for student work for fifteen years. Then for the next fifteen years, as Secretary for Asia of the Y.M.C.A., my work carried me from Japan, Korea, and China to India, Turkey, Egypt, and the

Middle East. In India I lived for ten days in the house of Gandhi, and more briefly still with Nehru. Nehru had already been eight years in prison, with almost every member of his family, three of whom came out of their imprisonment to die. I little dreamed when I was a guest in his home that he would so soon be the successful prime minister of a free, self-governing India. Nor did I dream that Gandhi, single-handed and unarmed, with no weapon but love, would, by nonviolent means alone, set free 400,000,000 of his fellow Indians from the world's strongest empire. I shall describe later some of the profound changes I have seen taking place over the whole of Asia.

During the summer of 1947 I visited the crucial countries of Europe and tried to make a study of the European crisis. I shall now endeavor to pass hastily in review some of the principal countries in this world neighborhood.

I found Europe wartorn, devastated, and demoralized, with many of its cities bombed into rubble. As my wife and I motored for a thousand miles in Germany, great areas of every city we saw were in rubble and ashes, except unscathed Heidelberg. Not only the buildings but the character of the German people seemed to be in rubble. The German masses seem to have lost their integrity. All Europe is engaged in the brute struggle for survival. At one time there were in Europe forty million homeless, twelve million displaced persons who feared to return to the land of their birth, and several million refugees driven back to impoverished Germany after it had lost a quarter of its arable land. Over wide areas of continental Europe we found demoralization and an increase of gambling, betting, thieving, and prostitution. Europe is now largely materialistic, and often pagan. J. Hutchinson Cockburn, of the World Council of Churches, in Geneva said: "Europe has now become a mission field like Asia." Europe today is in the midst of another Dark Age. There is widespread fear, hate, division, and distrust, rending Europe into two blocs, two worlds, two conflicting ideologies. There is as yet no sign of lasting peace, but the desperate fear of World War III.

We found also widespread signs of world revolution. All Europe, most of Asia, and some of the awakening continent of Africa, are swinging to the left. The hitherto underprivileged classes are now frequently in power. We found France, Italy, and Germany desperate, drifting perilously near the edge of the precipice of chaos, civil war, and revolution, which might make possible a Communist dictatorship.

We found evidence of the universal guilt of the Nazis and of the atrocities of Hitler's SS troops in Germany and in every country they had occupied. We visited the concentration camp of Dachau, where 238,000 persons had been put to death by every known means of torture, disease, and poison gas. Here one boy of fourteen, named Zieries, whose father, a camp commander, had given him a birthday rifle, with parental approval had practiced on the prisoners until he had shot fifty! He had no sense of guilt, but even after the priest had labored with him said: "Father, I did no wrong. They were only prisoners." With the exception of two liberal anti-Nazi resisters, we did not meet a single German in any interview who showed any adequate sense of responsibility or any sense of national guilt. We attended the trial of thirty keepers of the Buchenwald camp, who had put to death 51,000 prisoners. In Czechoslovakia we saw evidences of 350,000 Czechs who had died in German concentration camps under conditions of barbarous cruelty.

THE FUTURE OF GERMANY

We were, nevertheless, convinced of the futility and utter fatality of the Potsdam Agreement based on the morbid Morgenthau plan to keep Germany artificially pauperized in semistarvation, where the capacity for work and hope for the future were disappearing. Nearly all agreed that communism cannot be combated if we let Germany starve. As the people believed Hitler's false promises when they were hungry and desperate in 1932, they may believe Russia's false promises and turn communistic if we blindly try to crush Germany down to a dangerous standard of semistarvation and prevent the economic recovery of all central Europe. All agreed, however, on rigid inspection and continued control to prevent the military recovery of Germany. If the United States insists, however, that all recovery must be under monopolistic capitalism through the big cartels that financed Hitler, it will, of course, increase the danger of war.

The Potsdam plan abandoned the Atlantic Charter and set out to lower the standard of life in Germany and destroy its industry and trade. Germany was to lose a fourth of her arable land, and was not allowed enough fertilizer even for her own need. Her export of machinery was arbitrarily restricted to 31 percent of her 1938 total, machine tools to 38 per cent, chemicals to 40 per cent, dye stuffs to 58 per cent, precision instruments to 70 per cent. Germany is the keystone of the economy of Europe. Yet when all Europe needs unlimited steel for reconstruction, Potsdam would slash German steel output from 19,000,000 tons to a maxium production of 5,800,000, for which only her older plants could be used. When all Europe lacked rolling stock, Germany was allowed to manufacture none whatever. Above all, she must not export coal, when only three countries even in prewar Europe could supply it—Britain and Poland, which can supply but little; and Germany, now the only hope of reconstruction for central Europe. The Potsdam document fixed the permanent industrial output of Germany at about the figure of 1932, the year of mass unemployment that produced Hitler. As a cure for Nazism, Potsdam prescribed the permanent reproduction of economic misery and despair that brought Hitler into power!

It is to be hoped that the Allies have now learned that the Potsdam policy was fatal, though France fears German recovery and Russia will try to prevent it unless she can control Germany for her own ends. The United States and Britain are left with four alternatives: We might propose that 25,000,000 emigrate from Germany; but who would take them? We might starve that many and reduce the population; America might provide several billion dollars a year to subsidize an undernourished Germany in perpetual unemployment; or, subject to strict control against remilitarization, we might allow Germany to save herself and all central Europe from being a congested slum and a perpetual poorhouse. This is the wise conclusion to which the Americans and the British have finally been driven.

A Look at Britain and France

Among the neediest countries we visited in Europe, Great Britain is in unbelievable poverty. A few years ago the British Empire covered a quarter of the globe, with 500,000,000 population, and Britain was the great exporting industrial nation with the largest foreign investments in the world, twenty billion dollars. But Britain suffered the most colossal losses in the war. When India and Burma are independent, she will have lost four fifths of the population of the empire. Figuring in dollars, Britain lost in the war over thirty billion dollars, or a quarter of her wealth. Britain's present wealth of ninety billions is less than half the gross *income* of the United States in the year 1947.

Britain lost seventeen out of her twenty billions in foreign investments, while her external debt was increased from two to fifteen billion dollars. She must increase her exports to 175 per cent to survive, yet she now has only half her prewar export trade, with an annual deficit of two billion dollars; while the United States has a surplus of some twelve billions. Four million buildings were destroyed or damaged during the war with a property loss of six billions, and Britain lost over half her shipping. Food Minister John Strachey denied Dr. Bicknell's charge that the British people are being slowly starved, "dying from lack of crude calories," but personally I found the food in Britain the poorest and most tasteless of any country we visited in Europe. Ernest Bevin told us Britain had only six-weeks' food supply on hand instead of the usual four-months' supply.

The United Kingdom now finds herself with 48,000,000 people overcrowded in an area the size of Oregon, with few natural resources. Britain's economy was always based on coal, yet the coal mines were depleted by centuries of private profiteering, and annual production has fallen from 240,000,000 tons to 189,000,000. Although she used to export 40,000,000 tons annually, today there is little more than enough for domestic use. Only in January, 1948, could Britain begin to export coal. The average American miner produces five times as much as a miner in the unmechanized British mines. In textiles, with only 5 per cent of British looms automatic, the American weaver can handle ten times as many looms as the British. British machinery is worn and old-fashioned, and the workers are weary, physically and psychologically. In the present desperate crisis Britain must either cease to be a great power, encourage ten million of her population to emigrate, or she must modernize her whole industrial plant, which will take time and will cost several billion dollars—which she does not possess. Despite this desperate economic situation we found amazing courage in the British people. The heart of Britain is as sound as English oak. Great Britain has only a fraction of America's graft and crime. The Labor Government is doing as well as any government could possibly do under almost impossible circumstances.

We found many of our old friends in England shabbily dressed, but no one complained. When we lunched with Lord Astor, it was not like the old days on his beautiful estate at Cliveden. He apologized for asking us to a restaurant, as he had not enough ration points to provide a meal for guests at home. We drove out for tea to the beautiful estate of one of the two British tobacco millionnaires. He complained bitterly of the income tax that was compelling them to cut into their remaining capital every year. There are now only fifty families in Britain with a yearly income of $400,000. In the higher brackets nearly nineteen out of every twenty shillings are taken in income tax; that leaves the richest families a net income of only about $25,000 a year, on which they can no longer keep up their estates. There has been a wide redistribution of income, however. Few are left very rich, and fewer are destitute as formerly. Britain's plight is due to the war, not to her modest plans of socialization, which were for her an absolute necessity and which are succeeding on the whole very well. But her economic situation is none the less serious.

The situation in France is far more desperate. France never recovered from the losses of World War I, while the greater moral losses of World War II have left deep scars upon her soul. She was betrayed by her own "grave diggers," who were more eager to appease Hitler and believe his false promises than they were to give justice to labor under Leon Blum's "New Deal." The French people today lack bread; they lack coal; they lack steel; they have not recovered their prewar standard of either production or consumption. With their rampant individualism, in which liberty has often turned the license, the French lack the disciplined character of the British and the Dutch. We were told by a member of the cabinet that if France cannot stabilize prices within a few months and quickly rebuild her industry, she will sink into civil war and chaos. The Communists, who are the second largest party in France, seek to weaken the country by a chain reaction of endless strikes, to prevent recovery, and to plunge France into civil war that may enable them to seize the government as Lenin did in Russia in 1917. Conditions in Italy are very similar to those in France, but they are more advanced toward a possible revolution.

THE SITUATION IN THE UNITED STATES

When we returned from devastated Europe, we found the United States the only country left in the world with fabulous mass production, prosperity, and wealth. Our country alone has emerged from the war enriched, amid an impoverished world. The United States has now about two thirds of the industrial production of the world, twenty billion dollars worth of streamlined industrial plants that were never bombed, and two thirds of the gold supply of the world. According to the Department of Commerce, our exports for 1947 were over nineteen billion dollars, our imports eight billion, with a staggering balance of over eleven billion, or nearly a billion dollars a month. If we could utilize half this sum—only six billion a year for three years, or better, divided over a four-year period—it would, I believe, make possible the recovery of western Europe, avert communist dictatorship, and incidentally save America herself from a depression that might drag the world down with her in ruin.

We returned from Europe with the deepening conviction that the Marshall Plan is the last hope of saving France, Italy, and Germany, the only hope for the recovery of western Europe, and of averting a depression in the United States. If this is true, I fear that, in the words of Lincoln, "*We* shall nobly save or meanly lose the last, best hope of earth." I believe that it is a matter of life and death and that the time is short. We can save the world, avert a communist revolution and a world depression, or we can lose our own souls and perish amid our miser's gold.

During the summer of 1947 in Europe I was driven to hope in the Marshall Plan for several reasons: In the first place Europe was hungry. For Christians there was the word of Christ: "I was hungry and you fed me." Much more serious, the sixteen nations of western Europe that were eager to participate in the Marshall Plan needed industrial reconditioning even more than they needed food. Although the United States emerged from the war with twenty billion dollars worth of the most modern streamlined industrial plants, the machinery of Europe was outworn, or obsolete, or had been bombed, or had suffered devastation from the long war. If these sixteen nations could modernize their industrial equipment, they would not only be able to feed and clothe themselves, but they could defend themselves from communist revolution from within, or from the invasion of Soviet armies from without. If, on the other hand, these nations were left to sink in despair, if the keystone nations in Europe collapsed and

Europe began to go communist, our stockpile of bombs would be dropped, and World War III, as an atomic war and planetary catastrophe, would begin—because of our short-sighted selfishness.

If the plan were not adopted and the sixteen nations of western Europe, which were the great trading nations of the world, were allowed to sink unrecovered in poverty, our foreign trade would almost cease. Already threatened by the dangerous spiral of inflation and having already broken so many economic laws, we would be headed for another depression of vast unemployment. We would then drag down the other nations of an already war-impoverished world into a depression, caused by the only rich and prosperous nation left, a nation that could have saved the world if it would. Of course the monopolistic profiteers that had emerged from the war with fifty-two billion dollars in war profits, and who demanded an immediate reduction of taxes so that they could make fifty-two billion more in peace profiteering, would be so blinded by their own greed that they could not see this.

What About Russia?

We found Russia the unsolved problem of the world. Western Europe is convinced that the Politburo has decided that it does not want a recovered, prosperous, or united Europe, but would prefer starvation, desperation, and chaos, that might lead to civil war and a communist dictatorship in countries like France, Italy, and Germany. There was evidence, however, that the attitude of Molotov, intransigent and sometimes insulting at Paris, London, and other conferences, is due to his personal ambition to succeed Stalin, whose choice is Zhdanov, a much better man. Molotov's ambition threatens Europe with World War III, despite the fact that eighteen million are dead and twenty million said to be crippled in devastated Russia, which is at present too weak to win a war but yet might gain country after country if they sank into revolution.

The crux of the whole world situation—the question of a devastating atomic war or a creative atomic age of peace, prosperity, and abundance for all—centers in our relation with Russia. There is no country that is so important for us to understand, or that is so hard to understand, as Russia. Therefore let us try sympathetically to understand it and only then to judge it. In my fifteen visits to Russia—

twice under the czar and thirteen times under the communist regime
—I have tried to understand the Russian enigma. Russia matters to
the world profoundly. Its vast area is four times the size of Europe,
more than two and a half times the size of the United States, and
nearly a sixth of the area of the habitable globe. When the largest
country in the world, with vast undeveloped resources, attempts the
first total revolution in history, something is bound to happen, both
for good and evil.

Personally I am proud to be an American and would not change
my country for any other in the world. Russia is the last country
on earth where I would want to live. I have seen the Soviet Union
pass through three awful purges, in which millions have perished;
and there are even now unnumbered multitudes in slave labor camps
behind the iron curtain in that police state that denies all our four
freedoms.

To understand the Soviet Union we must look on both sides of
the shield, their side and ours. After fifteen visits to Russia I came
to the conclusion that, relative to the four Christian principles of
justice, brotherhood, liberty, and love expressed in loyalty to religion,
as truly as the leaders of the Anglo-Saxon nations stand consistently
for liberty and loyalty to religion but fail in the matter of economic
justice and racial brotherhood, so the leaders of Soviet Russia fail to
give full liberty or to support vital religion, but they stand consistently for their own interpretation of what we call economic justice
and racial brotherhood.

Let us recall the high idealism on which the Russian Revolution
was established in October, 1917. It was probably the most bloodless
in all history. Yet all the reactionary forces within and without the
Soviet Union rose at once to crush it. The vast powers of counter-
revolution finally represented by seven White Russian armies were
often aided and financed in London, Paris, Tokyo, Warsaw, and
at times even in Washington. Soviet tolerance was driven to intolerance; an infant democracy was changed to dictatorship; and evolutionary gradualism into "war communism."

Under Stalin, as Commissar for Nationalities, they sought to wipe
out all racial, religious, national, and class animosities. Here was the
largest country in the world attempting the boldest experiment in all
history. They sought to build a new society in every department of

life in the first total revolution ever attempted. There is no question about the early idealism that lay at the heart of that great experiment that climaxed a hundred years of revolutionary revolt against czarism, any more than there is of the ideals of the American Revolution. Soviet Russia, whatever its failures, abolished child labor and took the most advanced stand in the care of children. It stood for the equality of women in all walks of life; it abolished all unemployment during its three five-year plans and eliminated the periodic business cycle of "boom and bust." It provided an elaborate system of social insurance; it went in for universal education, and finally promoted the cultural and aesthetic advance of the whole population. After a thousand years of despotic autocracy and tyranny the Soviet Union took the boldest move ever known in history for economic justice and social planning. Although ruthless in its suppression of political enemies, it pioneered in its redemptive treatment of criminals. It stood passionately for the emancipation of the hitherto enslaved portion of its peasants and workers. All who have heard thousands of voices sing with deep religious fervor the "International" will never forget it:

> Arise ye prisoners of starvation!
> Arise, ye wretched of the earth!
> For justice thunders condemnation,
> A better world's in birth.
> No more tradition's chain shall bind you.
> Arise ye slaves! No more in thrall.
> The world shall rise on new foundations.
> You have been nought: You shall be all.

But for some reason Russia has got away from its early idealism and is now advancing across Europe and Asia by a gradual extension of its sphere of control, based on two contradictory principles. The first is the Marxian principle of *revolution from within;* as each country becomes rotten-ripe with injustice, they seize the government and establish a "dictatorship of the proletariat" upon the Russian model. The second is the principle of Peter the Great and Ivan the Terrible of *invasion from without.* By the invasion of Russian armies, by an expanding imperialism, by annexation after annexation, they aim to take and control country after country.

Hungary is the type of this new imperialism. This was not one of the border satellite states counted necessary to Russia's security against invasion. When Russia took control of Hungary, she allowed one fair and free election. The most democratic party in Hungary, the Smallholders (Peasant) Party, won 57 per cent of the total vote and half the places in the cabinet, while the Communists, to their surprise, won but 17 per cent. The Protestant Christian statesman Ferenc Nagy became president of the parliament and finally premier of Hungary. After trying to work with the Communists, who were backed by the Russian army of occupation, with their undisciplined excesses of robbery and rape visited upon the helpless population, Premier Nagy fled for his life to Britain and finally to the United States. He told in three frank articles in the *Saturday Evening Post*, beginning August 30, 1947, "How the Russians Grabbed My Government." It is a sorry tale of blackmail, extortion, bribery, intimidation, and torture, followed by the assassination of anti-Russian opponents. The Communists, backed by the Russian army, took over the government by the complete autocratic control of a police state of once-free Hungary.

How Shall We Deal With Russia?

The significant fact is that following that exact blueprint Russia is at this moment operating in eight countries in Europe and Asia, including northern Korea. In addition, she is taking a bolder and more advanced stand in France, Italy, and Germany, looking toward civil war and seizure of power by a communist "dictatorship of the proletariat."

If we ask what should be our policy in the face of the Soviet Union's imperialistic expansion, strangely enough we find the answer from Karl Marx himself as he warned Europe of the danger of expanding czarist imperialism that then menaced the world. Writing in poverty in his garret in London in 1853, in a series of articles for the *New York Tribune*, Marx said:

The total acquisitions of Russia during the last sixty years are equal in extent and importance to the whole Empire she had in Europe before that time. . . . And as sure as conquest follows conquest, and annexation follows annexation, so sure would the conquest of Turkey by Russia be only the prelude for the annexation of Hungary, Prussia, Galicia, and for the ultimate realization of the Slavonic Empire which certain fanatical Pan-Slavistic philosophers have dreamed of. . . . *The arrest of the Russian scheme of annexation is a matter of the highest moment. . . .* It would have been impossible for Russia to make more extensive demands upon Turkey after a series of signal victories. . . . *If the other powers hold firm, Russia is sure to retire in a very decent manner.*

Now that the Soviet Union is advancing by the same ruthless imperialism as the former czarist empire, what can we better do than follow Marx's advice to "hold firm" the line against Russia to prevent her dominance of all Europe. Let us not underestimate our own strength. In the present "cold war" of diplomacy carried on by Russia by Molotov's torrents of abuse, we do not realize that we are holding most of the trump cards. Even Hungary is not yet lost. When the time comes, at the psychological moment, Secretary Marshall will doubtless raise the case of Hungary, first before the Security Council, and if Russia once again uses the much-abused veto power, before the General Assembly. Former Premier Nagy's three articles in pamphlet form in English, French, and Russian will be a valuable document to lay before the United Nations, where many smaller nations fear absorption by advancing Soviet imperialism. Nagy and many others will be invaluable witnesses. Will Russia admit that the one election she permitted was fair and free and that the Small-holders Party won 57 per cent of the votes and half the seats in the cabinet? If so, where are those officials today? Are they living or dead, and who put them to death? Should not Hungary be restored to the government of the Smallholders Party democratically elected by the people? Should not the United Nations follow the advice of Marx and "hold firm" against this imperialistic advance of the Soviet Union, which is more ruthless and inexcusable than the advance of czarist Russia ever was? Lenin wrote: "We must be ready for trickery, deceit, lawbreaking, withholding and concealing truth." Reinhold Niebuhr, after a study of the situation in Germany, wrote in *Life* magazine, October 15, 1946: "Russian truculence cannot be mitigated by further concessions. . . . A trip through Europe . . . has convinced me that the Russians are not, and will not be, satisfied with any system of eastern Europe defenses but are seeking to extend their power over the whole of Europe." James Byrnes, after facing Molotov for two years, concluded in regard to Russia's attitude: "I do not doubt that *their ultimate goal is to dominate, in one way or another, all of Europe."* Russia's policy under Molotov has driven all our realistic statesmen to this conclusion.

A STANDARD FOR JUDGMENT

Have we any standard of judgment by which we may test or judge these two conflicting and contrasting nations—the U.S.A. and the U.S.S.R.? Let us apply our four Christian principles: justice, brotherhood, liberty, and love—the love of God and man embodied in vital religion, individual and social, that must build a new man within each of us and a new world without. We shall find that throughout a thousand years of history the Anglo-Saxon nations have always stood for two of these principles: for liberty and, by our leaders at least, for love expressed in vital religion, for our missions are the greatest on earth. For reasons that we can show we always fail, however, to give economic justice, and we fail to recognize racial brotherhood.

Russia, on the other hand, always fails on the two where we succeed. She fails in liberty, in all the four freedoms, for liberty she never knew in czarist or in Soviet Russia. And her leaders do not understand the meaning of religion. But despite these evils, the Soviet Union stands passionately—in aim and ideal at least—for economic justice, based on the social ownership of all means of production, and for equal brotherhood, or what they call "the equality and sovereignty of all races."

Where does our own country stand in the matter of economic justice? Over a thousand years ago the prophet Amos thundered God's demand for justice, that the rich stop robbing the poor. But in the United States today we have a thousand millionaires and multimillionaires, four billionaires, side by side with a third of our people ill-fed, ill-clad, and ill-housed. We have left over ten million of our people in rotting slums, urban and rural. If a Democrat or a Republican has a plan for public housing, to rebuild those slums, he is not only thwarted and defeated in his public housing program, as Franklin Roosevelt was and as Fiorello La Guardia was, but he is hated and called a "Communist," by church members in good standing—Protestant, Catholic, or Jewish—because Christian people will not stop robbing the poor! Not that we do it individually. When a blind beggar comes along the street, I do not take a penny or a dime out of his cup. But by our economic system we do it ten times more efficiently than if individually we should rob beggars.

Christ stood always for equal brotherhood. We are to love our neighbor as ourselves. But there are two nations that stand pre-eminently today for "white supremacy" over wide areas, for the segregation, and at times the degradation and robbery, of the Negro —the United States and the Union of South Africa. When I attend the United Nations Assembly, I realize that two thirds of the world's people are colored; which are these nations likely to follow at this point, the nations that stand for white supremacy and segregation, or those that stand for the "equality and sovereignty of all nations"? Did they vote with General Smuts of South Africa and his "color bar" to exploit the natives of Southwest Africa, or did they follow Mrs. Pandit of India, Nehru's sister, in the expectation that some day the colored races might attain genuine equality in the hope of life, liberty, and the pursuit of happiness?

In the Soviet Union, where they have some 180 races speaking 149 languages, with thirty principal nationalities, all are treated equally in principle and in practice. We raise now the question whether if all four Christian principles are absolutely necessary for the building of a better world, or achieving a just and lasting peace, God may not be compelled to use Russia in the matter of economic justice and brotherhood, just as he used the pagan idolater Cyrus, king of Persia, when the chosen people of Israel had failed him. We therefore conclude that God is indeed working and working effectively in Soviet Russia today. Perhaps these are among the signs of the times and the meanings of this era that the followers of Christ are called to understand.

If I am asked for the solution of the unsolved problem in our relation to Soviet Russia in the present "cold war," I would suggest these conditions: First, let us strive to put our own house in order in the matter of giving economic justice to all and recognizing equal brotherhood among all races. Second, I would seek an over-all understanding with Soviet Russia, especially on the two great danger zones where, if it comes at all, World War III will probably arise—Germany and China. One of the leading statesmen of Europe said to me that if war came at all it would arise over China. There is a great vacuum of poverty, famine, graft, the most shameful robbery of the poor by the rich known in all the world, or in all history. And there beside that vacuum in China is Russia, the high-powered storm-center, ready to rush into that vacuum. If, after the enlightening report of Secretary Marshall, and later of General Wedemeyer, of this awful graft and robbery in China, the corrupt Kuomintang will not put its house in order, and if Washington pours in more money without insisting upon thoroughgoing reform, the abysmal corruption of China may be the cause of World War III. And not only the corrupt government of China but the United States must bear the chief responsibility for this.

In the meantime, while seeking an over-all understanding and agreement with the Soviet Union, I would hold the line against the advance of the Russians in their effort to dominate Germany, Austria, Hungary, and increasing areas in Europe and Asia. I would do exactly as Marx advised Europe to do against the imperialistic expansion of czarist Russia. And I believe if we do so, they will retire just as Marx was sure czarist Russia would. If the sixteen nations of western Europe are saved by the Marshall Plan and can defend themselves against the Russian advance, then we shall win the cold war, and no shooting war need begin. I believe we should not appease Stalin and Molotov as we did Hitler. We fell back before Hitler in eight cowardly compromising retreats, culminating in the Pact of Munich. That made World II inevitable.

Personally I am not discouraged over the present world situation, nor over the United Nations. We shall learn only slowly to trust one another to the extent that we shall get beyond the abuse of the veto. We all look forward in the end to a federally organized world. But even now, with all our setbacks and failures, I believe we can see in the very imperfect functioning of fifty-seven governments in the United Nations the slow evolutionary process that is bearing us toward the great day:

> Till the war-drum throbb'd no longer, and the battle-flags were furl'd
> In the Parliament of man, the Federation of the world.

SECULARISM AND WORLD ORDER

Luman J. Shafer

I HAVE SUBSTITUTED THE WORDS "WORLD ORDER" FOR "PERMANENT peace" in the topic assigned, not because of a mere personal preference for a certain set of words, but because to me this change represents a radically different approach to the problem being discussed. The phrase "permanent peace" seems to indicate that what we seek to attain is a kind of static situation in which conflict will be eliminated. This does not adequately describe the state of affairs even within a given national community. Conflicts between social groupings in such a community have not been eliminated, but they have been channeled so that they only rarely result in actual physical combat. Peace is not, even in the national community, a "condition of quiescence where all is static," to use John Foster Dulles' phrase in his discussion of international war. What is being sought in the international field is not primarily the absence of war, to be secured by damming up the mass energies of groups in some rigid framework of peace obtained by a concert of power, but a method by which inevitable conflicts may be channeled constructively so that dynamic development can be effected without violent revolution with its accompanying bloodshed and destruction. What we are seeking is an orderly world, not a static world of permanent peace.

In attempting to achieve such an orderly world we come squarely up against the basic political factor in world life today, namely, the nation-state. The state gathers up the interests of the group within the geographical territory governed by it, secures order within that area, and regards itself as responsible for conserving the well-being of the group it embodies. To achieve this it must be prepared to defend itself against all assaults from groups without or within. It is essentially egoistic and egocentric. It would appear immoral for it to sacrifice any of its supposed interest to secure the well-being of any other state or of humanity as a whole. It is thus the apex of political life, and there is nothing above it to which it turns to conserve its own well-being or ensure its development.

Conflict of interest is certain to arise among these national groupings, as it arises among groups within states. Furthermore, situations will arise in which the *status in quo* is viewed as oppressive and intolerable, and a state or group of states will move for the alteration of this situation. Neither of these situations can be obviated in the international field any more than within individual states. Conflict of interest arises, and discontent with the *status in quo* produces dynamic situations within states. The difference in the resultant situation within states and among states lies not in the absence of conflict or lack of dynamism, but in the way these inevitable situations are met. In the national community local interests are subordinated to the well-being of the national community, and conflicts are resolved through reasonable adjustment and the progressive application of law. In the international field the state embodies the self-interest of the group and yields to no overarching interest or concern above its own will. It may be argued that it must necessarily do so, so long as there is no international instrument to which it can look for satisfaction; but, at the same time, there can be no such instrument so long as the state remains the egocentric state. There are clearly two horns to this dilemma. International anarchy makes it necessary for the state to maintain its own interests with egocentric fervor, but the egocentric state makes international anarchy inevitable.

It should be clear that any solution of this dilemma which does not deal with this basic problem is no solution at all. Disarmament, for example, is no solution, since in a situation where each state is solely responsible for protecting its own well-being it would be, in a sense, immoral for it to give up the means for this protection. The renouncing of war as an instrument of national policy is no solution so long as this nation-state relationship remains unmodified, for in that situation war is, in the last analysis, the only method of resolving a conflict of interest among the states.

What is required is some international instrument which will do for the no man's land of conflicting interest which lies among the sovereign states what has been done by the sovereign state in its own territory. This is what was sought in the League of Nations and what lies behind the United Nations. It is what is contemplated by those who insist that the only adequate organization for this purpose is a world state. This chapter cannot be a discussion of particular organizations, past, present, or future. It can only attempt to outline some of the basic requirements for any organization capable of giving an ordered world, and then proceed to consider what help can be expected from secularism for furnishing these requirements.

Two Basic Requirements

We shall consider two of these basic requirements: (1) the organization must be supernational in character, involving definite limitations of national sovereignty; and (2) its operations must be based on international law.

As I have already said, in the world situation that has obtained up to the present, the nation-state has been the apex of political government, autonomous, self-centered, concerned only for its own welfare. This has left the area of interests that lie in the international field without political government. The nation has been its own judge of where its interests lie; and when interests have conflicted, the final arbitrament has been by force, producing international anarchy.

Thus, an international organization will need to be above the nation and so constituted that it can deal progressively and effectively with conflicts that arise, executing even-handed justice and guaranteeing to each nation fundamental and inalienable rights, such as the right to exist and make its contribution to the world community.

It is obvious that this cannot be done unless the international organization is something more than a consultative organization based on the full sovereignty of each individual state. It may not be possible to go much beyond this in the initial stages of the development, as when, in the founding of the United States, federation preceded union. But a league, as experience has shown, tends to become a system, not for bringing about change through orderly procedures, but an alliance system of those interested in maintaining the *status in quo*. The international organization will need to be something other and beyond the sovereign state, deriving its authority from considerations more all-inclusive than the individual states alone. Just as the social group is something more than the sum of the individuals who make it up, the world organization will need to be something more than the sum of the nations which compose it. Each individual unit will possess its own rights; it will not be absorbed in the whole, nor lose its unique identity, but each unit will, at the same time, be limited by the larger interests of the whole. In other words, world organization, to be capable of resolving the dilemma in which we find ourselves, will need to be concerned with the total human situation in which each particular grouping will have its proper place, its own peculiar rights and duties.

It is at this point that many contend that no such organization can be successful unless it is based, not on the nation as such, but on the people themselves. This is pressed still further by those who contend that individuals within states must be subject to the jurisdiction of the world organization and not under its control through the medium of the state. This principle was introduced, for example, in the trials of the German war criminals in the interpretation of "crimes against humanity." This is an important consideration; but whether representation in the world organization be based on states or on populations, in either case the organization will need to be grounded in principle on the concept of the human community, concerned for the welfare, not of a particular group, but of the totality of which each group is a necessary and legitimate part.

This means the limitation of national sovereignty. The nation will need to relinquish the right to decide what its own interests are in the light of those interests alone, and instead will have to allow those interests to be accommodated to the interests of the larger community of which it is a part; it will need to pool its interests with those of others in all matters where there is common concern.

This leads us to the next consideration. It is obvious that this limitation of existing national prerogatives cannot safely be done if the international organization seeks to effect the accommodation of national interests by a balancing of self-interests on the basis of the relative power of states. In other words, the international organization will need to bring into focus in its operation something more than the self-interest of the individual state backed by power. An organization which brings states together, each resting back on its sovereignty and each backed by military power, in order to effect a balancing of interests is a great advance over the sporadic unilateral arrangements brought about through the initiation of individual states. The mutual agreement of states to continue in open conference in an organization such as the United Nations, in order to prevent conflict from issuing in war, is a great advance over the old method of unilateral secret diplomacy and unilateral or multilateral treaties; but unless progressively the decisions of the world organization are made on the basis of a common opinion of mankind, and some concept of justice, it will be difficult to achieve a peaceful world order. There will need to be back of all decisions a respect for that which flows, not from individual interest or balance of power, but from the demands of a common humanity. Decisions made in the endeavor to arrive at some kind of rough approximation of justice for all should progressively create precedents and gradually issue in a kind of statute law for the international community. A world state with a properly constituted legislature would be the logical demand of the situation. It is a question whether this is either practicable or desirable; but whatever the form of the organization, it would seem to be clear that a basic requisite for world order is the development of a body of international law which would bear equally on all states and which would put the broad concept of justice for humanity over the self-interest of individual states.

THE WORLD COMMUNITY

Both of these requirements for world order which we have been discussing have revealed something basic to each, namely, world community. Unless the fact of world community becomes a living and powerful reality, the supernational aspect of world organization with the accompanying modification of national sovereignty cannot be realized; and similarly international law must rest solidly on a concept of a larger community whose interests overshadow and outweigh the alleged interests of any one group.

But this world community can scarcely be said to exist today, and it certainly does not exist in the real and vital sense required to sustain the world organization requisite for world order. Attempts to create a world organization indicate an embryonic sense of the need of such a community, but unless it can become a vital reality, adequate world organization cannot be maintained. Political organization rises out of the community, not the community out of organization; and world political organization must have its corresponding world community if it is to be sustained.

In all communities there are certain characteristics. When we look for these in the international field, we do not find them in the degree required. Let us take three of these: (1) the recognition of the equality of the members of the community; (2) the recognition that the good of the whole takes precedence over the good of the part; and (3) an acceptance of a minimum common view.

In common thinking today this recognition of the equality of different national groupings scarcely exists. We make a clear distinction in our minds between our particular national group and all others. The word "foreigner" is indicative of this distinction. Bergson has maintained that world community is biologically impossible because man by nature is not made to live in large-scale society. Men, he contends, are fitted by nature to live in small-scale society and can therefore never make all humanity members of their own social group on an equal basis. It is, of course, inevitable that the sense of common interest and responsibility is strongest in the small, face-to-face group; but by common tradition and common education this sense of community has nevertheless been extended to include the national group. There is a common picture in our mind of an American, and we have a sense of community with all Americans. The nation has become for us the "in" group, but all others outside the nation are still regarded as members of the "out" group. They are not in the same category with us, and for them we do not feel the same sense of responsibility as we do for our own group. A disaster in China does not move us as much as a lesser calamity at home. E. H. Carr reports that an American newspaper correspondent in Europe is said to have laid down the rule that an accident was worth reporting from abroad if it involved the death of one American, five Englishmen, ten Europeans, or a thousand Orientals. This "in" group feeling, already expanded from the small face-to-face group to the larger national group, will need to be further expanded to take in all other groups if world community is to be achieved.

The second characteristic of community to be considered is the recognition that the good of the whole takes precedence over the good of the part. In the national community local interests are strong and often blur the larger interest, but in the last analysis these local or related interests are subordinated to the general welfare. This has not yet taken place to any great extent in the international field. The current discussion in this country of the needs of the outside world is a case in point. Individuals are making real sacrifices to meet the needs of others outside our own national group, but on the level of the nation the discussion tends to emphasize the self-interest aspect of the problem. It is not thought that the needs of Europeans or Orientals, or the needs of humanity as a whole, have equal rights with the needs of Americans. It would appear to be difficult to carry out the Marshall Plan, for example, unless it can be shown that the self-interest of the American people is served thereby. Furthermore, instead of modifying its supposed self-interest for the good of humanity, a nation rather tends to identify its own self-interest with the good of the whole. For example, we tend in this country to justify any and all steps which we regard as necessary to maintain American prosperity and the American standard of living, including tariff schedules detrimental to world trade, on the ground that the well-being of the world depends on American prosperity.

The third requirement for community is a minimum common view. It does not need to be argued that this is the basis of unity in the national community. It is difficult to see how world community can be possible without what the Oxford Conference called a world ethos. In the wide diversity of peoples and cultures in the world this common view must necessarily be on a lowest common denominator basis; but unless there is some minimum agreement on basic concepts of right and wrong—for example, on the idea of justice and the relation of means to ends—real community cannot exist.

To sum up so far as we have gone: If national sovereignty is to be modified and a supernational world organization developed, a world community in the presence of which all members are regarded as equal and in which the good of the whole takes precedence over the good of the part will have to be created. Furthermore, for such an organization to be under law, there will need to be a minimum common consensus on which law can rest and by means of which it can be enforced.

What Does Secularism Offer?

What help can secularism give us in the creation of such a world community? Secularism, having cast loose from God, must find its motive power within the human framework in the well-being of mankind. But the dilemma is this: the welfare of mankind is the very concept which must be introduced into the situation if world community is to be achieved; and so long as there is nothing more powerful than the idea of that welfare itself with which to introduce it, there seems scant chance of success. What actually happens is that these self-centered national groups take over the concept of general human welfare and make the welfare of mankind mean the welfare of the particular group or groups concerned. The general welfare is quickly prostituted into particular welfare by those very national groupings which must be subordinated to the welfare of humanity as a whole if world community is to be realized. In the quotation from Robert S. Lynd in Leroy Loemker's chapter, Lynd is discussing the problem of American culture cut loose from traditional religious presuppositions. In trying to find a new ground for our culture in the general concept of human welfare he very easily assumes that American culture must discover its "richly evocative common purposes," not in any overarching considerations, human or otherwise, but in the "personality needs of the great mass of the people." Similarly, in discussing education for democracy Alexander Meiklejohn, in his book *Education Between Two Worlds*, asks: "Why educate for democracy?" He writes that we used to believe in democracy because we believed that that was the way God wanted it, but that this is no longer possible because we no longer believe that way. Consequently, he goes on to say, the only way out is for us to decide that we prefer democracy because we prefer it, and then set zealously to educate for it.

But on this basis soviet culture finds its ground in what the soviet man believes to be the needs of the Russian people, and so on through the gamut of the world's peoples. Each group may choose a quite different system with quite different moral presuppositions behind it, and there is no ground from which to view the value of any system so long as it is the system thought to be the best for the well-being of the people concerned. One group may regard the well-being of the individual person as of supreme importance; another may conclude that the individual person has no importance, except as he is a member of the collective; one group may insist that means and ends have definite moral relationship, and that justifiable means are as important as justifiable ends; another may contend that any means are justifiable in order to achieve ends that are regarded as necessary. One group may insist that justice for individuals and groups in society is a ruling concept; another may contend that justice for the individual is determined, not by a consideration of the rights of the individual, but of the demands of the state.

Thus what we actually get from secularism is not integration and universality or minimum common view, but a further disintegration and disunity with one culture grounded on human welfare, interpreted from the viewpoint of the national group, set over against another culture as firmly grounded in what is thought best for that group. Secularism, cast loose from God, offers no hope for the attainment of world community but rather contributes still further to the breakup of the world into different national groupings with no common meeting ground among them. This is quite in line with Dr. Loemker's discussion in which he concludes that one of the fruits of secularism is disunity and conflict within the person himself and in society as a whole.

It is hard to see how it will be possible to move from the present situation to world community and the world political instruments necessary to peace unless the problem of self-centeredness is radically dealt with. The self-centeredness of the nation-state has so far thwarted the development of world community. We have seen that the nation cannot "morally" yield its right to decide what is in its own interest until there is an international system that will guarantee each nation its just right, but, conversely, that such an international system cannot come into being until this national self-assertiveness surrenders to the general will. Secularism, moving within the human framework and relying on a naïve faith in the general reasonableness of mankind, must hope that there will be a gradual accommodation of these self-interests, that it will gradually come to be seen that a higher interest requires the modification of self-interest. It certainly will be futile, as Reinhold Niebuhr has pointed out in *The Children of Light and the Children of Darkness*, to "ignore the power of self-interest in human society." But if it is futile to ignore self-interest, it is equally futile to ignore its stubborn character. For a considerable period there was a hope that the interdependence of the world, the fact that the world is a physical neighborhood, would gradually issue in world community. World neighborhood was loosely equated with world community. But experience has amply shown that physical interdependence, economic interchange, and mutual acquaintance among peoples do not automatically issue in social cohesion. The world-wide links of communication and trade established in the nineteenth century were the result of a coincidence of separate self-interests, and not a process of social integration. The cohesive social integration of the national group, developing into economic nationalism, has proven again and again a more powerful force than any supposed international cohesion resulting from the casual relationships of world trade. It is rather clear today that an infinite number of individual interests added together will not necessarily produce that sense of social solidarity which is required for world community.

Secularism provides little discernible possibility for the modification of the self-centeredness of man. As we have seen, this self-centeredness tends to limit the application of the concept of human welfare to the welfare of the particular nation or group of which the individual may be a member. The motive power for its modification available to secularism is reliance upon humanity itself, and finally, therefore, on the resources within the person himself, namely on self-reliance. This self-reliance tends itself to be transmuted into self-centeredness. It is hard to see how such a stubborn reality as national sovereignty grounded in self-centeredness is to be modified by a viewpoint which, so far from dealing radically with this principle, tends itself to be transmuted into the very thing which must be radically altered if world community is to develop.

What Christians Must Do?

As Christians we shall need to work through the self-interest principle to wrest what we can of order out of the stubborn facts of the immediate scene; but we shall need, at the same time, to recognize that it is our duty to take a radically realistic view of the nature of the problem, so that we can make our maximum contribution through our faith. For the Christian the tragic divisions among men are not to be thought of as incidents to historical development which can be easily overcome by introducing an idealistic concept of the essential unity of mankind and a right consideration of human welfare as a whole. The world does not develop with an inherent necessity toward the unity which is required. The very choice of secularism to live without God and to regard mankind as the sole agent of history invites man's self-centeredness to take the helm and produces those very divisions which must be overcome if world order is to be achieved. To the Christian what is actually given in an unredeemed world is not unity, but division. Unity cannot be restored by good will or by human commands. "The powers of disruption destroy all well-meaning efforts to achieve unity."

The nation-state as we have it today is an embodiment of the will to dominate which is characteristic of unredeemed man. It is a kind of demonic incarnation of the self-interest principle, which is native to man in rebellion against God. As such it is doomed by an inner necessity to destroy itself. In the naked pursuit of self-interest it comes into conflict with other like incarnations of this principle; and, even though victorious in the ensuing struggle, it emerges with its resources wasted and with new strains and stresses which endanger its whole economic and social life. No one seriously questions that a continuation of this process means the ultimate destruction of modern civilization. Thus is demonstrated the inexorable law that "whosoever shall seek to save his life shall lose it." Surely it is the height of futility to expect to effect a basic cure of this disease by small or large doses of that which produces the disease in the first place. Secularism, grounded in man and cut loose from God, cannot be expected to alter a situation which is clearly due to man's rebellion against God and the incarnation of his own selfish will to dominate.

For us as Christians, therefore, our hope lies in our Christian faith, in a new creative power which has entered the world in Christ, able to redeem men from the worship of self and to furnish that unity which God himself can create as he wakens belief in the gospel. Christ can, and has, redeemed men from a slavish following of self-interest into a community of the faithful. This community has given, and is giving, amazing demonstration of its ability to surmount national boundaries and become indeed a world community. Our ultimate hope, therefore, lies in the creation of world community, not from within the unredeemed human framework, but by the emergence into history through Christ of a new creative power able to redeem man from himself and to create that true community which is requisite for world order.

That some such creative force grounded in religious faith is required if we are to resolve the dilemma created by national self-interest is recognized even by such an avowed secularist as Albert Einstein. In the *Atlantic Monthly* for November, 1947, he says:

> Those to whom the moral teaching of the human race is entrusted surely have a great duty and a great opportunity. The atomic scientists, I think, have become convinced that they cannot arouse the American people to the truths of the atomic era by logic alone. There must be added that deep power of emotion which is a basic ingredient of religion.

This "deep power" cannot be evoked by saying so. One cannot lift himself up by his own bootstraps. It can become vital only as man bows in humility to the terrible reality of God and his will, places the nation-state under God and makes it subject to his government, and allows the beneficent ministry of Christ to save him from himself. Whatever else the Christian does, he is primarily responsible for seeking to mediate this saving power of Christ to the world.

If, then, we have to wait for world order until the Kingdom of God becomes a reality and a common faith creates a world community with a common world view, it would seem to make its realization unlikely, if not impossible, within history. Whether or not this is so, as Christians we are in duty bound to view the task from within the framework of Christianity, and only as the stubborn nature of the problem is deeply realized can we work profitably through all the means at our disposal, and with the existing human situation for such measure of world order as is immediately achievable.

Part

IV

SECULARISM
IN ECONOMIC
AND SOCIAL ISSUES

SECULARISM AND ORGANIZED LABOR

Don D. Lescohier

The achievements of science and technology, of the arts, of national power and world-wide economic structures, being more conspicuous than is the experience of God, offer themselves as tempting substitutes for him. Our language is better fitted to discuss them. . . . The cults of state or of a vague "humanity," of science or of beauty, of social reform or of revolt, tempt us as sources of moral inspiration and human betterment in which every just interest shall have its place. And under limited circumstances, for a limited time, and involving a restricted social range of values, such loyalties do in fact arouse a personal and a social response which leaves no value untouched, and which gives power, and even some unity and plan to life.

THIS PASSAGE FROM LEROY LOEMKER'S CHAPTER "THE NATURE OF Secularism" seems to be where he touches most pointedly the ideologies, objectives, and activities characteristic of organized labor.

Christianity has been a religion of revolutions. Christ visualized himself as one who came to disrupt much of what was characteristic of human life and to produce reconstructions and new orientations which would give man peace in his soul and in his social order. But only after man had endured conflicts and sacrifices, and made efforts and personal reorientations from which peace would emerge as the product of life that was *right*.

Revolutions, whether inspired by lofty aspirations or base motives and desires, have a habit of getting out of hand. Religious and ethical reform movements, no less than secular, have historically become entangled in a myriad of personal, class, and group desires. The struggles by which social classes have fought their way up into the sun and advanced their secular interests have been particularly liable to be characterized by human selfishness, shortsightedness, greed, rancor, and the efforts of individuals and groups to achieve power and its emoluments. This was true when the capitalist class partially broke the combined power of the landlord-church-military coalitions in various countries from the fourteenth to the nineteenth centuries. It has been true, likewise, of the organized labor movements as the submerged wage earners have fought their way up to greater political, economic, and social position and advantages. Even in societies where most of the manual labor was done by slaves, some free labor existed. The gradual breakdown of slavery and serfdom, and the slow processes through which the agricultural and urban laborers, formerly bound by custom and law to the service of particular masters, won the universal status of a free wage earning population is too long a story to be even summarized here; but it must not be forgotten that the labor movement today gets some of its glamour from the contrast between the wage earner's present state and his lot in that grim past when the laborer was pitifully poor, pitifully ignorant, and the helpless victim of unbelievably unjust laws and customs. The men who were hanged in former times for stealing a loaf of bread were most of them free men, but their freedom was an empty eggshell.

The first authentic record of a strike in the United States was in 1786; and the first union which lasted for a period of years was formed by the printers of Philadelphia in 1792. Between then and 1821 there were sporadic organization of local unions and some strikes. From 1821 to the present time the United States has had a continuous labor movement which has moved forward through various ups and downs into the strength and influence it has in our times, in spite of the powerful resistance of employers, courts, a largely hostile press, and adverse laws and legal principles. Only during the last generation have labor unions achieved a position of respectability in the eyes of the law and general public opinion, and only since 1934 has federal legislation unequivocally recognized labor organizations as legitimate and essential social institutions deserving legal protection and given them full freedom to carry out lawful purposes.

Historical Background

The labor movement has consisted of three somewhat separate and yet interwoven ideologies and processes. Labor organizations were developed in the first place to bargain more effectively with employers, particularly over wages and hours. The individual employee was at a disadvantage in bargaining because ordinarily it made little

difference to the employer whether or not he hired a particular workman but a great deal of difference to the individual workman whether
or not he obtained that particular job. Unless he worked, he could
not eat. If he and the employer did not come to a bargain quickly,
he lost forever those hours, days, weeks, or months that he might have
been working. A wage earner cannot go back and earn the wages
he might have earned yesterday; an employer, on the other hand, by
hiring extra workers, working overtime, or speeding up his production processes in some other way, can make up the production which
should have been accomplished yesterday, or in past weeks or even
months.

Labor's bargaining position was essentially weaker than the employer's unless and until wage earners could get a control over the
labor supply comparable with the employer's control over the demand
for labor. Under the legal principles and institutions that we inherited
from Great Britain an employer was recognized, in former times,
as having complete autocratic control over his business enterprise and
the working conditions in his establishment. He owned the plant,
the equipment, the materials, the orders of the customers, and controlled the relations of the business with those from whom he bought
and to whom he sold. The wage earners had no rights on his premises
except by his permission and sufferance. When a wage earner accepted a job, the courts presumed that he was satisfied with the
wages, hours, safety and health conditions, speed of work, and all
other characteristics of the work place. The judges reasoned that
a workman didn't need to take a particular job unless he wanted to.
He was free to go and work for someone else, and they were curiously
blind to the fact that a wage earner must work somewhere and one
employer's place was much like another's. The wage earner, under
individual bargaining, was in effect forced to accept such employment as he could get, regardless of the fact that the working conditions might be very unsatisfactory.

The early unions, both in this country and Europe, therefore concentrated first upon getting better wages and limitation of working
hours below the "sunrise to sunset" hours which were customary
150 years ago and far into the nineteenth century. The resistance of
the social classes, who were in political and economic control during
that early period, was terrific; and wage earners in Britain were

given what amounted to life sentences in many cases for attempting to bargain about wages and hours. This was during the period when the formation of unions was considered in law to be a conspiracy against the public welfare.

The second major objective which developed in the labor movement and began to be crystallized into law in the United States after the 1860's was to limit the autocratic controls of the employer over his employees and to require that working conditions conform to certain minimum standards. Restraints were sought through legislation, collective bargaining agreements, and public opinion, though the American labor movement did not attempt, until recent years, to use legislation as extensively as did the unions in Great Britain and Europe. The American labor movement did work, however, for laws to protect women and children, regulate immigration, require safety and health protection in working places, and legalize a shorter working day. But they did not attempt to use the government, either state or federal, extensively to advance their interests until during the last twenty-five years.

The third objective of the labor movement has been the social betterment of the wage earning classes. It has been *the* agency through which they have tried to relieve themselves from specific social disadvantages and to attain their "place in the sun." In the early nineteenth century imprisonment for debt still existed in this country. It was one of the most idiotic of legal principles: a man was put into prison because he couldn't pay his debts; and while he was in prison, he couldn't work and earn money with which to pay them. One of the first social changes sought by the growing labor movement was abolition of imprisonment for debts, since wage earners were among those who suffered most from the debtor laws.

Again, 150 years ago there were some employers who failed to pay the wages of their employees, just as there is an occasional one who would act the same way today. A second "cause" espoused by the early American labor movement, therefore, was the enactment of mechanics' lien laws to give the wage earners a claim against the goods or property upon which they worked in case the employer failed to pay them their wages. Today we look upon mechanics' lien laws as an integral part of our social system, but a century ago they were a social justice which the labor movement had to struggle to obtain.

A hundred years ago it was the labor movement, more than any other social group, which was applying pressure for the creation of a free public-school system in the United States. It was not the educators of the early nineteenth century or the middle classes or the so-called cultured classes which were promoting universal education. Neither was it the farmers. A large part of the people in those groups were indifferent, and many were opposed to the idea of free public schools.

Manhood suffrage and later woman suffrage were issues vigorously promoted by the labor movement. In our so-called democratic society, during the first half century after the adoption of our Constitution, property qualifications of various types were used to disqualify large numbers of men otherwise eligible to vote.

In recent decades efforts to develop a comprehensive system of social insurance, the prevention of unemployment so far as practicable, and sound policies for relieving the needs of the unemployed, as well as the putting of floors under wages and the legal recognition of the right to carry on collective bargaining and require employers to bargain with unions, have been major objectives designed to make the political and economic freedoms of wage earners realities rather than phrases. These and many other activities fall into what I have called the effort of labor to advance its social status and rights.

The wage earners and their leaders would be more than human if they could have carried on these varied struggles and efforts during the last hundred years without at times committing acts which were illegal or were unfair to other social groups. No social movement has conducted itself irreproachably, and those friends of the labor movement who blind their eyes to its shortcomings and mistakes do it a disservice.

The rise of the labor movement unquestionably diverted the reliance of the wage earners for their economic, social, and cultural betterment from religion and the church to a very considerable extent. Many people in the labor movement even became extremely critical of the church, because historically the church had been tied up in all countries with the ruling classes and their institutions and during most of the nineteenth century the church did not take a strong position in favor of the rights which labor eventually won by its own efforts and through secular agencies. Labor felt that the church's typical advice was to obey and submit to those in superior social position rather than to attempt to force changes in the social order. The impetus to correct social injustice, which was so characteristic of the teachings of Christ and the Jewish prophets, they believed to be singularly lacking in the attitude of the church of the nineteenth century toward social questions. Although that emphasis was not entirely absent from religion, most of the clergy and most of the church organizations concentrated their attention upon individual religion and the hereafter more than upon vigorous support for the establishment of the Kingdom of God on earth. During the later years of the nineteenth century and the early part of the twentieth, such spokesmen as Walter Rauschenbusch sounded a clarion call to the church to insist upon the establishment of righteousness in the relations of employers and employees, as well as in other types of social relationships, but the church had missed its opportunity for so long that the place of the church had been preempted to a large extent by the labor movement.

I distinguish at this point between religion and the religious institutions of society. Religion's interest in the correction of social injustice goes far back into history. The Code of Hammurabi and the Laws of Moses, while not entirely religious codes, contained many requirements for justice to wage earners and even to slaves. They even attempted to require decent treatment of animals. A certain social vision has been embodied in the stream of religious and ethical thought since far back in human history; but the church, both Christian and Jewish, failed to seize, in any adequate manner, its opportunities to apply those principles vigorously down through the ages. It is not strange that today organized religion finds it hard to do more than use its influence on the fringe of social movements or to do more than co-operate with secular groups which have taken over the leadership of movements for social betterment. It is possible that had organized religion played a larger part in bringing about the social changes the labor movement has promoted, there might be a less secular cast today to the movements promoting labor's welfare.

So much for background. We have today some fourteen million wage earners who are members of labor organizations. The largest proportion are affiliated with the A.F. of L., the C.I.O., or the railroad brotherhoods. The independent unions, though not affiliated with the federations, pursue similar objectives. The various unions differ more in their degree of emphasis upon particular provisions in their collective agreements than in their basic objectives.

MAJOR ISSUES OF THE MOVEMENT

The major issues of the present time center around wages, productivity, discipline, employment rights, and the rights and privileges of union representatives when on the employe's premises and engaged in union work. Hours of labor, a major issue for nearly a century, is no longer a real issue. The battle for reasonable hours of labor has been won. When the question of hours comes up again, it will probably be during an industrial depression when labor will ask for a shorter work week without reduction in wages in order to spread the available employment over the maximum number of wage earners and still preserve the national standard of living.

Wages are the fundamental objective in accepting a job. They are what determines the ability of a wage earner and his family to live at all. They determine their standard of living and the kind of life the members of the family can live. Education, culture, recreation, and religion—as well as food, clothing, and housing—are available only at a price. Ministers may say that religion is free, but it isn't except for individuals who acquire it in the same way they may acquire poor relief—at someone else's cost. Normally, those who want the services of religious institutions must participate in carrying the necessary costs of maintaining them. Religion is not sold at a price, but it has to be supported through contributions determined by each individual's economic resources and degree of interest. Unless wage earners can support churches, they won't have churches. The same is true of all the other types of influences that contribute to personal and family culture. Essentially, then, the incomes that wage earners can earn determine most of the possibilities that life holds out to their families.

The things that we consume may be grouped under three classes: necessities, conventional necessities, and optional goods. We must have food, clothing, housing, medicine at times, and a few other things that are absolutely indispensable. Those are necessities. We think we need neckties, bobby pins, personalized clothing, furniture that has beauty as well as utility, and many other things that are conventional necessities in our stations of life. A university professor cannot live exactly the same way that he did when he was a student. There are certain things that a professor is conventionally expected to include in his standard of living that a student does not feel under pressure to include. Sometimes we speak of this as "keeping up with Joneses." We laugh at it at times, but it is a tremendously important thing in our social lives. Each person and family feels the necessity of upholding certain conventional standards, and often they sacrifice on necessities to buy the things which they think people expect them to have. The third group of commodities, optional goods, consists of those things that we buy of our own free choice and not in response to either necessity or convention. I don't own any golf clubs, and no one thinks the less of me because of that. Whether you own fishing tackle, a gun, various kinds of jewelry, and many other things is entirely a matter of your own free choice and your ability and willingness to buy them.

The employment of the wage earners of the United States depends as vitally upon a demand for conventional necessities and optional goods as upon the demand for the bare necessities of life. Our civilization is wound around these three classes of wants, and the fact that some of them are silly wants or even injurious to us individually does not change the fact that they are characteristic of our stage of social development. Wage earners and farmers, like businessmen and professional people, want to satisfy these three classes of wants in the lives of their own families, and one of the powerful pressures toward higher wages comes from the constantly widening area of our wants as the commodities available to us multiply in number and variety.

Mass production and the wide variety of commodities produced in our land must be complemented by mass ability to buy what is made and offered for sale. Down to the time of World War I the labor movement emphasized, first, subsistence, frugal comfort, and then real comfort when bargaining for wage adjustments. In the railroad shopmen's dispute of 1919 the government board arbitrating the dispute was told that the railroad men had raised their sights and aspired to what they called a "cultural standard of life" and not merely a comfortable standard. In the years since, this point of view has spread widely among the manufacturing, mercantile, and other types of wage earners. Labor is working for wage standards that will enable families to give their children educational and other advantages far above those they dreamed about even thirty years ago. A deep fundamental desire like this cannot be brushed aside. It represents an upsurge of millions of people toward new concepts of life and living, and labor feels that these higher concepts and objectives are in tune with the basic concepts of religion and with the ideals that religion has contributed to society. Here is a point where secularism and religion can find some common ground.

Many of the wage problems which have been bargained in the labor disputes of recent years involved technical matters about production and working methods which lie outside the area of religion. Outsiders cannot have even an intelligent understanding of many of these problems. They are matters concerning which religion need not attempt to intervene. The question, for instance, of whether certain wage earners on certain particular jobs ought to be paid an hourly wage or through some sort of incentive system is a technical question involving time study, job evaluation, and understanding of the technical details of the job. Such matters are technical rather than ethical, and their solution must be accomplished partly by engineering and partly by practical business and wage-earner experience. They have to be thrashed out by the people who are working in the industry and upon the basis of industrial rather than ethical or spiritual conceptions.

RELIGION AND WAGES

But the basic wage problems involve religious ethics. There are three basic lines of reasoning along which labor has pressed for wage increases. First, during the last seventy years prices have been more fluctuating than was true formerly. We have had prolonged downward and upward trends of prices which have materially affected both the purchasing power of the dollar and employment. Wage earners have pressed for wage adjustments to keep real wages, i.e., the purchasing power of wages, from deteriorating in times when prices were falling and employment was slack. But adjustment of wages to the changes of the cost of living, whether on a rising or falling market, does nothing more than keep real wages constant. It does not provide increase in real income to enable a family to progress in its standard of living and economic welfare. The second objective has been to raise real wages so that families could make economic and social progress. At the end of World War I, when it was certain that prices were going to fall, Samuel Gompers led the A.F.of L. in a vigorous campaign to retain the wartime money wages in the face of falling prices and thereby raise real wages. He said real wages were too low in 1914 and that when prices broke in 1921, labor should be allowed to raise its real wages and real standard of living by the retention of wartime money wages. The same thing is occurring now. In the last two years labor has been emphasizing the two ideas that they should get wage increases commensurate with the increases in the cost of living and retain their present money take-home when prices start downward so that there can be another lift in the national standard of living. In other words, that when the present inflationary movement of prices is checked and prices turn downward, labor should retain its present high wage level and thereby obtain another advance in real wages. This is but a current manifestation on a large scale of the effort which labor has been making for the last century, at first feebly and later powerfully, to raise the wage earners to a higher level of living, of life, and of citizenship.

The third reason for demands for higher wages has been to give the employee a part of the benefits from the increases in man-hour productivity which are going forward because of improved technology and new applications of science. Most of the increases in man-hour productivity have not been the result of wage earners working harder, but of the whole complex of improvements in methods of production. The application of science and engineering, the invention constantly of new and better machines, the development of better transportation facilities, the increasingly effective use of man-power through line methods of production, and many other technical changes have combined to make the labor of the American workman more productive regardless of whether he has worked harder or not, and regardless of whether he has attained a higher degree of skill. The splitting of occupations into specialized tasks and the grouping together of many workmen into production processes where each does but a small part of a total task—but does it faster and more effectively than the workman with generalized skill can do—have resulted in a continuing increase in man-hour productivity. Labor looks upon this advancing man-hour productivity as a social product from which all who are involved in the production processes have a right to benefit—ownership, management, labor, and the consumer. Nearly all businessmen agree that as our industrial system becomes more efficient, labor should share in the benefits of that efficiency even when the more efficient methods are the result of management's ingenuity and investment.

The controversies over wage problems during recent years have involved a wide variety of detailed issues, but basically they fall within the general pattern which I have described. I think it is safe to say that we are in the midst of some almost revolutionary developments in this area. Formerly wage earners consisted for the most part of two groups, the skilled workmen and the laborers. The skilled workmen were paid higher wages partly because of their skill and ability and partly because of the limited supply of such workmen. The laborers were paid low wages because anyone could be a laborer and there were so many of them that typically the market was glutted. During the last twenty years particularly, a vast army of the unskilled have become semiskilled workmen using modern machine tools and equipment and able to produce a large quantity of work of standard and often fine quality. Whereas the skilled mechanic was paid for the quality of his work, the semiskilled operator in modern industry is paid for turning out a large quantity of standard-quality work. He has become as valuable as a quantity producer of good work as the skilled mechanic is for his knowledge and skill. Millions of wage earners in this semiskilled group now see how vitally important they are to industry and maintain that their quantity production makes them as valuable as the skilled mechanic's knowledge makes him. The drive of such great unions as the automobile workers, electrical workers, rubber workers, and farm implement workers is largely for the development of wage stuctures which satisfy their conceptions of the kind of wages that such operators should be paid.

THE PRODUCTION QUESTION

The approach of the employer and the wage earner to the question of man-output differs at some significant points. An employer's interest in work is essentially in quality and quantity of output. He is not interested in having his workmen get tired; that of itself does not get him anything. What he wants is to have their efforts result in production. When he thinks of the value of a workman or a class of workmen, he thinks in terms of the value they create in a given number of hours. The presence of the workmen in the plant, the number of hours that they put in, the extent to which they get tired, are all matters which involve no benefit to him; rather they make problems for him. What he pays wages for is production and nothing else.

The workman, on the other hand, is very much interested in the fact that he has to remain in the plant for a given number of hours, that he gets tired, that he likes or dislikes what he is doing, and whom he is associating with while at work. Ordinarily the amount and quality of the output he creates, though vitally important to the employer, are of only incidental interest to him. His sphere of interest is the effect of his job upon him personally. Inevitably, therefore, the employer and employee approach the matter of productivity from different angles and often with conflicting interests. The employer wants to pay for results; the workman wants to be paid for time and effort regardless of results. Inherent in such a situation are unlimited possibilities for dispute, with just as good arguments on one side as the other.

There is no way of determining the amount of work that a person ought to do on a particular job with such certainty and precision that both the employer and employee will accept the decision without question. The employers typically think that a large number of their employees do not produce as much as they ought to, and a large number of wage earners feel that their employers are trying to speed them up and make them work harder than it is reasonable to expect them to work. Consequently, the conflict arises between employers and unions over questions and man-hour output.

But there are other causes of conflict involved in the question of productivity. Labor has found by experience that many workmen cannot depend upon having steady, year-round, and life-long employment. They are constantly afraid of getting out of a job. Is it strange, then, that they wish to set work standards under which they will not work themselves out of a job and under which the maximum number of workmen will be employed? Since there is no way of proving that the wages paid for given work are exactly right, nor exactly what is a reasonable day's output, the employer is apt to think that he pays too much and the workman that he receives too little. If the workman is not fully satisfied with his wages, that dissatisfaction easily rationalizes into a justification for holding back on output. The church has said repeatedly since the Middle Ages that the employer ought to pay a fair day's wage for an honest day's work. Neither industry nor labor disputes the statement. But when it comes to defining what is "a fair day's wage" and what is "an honest day's work" in a given occupation, there is a possibility of conflicting views. Such are some of the vital issues about which labor and industry are disputing and bargaining incessantly. Religion can lay down general principles, but it cannot resolve the practical situations. The ethics which religion contributes must be supplemented by analyses and decisions which are essentially technical.

DISCIPLINE

The problem of discipline has been more difficult in the last few years than ever before. Discipline is not punishment; it is orderly procedure. Soldiers are well disciplined when they carry out their orders and duties fully. The ones who get into the guardhouse are the ones who violate discipline. In former generations the right of an employer to establish and enforce discipline was hardly questioned. With the growth of our large industrial organizations employing thousands of men and managed by hundreds of thousands of foremen, superintendents, and managers, impersonality and the errors made by some of the many supervisors complicate such questions as discipline. This is another area where religion can emphasize principles, such as justice and right dealing, but where hardheaded, practical common sense, sound psychology, and often legal principles have to be applied to the specific situation.

The other matters I listed as major issues need not detain us here. Their solution depends largely upon sound practical policies and intelligent discussions between industry and labor. Technical considerations constitute a large part of the subject matter which comes into their discussion and disposition. Religion can emphasize the importance of righteousness and kindness in the working out of the answers, but it cannot furnish the answers. The greatest contribution which religion can make, probably, to the problem of industry-labor relations would come from an even stronger insistence upon the application of Christian ethics to problems of our complex industrial order which have to be resolved principally by secular agencies.

In closing, permit me to make one further observation: there is no such thing as a "solution" for these labor problems. Human beings living together in industry, and particularly in an evolving, ever-changing industrial system, will have the problem of mutual relations and the solution of day-to-day problems ever before them. No capsules can be administered. No conclusive operations can be performed. At best, industry and labor can achieve more perfect principles and procedures and accept or develop a more precise code of ethics, which will facilitate peaceful solution of their problems. But they cannot hope for permanent "solutions" for their ever-developing and changing problems.

SECULARISM IN BUSINESS AND INDUSTRY

F. Ernest Johnson

IN APPROACHING THIS SUBJECT WE SHOULD HAVE IN MIND LEROY Loemker's remark in his introductory chapter that the nature of secularism "is neither to affirm nor to deny religious faith, but to live indifferently to it." In other words, secularism is "irreligion"—a kind of living to which religion is irrelevant. It is given classic expression in Studdert-Kennedy's lines:

> When Jesus came to Birmingham they simply passed Him by,
> They never hurt a hair of Him, they only let Him die.

The bearing of secularism upon business and industry is an especially important phase of the subject because of the way in which the secularist movement developed. Indeed the topic might be the bearing of business and industry upon secularism. For as Canon Lilley has said concerning the economic and industrial developments between the thirteenth and the fifteenth centuries:

> Industry and commerce, in extending the range and complexity of their operations, had unconsciously developed an autonomy of their own. All that the spiritual authority could do was to accept that autonomy and to humanize or Christianize it in the widest measure of its power.

We must not, of course, underestimate the intellectual factors in the growth of secularism, and in particular the rise of modern science and of romantic humanism. Yet it may well be argued that the lure of gain was the strongest single factor in undermining the religious sanctions erected during the Middle Ages for the regulation of economic life. To be sure, these sanctions were often honored in the breach rather than in the observance, but they were recognized as having moral validity. Today if a group of churchmen should submit to businessmen a formula embodying the medieval principle of the "just price," they would probably be told to go chase themselves—if not admonished in stronger language.

155

The slogan "Business is business" is an accurate expression of the modern secular mood in the Western world, so far as the majority of the people are concerned. To criticize it is not to say that what is put in the secular category is in any sense unholy. It is a question whether the use of the word "secular" to denote an area of interest and activity can be dispensed with. It is employed in ways that have no derogatory connotation, as when Roman Catholic priests who minister to parishes are called "secular clergy" to distinguish them from the "regular clergy," who belong to religious communities. It would seem, however, that a truly religious view of life is better expressed by giving the word secular a meaning identical with that of the word "temporal," which denotes, not a sphere beyond the reach of religious sanctions, but those interests and concerns arising out of the conditions of man's existence. The subordination of the temporal to the spiritual is a basic requirement of all ethical religion. We Protestants differ from Roman Catholics in this respect only in disputing the authority imputed to ecclesiastical institutions. We, on our part, may well ponder, however, the consequences of the wide separation that has taken place, in cultures where Protestantism is the dominant religious influence, between spiritual and temporal affairs. It can hardly be denied that the Protestant ethic itself reflects the secularist trend in its failure to challenge the unchristian aspects of the economic order.

Indeed, Milton Yinger, in his book *Religion in the Struggle for Power*, maintains that even the modern development of what is called social Christianity was for the most part

not the triumph of radical Christian doctrine forcing society to justice, but the emergence of a new power to which the churches had to adjust— as they adjusted to the bourgeoisie in the seventeenth century—if they were not to lose what influence they yet maintained over a large group of people.

The temptation to underestimate the influence of secular forces upon the church itself is one against which we should always be on guard.

It is an ironic aspect of the laissez-faire philosophy that it rested, in its original form, on religious sanctions. Adam Smith was primarily a moral philosopher who had no difficulty in seeing the hand of God behind the mechanism of the market. Indeed, the entire competitive system was envisaged as a divinely ordained device, based on a sort of calculus of human purposes, each of which taken separately was egocentric, but which in the aggregate assured collective well-being. Thus the individual might go all out for his own ends undisturbed by the disparities in human fortunes, and even finding in his own prosperity—if fortune favored him—an evidence that he was operating in accord with a divine plan.

THE LAISSEZ-FAIRE PHILOSOPHY

The laissez-faire philosophy as thus formulated was therefore not antireligious. In intention it was not even irreligious. But it fostered that autonomous development of economic life of which Canon Lilley speaks by postulating an automatically operating benevolent purpose which the human beings concerned did not need to share. To be sure, the Christian businessman was supposed to do all to the glory of God. But the burden of this responsibility was vastly lightened by the assurance that God was looking out for his own glory. An inscrutable Providence was balancing all the competitive thrusts of man's economic effort. How should he who makes even the wrath of men to praise him fail to subdue to order the competitive deeds of mere human beings who lack the wisdom to create order themselves?

My references to the laissez-faire philosophy have been in the past tense. This is due to the fact that many modifications of the laissez-faire system have been effected, as everyone knows. Completely free competition is advocated today by few people. Indeed it probably never existed anywhere. But there is a striking resemblance between the historical argument that I have briefly sketched and much of the contemporary argument for free private enterprise. Although the facts of life have compelled a resort to one legal limitation after another upon business practices, the nerve center of our economy is still generally assumed to be the competitive struggle for private gain. The opposition to economic planning is the counterpart of the classical theory that only the Almighty can preside over the economic process and direct it to a noble end. But in our time the economic sphere has become secularized in a way contrary to the intention of the first vintage of classical economists and of their devout religious adherents by making economic process a law unto itself. A God who runs the affairs of men by remote mechanical control is on the way to becoming "God emeritus"—Shailer Mathews' apt term.

A curious fact about this appeal to a mechanistic principle as justification for rejecting ethical criticism of the economic order is the widespread departure from it in practice by business corporations. The operation of the competitive price system is on every hand interfered with by the substitution of "administered" prices for prices fixed by the "law of supply and demand." Again and again, when the market begins to fall, instead of letting the laissez-faire theory operate, business has curtailed production. This is the essence of the "economy of scarcity." Theoretically, at such a time an increase in demand due to the lowered price should press upward on the price level and restore equilibrium. Instead of this, what commonly happens is that business executives decide to meet the situation by shutting down or at least slowing down production. This is what happens with the onset of a depression. Reducing output reduces employment, which further reduces demand, and the spiral begins.

The meaning of all this I take to be that the austerity of the supply-and-demand system is too severe for business to take and in the pinch it is avoided by stopping the game. Businessmen say, reasonably enough: "We can't be expected to operate at a loss." But there is the rub. They remind us that the so-called profit system is really a profit-and-loss system. That is quite true. And, of course, this is the reason why business demands high profits in good times. But my point is that appeal cannot logically be made to an "inexorable" law of supply and demand if, when it begins to operate adversely to business, supply is arbitrarily cut off. Administered price is really a form of planning. Studies of the Brookings Institution have made this point clear. The mechanism of the market is proclaimed as the governor of price in a profit-and-loss economy, but business itself finds the game much too rough to play through on the loss end.

Please note that I am not here passing judgment on the validity of a free enterprise economy. The extent to which it can, or should, be modified is a difficult question. We lack knowledge of the capacity of human beings, collectively considered, to subordinate self-interest to the point necessary for elimination of the austerities of our economic system while at the same time avoiding the evils of coercion by an omnicompetent state. I am often struck by the

similarity, at least on the surface, between the discourses on the
nature of man given us by the "realistic" theologians and the business
arguments for economic individualism on the ground that "you can't
change human. nature." My chief complaint is that in our times the
defense of free enterprise, even by churchmen, is so largely quite
complacent, reflecting no concern over the fact that the economic
system with its recurrent depressions and its grievous hazards to the
lives and the security of the masses of the people finds its orthodox
defense in the impersonal operations of market mechanisms. Surely
the least a Christian, standing on a New Testament platform, can
say about it is that if the quest of private gain is necessary to motivate
adequate production of goods and services, this is to be taken not as
justification of self-seeking but as a moral compulsion to make a
progressively larger place in the economic order for the incentives
enjoined by him who "came not to be ministered unto, but to minister." The Christian indictment of the economic order is that it is
secularized: taken as a whole it tends to deny the relevance of religious sanctions to the sphere of economic incentives.

I hasten to add that many businessmen and industrialists do not
fall under this indictment. We all know many of them who keep
alive in their own souls the tension between the Christian ethic and
things as they are. But most of the current utterances by defenders
of our economic system are excessively adulatory and reflect no deep
ethical concern over the defects in its operation, no sense of individual or corporate responsibility for the hardships it entails upon
millions of families who never enjoy economic security and who are
periodically plunged into want and suffering. From a Christian point
of view this is a grievous lack.

Let me illustrate this point by reference to the controversy over
price controls. The demand for their continuance rested on the fear
of disastrous inflation. The argument for their removal was that
without greater incentives to production the disparity between demand and supply could not be overcome. Both contentions had a
factual foundation. The subsequent rise in prices justified the fears
of those who wanted the controls continued. Yet an elementary
knowledge of the way the market works makes it clear that such
restrictions do in fact discourage production. But if the demand for
maintenance of price controls may be called unrealistic, the insistence

on their removal involved the assumption that even in an emergency those who have goods to sell or facilities for manufacturing them will hold out for the price they want—or supply the black market. The financial editor of a great newspaper said that we need to recognize that "the so-called capitalistic or free-enterprise system appeals to one of the most universal characteristics of man, which is selfishness." He noted that many people "beat the bushes for a nicer description" and produce confusion, for "gross as it may seem, selfishness is the hub around which the wheel of our economy and the American way of life revolves."

The central difficulty here is that a social process, which is regarded as indispensable, is referred to an individual motive which Christianity has always regarded as inferior. Because a social process, namely, the regulation of production and distribution by the checks and balances operating between supply and demand, is adjudged necessary—in spite of the lapses in its operation already noted—in order to keep our system running, the play of incentive incident to it is rendered immune to criticism and removed from the sphere of Christian discipline. This, I maintain, is a nonsequitur. If it is true that economic life can be regulated in a free society only by the balancing of self-regarding interests, then from a Christian point of view it becomes all the more necessary to discipline and refine the profit motive. Today this has become such a delicate subject that even to mention it is to incur the charge of being subversive.

CHRISTIANS AND PROFITS

As I have already intimated, the ultimate verdict of the Christian conscience upon our profit-and-loss economy cannot be accurately anticipated, but of this I am convinced: Christianity can never be complacent about self-interest, for Christianity requires the transformation of the *self* until it is capable of no interest that is exclusively private. Whatever may be normative in economics, Christianity recognizes no private property in a *spiritual* sense. Its dominant economic concept is stewardship: God is the owner of all things. True enough, Jesus' advice to the rich young ruler affords no norm for economic relations, but not until a man has fortified his soul against the lure of private gain can he qualify as a steward unto God. A member of the editorial staff of one of the greatest American daily newspapers said to me: "The urgent question today is whether greed is to become the dominant force in our national life."

It seems to occur rarely to business leaders that it is one thing to expound the workings of a profit-and-loss economy and to contend that there is no practicable alternative, and quite another thing to glorify it as if it were ordained of God. No one but a doctrinaire can speak with assurance as to what economic innovations would work out in practice, but to be complacent about the social evils inherent in the present order is to deny the relevance of Christianity to the economic sphere.

A phase of this problem that gives me no end of concern is the secularization of the churches themselves with respect to their economic practices. It is sometimes easier to get churchmen aroused over antisocial practices in industry than over the responsibility of the church itself for scrutinizing its own practices in the investment of funds and the employment of labor. Progress has been made in this respect, but not enough. It is too easy for Christian men exercising fiduciary responsibility for church funds to take over uncritically secular standards of "safe" investments. I fear little progress has been made in developing criteria of *morally* safe investments. The fact that a church board has no liquor stocks in its portfolio does not indicate that its investment policy is exemplary from the Christian point of view. Also, in the matter of employment practices it is to be feared that our churches often lag behind the more enlightened industrial concerns.

In the course of a correspondence I have conducted during the past year or two with an eminent businessman who is also an active churchman, he wrote me this:

In my connection with religious, philanthropic and social organizations of a nonprofit character, I have been repeatedly struck with the fact that the profit-and-loss system operates almost identically in all of them. In nonprofit organizations, of course, somewhat different terms are used— "deficit" being more frequently used than "loss," and "surplus" more frequently used than "profit." . . . In their efforts to avoid deficits and *to create surplus resources for non-profit uses* [some] are more unreasonable, less considerate, and sometimes even less honest in the treatment of employees than are the commercial organizations, or at least the better half of them.

This is, of course, no basis for a generalization, but it is to be feared much other testimony could be elicited to the same effect, and that churches as well as other agencies are at fault. How contrary it is to what might be expected of an organization that enjoys tax exemption and is itself immune to the stern requirements of a competitive market—not that churches don't compete with each other, but that is a different subject; and anyhow it is in the category of things we may in our candid moments acknowledge but do not care to advertise. In the matter of employment practices we often yield to the insidious temptation to assume that the privilege of working for the Lord equates to a wage differential. That this is true of many servants of the church who find in their employment an outlet for creative spiritual energies may be taken for granted, but it is stretching imagination pretty far to assume that it is true of those who do routine work that is indistinguishable from that done by employees of secular organizations.

This reference to the corporate practices of the churches may seem like a digression from the main theme, and may perhaps infringe on the area assigned to another paper. Yet it is part of secularism in economic life as it presses in upon the church itself, and I have felt constrained to bring it into the picture.

THE FUNCTION OF MANAGEMENT

The next phase of the subject to claim our attention is the function of management in business and industry. I raise the question whether the present understanding of this function has an adequate ethical foundation. By common agreement management represents the owners of the enterprise. Indeed, with the wide distribution of ownership, management has become in large-scale enterprise almost the only visible symbol of ownership. These facts explain the changed usage whereby what were formerly called capital-labor relationships are now referred to as management-labor relationships. At the same time an effort is being made to raise management to a professional level. The full implication of the concept of professional management, I think, is that the manager should have more than the function of an employer's agent, that he should represent in some sense all the interests that are conceded to be involved. The word "profession" has a broad public connotation. It signifies a type of activity which the community at large has had a hand in standardizing. An occupation does not become a profession until it becomes amenable to standards that have a public reference, conformity to which signifies a broader loyalty than is comprehended in a contractual relationship or any money nexus.

I believe that many business and industrial managers, in their own conception of their function, have been making this transition. Also it is undoubtedly true that individual employers and corporations have recognized a responsibility to the public and to their employees which sets some limits to their concern for profits. But is it not still true that the majority of managers are hired men whose tenure rests upon their ability and readiness to defend the interests of the employer against all comers—interests that are defined within a competitive framework? To make management a profession would mean giving a definite and recognized responsibility for making and improving the standards of performance in its own field. When a company retains a lawyer—that is, a lawyer with a healthy conscience—it submits itself to guidance as to what legitimate behavior is in legal terms. The lawyer has to be listened to, not merely told. A professional business manager would have a body of approved practice to which to appeal and would be able to command respect for his authority in his own field.

A profession is afforded protection in its effort to build and maintain standards by the fact that its members serve different clients and do not ordinarily become the exclusive agents of one. Perhaps it is visionary to suggest that management, in order to become a profession, should be paid jointly by owners and workers. But at least the kind of relationship that this would symbolize is of the essence of the professional spirit. Through professional contact and interchange with other managers, representing public and private enterprises, the impact of the public interest might be preserved.

It will be apparent already that what all this means in terms of Christian ethics is the realization of Christian vocation. It is one of the conspicuous faults of a secularized society that it affords so little opportunity to make of one's occupation a vocation in the ethical sense. If time permitted, the application of this principle might be indicated over a considerable range of economic functions. A sadly neglected aspect of Christian education at the adult level is the bringing to bear on vocational practice, in specific functional terms, of Christian teaching. This is of especial importance in the economic sphere, where secularization has such profound and far-reaching effects. The church should educate all its people with respect to investment and consumer practices in the light of the Christian testimony; also it should give particular guidance to those of its members whose occupation is in the production of goods and services.

I cannot end without special reference to advertising. Here is an area in which, it seems to me, the application of Christian ethics leaves a great deal to be desired. I am quite aware that many improvements in advertising practices have been made over a long term of years. But while these improvements reflect a higher level of honesty and decency, I see little approximation to the ethical ideals taught by Christianity and Judaism. It is related that a church deacon once sold a horse to a man who later complained that he had been "done." To the deacon's protestations that he had done nothing illegal, the aggrieved buyer replied: "Deacon, if you're no better than the law makes you, you'll go to hell, sure pop!"

I am not referring now to liquor advertising. I am thinking of brazen efforts to convince prospective customers that a given product is better than all its competitors: "If everybody knew what X-users know, they'd all change to X." I am thinking of the enormous expenditure of money—customers' money—in the effort to make people buy what they don't need and can't afford, and the exploitation of the human weakness for display. This whole business seems to me to be at once infantile and exploitive. Advertising is undoubtedly indispensable in a free-enterprise economy. But if a crude and costly system of competitive advertising—which runs far beyond the economic function of marketing communication—is necessary to sustain business, then the restraints of social ethics would seem to be definitely outmoded.

I have attempted, all too sketchily, to indicate the impact of secularism upon business and industry. My purpose has been not to prescribe remedies but to plead for more use of the Christian searchlight upon the secular economic order.

SECULARISM AND SOCIAL ISSUES

Bertram W. Doyle

IN THE UNITED STATES APPROXIMATELY ONE TENTH OF THE POPU-
lation is enumerated in "colored minorities," that is, in groups characterized by skin color darker than that of the dominant white
group. There are approximately 13,000,000 Negroes, over 1,000,000
Mexicans, 130,000 Japanese—Issei, Nisei, and Sansei—45,000 Filipinos,
50,000 Chinese, and fewer than 1,000 Hindus. In addition, in "white
minority groups"—not different in skin color, but different in cultural characteristics from the dominant group—will be found about
one seventh of our population. Among these latter groups are Southern Europeans, Irish, Jews, Italians, Danes, Dutch, Finns, Swedes,
Germans, Greeks, Rumanians, Poles, Hungarians, Russians, Welsh,
Scots, Austrians, and Portuguese.[1]

Those groups, as Young has pointed out, are called "minorities"
not for the reason that they are statistical minorities, but because they
are members of another "race"—in the sense in which that term is
popularly used—or because, as James G. Leyburn observes, they are
"members of a group who have either recognizable physical characteristics or recognizable cultural characteristics that set them apart
from the dominant group."[2]

When dominant and minority groups meet in social contact, occasions tend to arise when neither understands the other. Minorities
are doubtless harmless enough when considered as statistical minorities, but they become a *problem* when

(a) the dominant group has a stereotyped opinion about such people
and (b) refuses to treat them as "we" treat people in "our" group, thus
(c) arousing on the part of the minority a feeling of discrimination, caus-
ing them (d) to have a grudge against the dominant group, or (e) strengthening their desire to remain a separate people.[3]

[1] Donald Young, *American Minority Peoples: A Study in Racial and Cultural
Conflicts in the United States,* pp. 152-94.
[2] *World Minority Problems* (Public Affairs Pamphlet No. 132), pp. 2, 5.
[3] *Ibid.*

Stereotyped opinions are a sort of social shorthand, saving time by classifying persons, generally in terms of derogation, into wide classes and allowing judgments about their status, from which appropriate action will proceed. They are socially infectious, however, and tend to spread and encompass groups not originally classified as "out-groups" or minorities—such as occurred, for example, in industrial communities of the North during World War II, when "old line, white Protestant, Anglo-Saxon Americans, migrants from the hill-country of West Virginia, Kentucky, and Tennessee were [sterotyped as] 'crickets' and 'hilligans.' " [4]

Although sterotypes tend, on the one hand, to reflect prevailing attitudes of dominant groups, they also symbolize exclusion, proscription, and the too often resultant mistreatment that occasionally determine, frequently change, and always debase the character and personality of individuals who comprise the minority group. Descriptions of the crippling, deadening, lasting effect upon a man's character of being required "to live in a country, with almost infinite room for development, and yet to be denied full acceptance," [5] have been given too often to need repeating here.

Social reactions as described hitherto we shall call antipathies. Race antipathies, then, are generally directed toward persons of an outgroup who are occasionally in a minority, and in addition are reactions of persons within minority groups to treatment by members of dominant groups.

Racial Antipathy

Racial antipathy originates in fundamental nature, says Robert E. Park, and is one of the bases, if not a source, of race prejudice. Moreover, though it is fundamental, it is not for that reason instinctive—that is to say, biological—since it may be influenced by convention, custom, or tradition, and consequently change its direction and emphasis if not its nature.

All our sentiments, love, loyalty, patriotism, homesickness, contempt, arrogance, hate, are based upon and supported by prejudices. . . . The thing reduces itself to this, that prejudice, defined in this broad and inclusive way, has its source and origin in the very nature of men and their

[4] Carey McWilliams, *Survey Graphic*, Jan., 1947, pp. 22-25; cf. pp. 106-7.
[5] Leyburn, *op. cit.*

relation to one another. It gets itself fixed and sublimated in the habits of individuals, and enters into the very structure of society.[6]

It seems to be understood and admitted, however, that before it is fixed and sublimated, it is undergirded by antipathy.

Former President John Grier Hibben, of Princeton, observed that prejudice is a "natural factor in thinking," not necessarily to be decried, and certainly "not to be regarded in any sense as an abnormal and disturbing element." Shall we then assume that racial antipathy is also natural to the extent that naturally, if not inevitably, from it issue springs of prejudice?

Race antipathy and race prejudice are the first two terms of a series of which "racial animosities" is a third. Racial antipathy seems original and biological; race prejudice is certainly social and derived; and racial animosity seems to develop and become more intense "where racial prejudices, and the social order which they perpetuated, are breaking down."[7]

In some respects and to some of us, at least, the social order appears to be dissolving when "our-group" begins to acquire members from groups dissimilar to our own. The very presence of such persons tends to create in us a sense of insecurity which, unless dispelled by more intimate acquaintance, crystallizes into an attitude. The attitude then is clustered about with sentiments that support and give it substance. Then if there is social or physical contact, the sentiments tend to become intensified and to establish physical, if not social, distances between us and the persons whom we fear, or who bring us a sense of insecurity.

To refrain from, if not to resent, and consequently to rationalize on withdrawal from close contact with outsiders—"strangers," as Park calls them—seems then to be an elemental human reaction. True, there may be instances where resentment may be overcome and in which interaction may proceed, but those contacts must be encountered upon socially approved levels.

Racial antipathy, then, as hostility toward the "other-group" exists fundamentally as a correlate of comradeship and peace within

[6] "The Bases of Race Prejudice," *Annals of the Academy of Political and Social Science*, Nov., 1928, p. 12.
[7] *Ibid.*

the "we-group." For, as Sumner has remarked, "loyalty to the group, sacrifice for it, hatred for outsiders, brotherhood within, warlikeness without—all grow together, common products of the same situation."

The incidence of racial antipathy and prejudice, as Louis Wirth [8] and Thomas Sancton[9] have had occasion to note, may be measured in terms of the economic costs needed to maintain the mores, customs, laws, and institutions in order to separate minority groups and to keep them "in their place." It seems, however, that the chiefest human liability consists of the frustrations and rejections to which minorities are subjected, not to mention the effect in character, personality, and development upon the dominant group. Indeed, relating such human costs to the treatment of the Negro in America, Sancton says:

> There has been at work an inner psychological corrosion in the American character as the cost of imposing this thing upon a part of our people. It has made us experts at self-deception—we who began as a people characterized by simplicity, enthusiasm, and a genuine belief in individual dignity. It has brought an overplus of cynical pessimism into our arts and letters, and into popularly accepted beliefs. It has brought an element of narrowness and rigidity into the character of the individual. It has diminished our interest in others, and in our ability to appreciate the inexhaustible wonders of the human spirit.[10]

Problems of Minority Groups

All minority groups in the United States have problems in relation to the dominant group, or in themselves alone, or frequently in both. In one way, however, white minorities differ from colored minorities. Their cultural characteristics may disappear with time, and they may be absorbed in the dominant group. The colored minorities, on the other hand, are marked generally by color that does not change. To that extent, then, so long as color is a value, the colored minorities represent a perennial problem. If, then, we have selected those minorities for discussion, it is largely due to the judgment that not only through them may race antipathy be dramatized more em-

[8] "The Price of Prejudice," *Survey Graphic*, Jan., 1947, pp. 19-21.
[9] "Segregation: The Pattern of Failure," *ibid*., pp. 7-8.
[10] *Ibid*.

phatically, but also that facets of the race problem, in all their seeming inevitability and pervasiveness, may be presented in sharper focus. There will be no intention to underestimate nor deny the relative universality of race antipathy in the United States, but rather to suggest that phases of the problem are very similar among all minorities.

Persons who are oppressed by the place which color plays in maladjustments may be heartened to observe the many points of similarity in the problems experienced by groups not materially different from the dominant white stock. Others will be disappointed to find disparagement so frequent, disruptive attitudes so pervasive, and misunderstanding so general in the human family.[11]

The Negro, from sheer weight of numbers, emerges as the minority whose problems assume pre-eminence in a discussion of racial antipathy. Discussions in regard to the problems that face him are certainly more widespread than for any other group, and the public mind seems more occupied with the implication of his problem than that of any other minority.

Selecting the field of social problems as a starting point and citing references from the Report of the President's Committee on Civil Rights—published under the title *To Secure These Rights*—we will find listed topics on "The Crime of Lynching," "Police Brutality," "The Jury No Protection," "Discrimination in the Armed Services," "Bigotry in the Schools," "The Right to Housing," and "Discriminations in Places of Public Accommodation." If, from the same publication, we extended the list to include economic problems, we could put on display discussions of "Involuntary Servitude," "The Threat of Peonage," "Discriminatory Hiring Practices," "On-the-Job Discrimination," and "Discrimination in the Federal Service, and in the District of Columbia."

That list in itself is formidable enough to defy consideration within the limits of this chapter, but is not too long to prevent our conceiving the problems of the Negro as ones that pervade practically every nook and cranny of American social life.

If we were to select housing in Chicago as an example, we would discover that, as Ernest A. Gray writes:

[11] Herman Feldman, *Racial Factors in American Industry*, p. 131.

Every square mile of Chicago's Black Ghetto, to which Negroes are virtually confined by social and legal pressure, is now choked with 55,000 to 90,000 inhabitants—when housing authorities set 35,000 as the maximum for decent living. . . . Negroes have had to make their homes in shacks, hovels abandoned by former owners as unfit for human habitation, with direct and incidental results of exorbitant rents, bad sanitation, inadequate schools and other public services, and a shortage of recreational facilities.[12]

If we examined the record of the experience of the Negro in the armed services, we would find a recent, extensive literature filled with stories of segregation, discrimination, frustration of talent, insinuations concerning lack of bravery, explanations of shortcomings, and only an occasional attempt to assess the entire situation in terms of truth, rumor, and stereotype. We would read, for example, that "the most important loss to the Negro was the frustration of the first-rate talent in the group;" or discover that "many Negro enlisted men knew that their abilities were wasted under a scheme where color determined assignment. Along with this frustration went a deepened sense of inferiority." [13] We might, however, better understand the author who explains:

The unfavorable position of the Negro minority in our national life results in its members coming into the Army greatly handicapped. By denying them the opportunity to become fully-developed citizens, we have succeeded, really, in blunting not only the desires but the ability of most colored Americans to be good combat soldiers.[14]

If, satiated with evidence of conflict and misunderstanding, we turned to schools and education to discover what progress the Negro had made, we should find that many of the best universities have a quota for Negro admissions. We might get some solace, however, from noting that practice is not confined to Negroes, but has been extended as well to one of the white minorities—the Jew. If we recoiled from consideration of basic injustice of applying such a system to anyone, we might nevertheless note that, according to the

[12] "Race Riots Can Be Prevented," *Harper's Magazine*, Dec., 1945, p. 489.
[13] Charles Dollard and Donald Young, "In the Armed Forces," *Survey Graphic*, Jan., 1947, pp. 111, 113-19.
[14] Warman Welliner, "Report on the Negro Soldier," *Harper's Magazine*, April, 1946, pp. 336-37.

formula, patterns of discrimination caused by racial antipathy, fostered by prejudice, and supported by animosity, would be general for minority groups. We would also find that examples of antipathy could be extended almost indefinitely.

However, to change the field of discussion, if not the pattern of relation, we may consider the interaction of economic relations and racial antipathy by examining Herman Feldman's *Racial Factors in American Industry*. In that treat se antipathies are presented in chapters on "Barricading Higher Position," "Last Hired, First Fired," "Unequal Pay for Equal Work," "Discriminations in Working Conditions," and "Housing and Environment." Racial animosities would appear in chapters that deal with stereotypes and rationalizations about the Negro, such as "Natural Laziness," "Irregularity and Irresponsibility," and "Adaptability to Hot and Hard Work."

Change again the field to race antipathy and labor unions, and we would find charges that when white and Negro workers are associated in conservative labor unions, like the American Federation of Labor, questions generally arise concerning differential wage, separate organizations, and differential rights and privileges; but in the Congress of Industrial Organizations, which Negroes have joined in large numbers, their status would be raised, wages increased, and some, if not all, animosities alleviated.[15]

In unorganized labor, and in the congested industrial cities, evidence concerning employment of Negroes could show differentials, on the basis of competitive capacity and distribution of employment, that would force the conclusion that the differentials would be "due almost entirely to race discrimination." [16]

We turn from the Negro to the Japanese only to find that each colored minority has some particular problem of its own. The Japanese in the United States, for example, have long been proscribed, socially and economically. However, after a long series of conflicts ranging from charge and countercharge through physical oppression to civil action, they had achieved a status on the West Coast—where indeed nine tenths of them lived prior to 1940—and "occupied a niche

[15] Charles S. Johnson, "Race Relations and Social Change," in Edgar Thompson, *Race Relations and the Race Problem*, pp. 296-97.
[16] Edward Nelson Palmer, "Discrimination in Urban Employment," *American Journal of Sociology*, Jan., 1947, p. 357.

considerably above Negroes, Chinese, Mexicans, and Filipinos." [17] Stereotypes concerning them included charges of inassimilability, in addition to some generally assessed against other races.

Their minority status was brought to the focus of attention, however, in the first six months of 1942, when they were evacuated from their homes on the West Coast and established in relocation centers. Such an action pointed up the status of all minority groups in the country, since it was assumed that what could be done to a group as numerous and powerful as the Japanese could be done to any other.

The Japanese had not been charged with laziness, unreliability, inadaptability to menial labor, but they seemed to progress too rapidly, and thus to offer competition to "we-group" members. The evacuation and relocation of an entire group of persons, two thirds of whom were citizens of the United States, constituted not only a distinct injustice, but also a distinct shock to the pride and faith of the Japanese in America.[18]

With respect to the Chinese, the "stereotype was basically nothing more than the Negro stereotype imported to the West Coast and fixed upon Chinese immigrants." [19] True, in 1947 they have seemed to be accepted as a comparatively docile group, inassimilable, of course, as antimarriage laws in several states attest, but nevertheless comparatively harmless. Their present status is an evolution, however, for once, when tempers were high and charges filled the air, they were represented as "immoral, criminal, treacherous, clannish, pagan, mentally inferior, and a menace to Americans because of their low-grade tastes and primitive needs." [20]

Mexicans comprise the second largest colored minority group in the country. They are generally migratory workers who return periodically to their homeland. Nevertheless, approximately 30 per cent of them are citizens of the United States. Their color, however, seems to be against them. For socially they tend to occupy a sort of halfway position between the Negro and the European, and their development is much the same.[21]

[17] Carey McWilliams, *What About Our Japanese-Americans?* (Public Affairs pamphlet), p. 24.
[18] *Ibid.*
[19] *Survey Graphic*, Jan., 1947, p. 24.
[20] Charles Johnson, *op. cit.*, p. 293.
[21] Feldman, *op. cit.*, p. 114.

Their social status is indicated by the following description of a Mexican neighborhood in a small Texas town: "Large semi-rural slum . . . crudely built and in very bad repair. Few have electricity or plumbing, . . . badly overcrowded, . . . low incomes, poor housing, bad sanitation, . . . tuberculosis and diarrhea, . . . education on a low level." [22] The so-called "zoot-suit riots" in Los Angeles a few years ago are an index to the low esteem in which they are held in that city, if not indeed in all the country.

The availability of large numbers of Mexicans, relatively poor, certainly migrant under the necessities of their condition, seems to offer opportunity to large farmers to exploit them. Although a whole family tends to work at menial tasks, Menefee reports from Texas that "most of the family incomes fell between $300 and $699." [23]

In industry the Mexican's experiences

differ not in kind, but only in degree, from the experiences of the Negro, the Oriental, or the unskilled European immigrant. . . . When there is a reduction of labor he is among the first to be laid off. . . . His work is irregular. . . . Not many Americans employ Mexicans as skilled laborers. . . . He has the reputation of being a floater.[24]

The Indian occupies perhaps the highest status of colored minority groups. His skin is colored, but his racial descent seems to place him between the Oriental and the white. In recent years, at least, intermarriage has not been interdicted. One view of his social condition holds that he is a reminder of the white man's cruelty and injustice, while another depicts him as shiftless, inassimilable, and socially undesirable. Certainly when his settlement on reservations, with the resulting social conditions, is considered, he represents one phase of the "white man's burden." [25] Relatively isolated in very small numbers, he doubtless presents more of a dramatic challenge to our sense of justice than to problems of social relationships. He is a symbol of the "warring elements of ruthlessness and idealism that have been present in our American culture from the very beginning." [26]

[22] Selden C. Menefee, *Mexican Migratory Workers of South Texas,* p. xv.
[23] *Ibid.,* p. xi.
[24] Feldman, *op. cit.,* pp. 114-15.
[25] Carey McWilliams, *Survey Graphic,* Jan., 1947, p. 22. Allan L. Hulsizer, "Indians Meet All Problems," in *Americans All: Studies in Intercultural Education,* pp. 113-31.
[26] Sancton, *op. cit.,* p. 10.

In summary, then, minorities are sources of, and are affected by, problems common to them all. On the other hand they seem in addition to have, and to be the subject of, problems that are peculiar to themselves. Feldman indeed has suggested, with regard to general economic relations:

When one looks at the history of American attitudes toward alien groups, one is struck with the recurrence of certain definite cycles of public feeling. First, there is an "eager welcome for cheap, docile, labor supply; second, mild contempt for a segregated group which will accept work refused by members of a dominant group; third, active bitterness against any who are able to escape from their economic status and threaten that of the dominant group; fourth, organized and determined propaganda based upon supposed racial antipathies and national rivalries, to prevent equal economic opportunity to the alien group." [27]

It has been remarked that there is also a "race relations cycle," through which all minority groups proceed before being admitted to complete participation in the American way of life. Such a cycle would doubtless be a counterpart of the economic cycle already described.

SECULARISM AND RELIGION IN COLORED MINORITY GROUPS

If we ask how religion has fared, and to what extent secularism has developed among the minorities discussed, or if we ask what effect have science and secularism had upon them, their status, and aspirations, answers would need to be largely qualified. Perhaps every group has been at one time an object of interest for both secular and religious organizations that have been stimulated by some philosophy of social relations and minorities. However, there is reason to say that both types of organizations have appreciated and sympathized, infrequently have alleviated, and too seldom have defined the problems of minorities or suggested dependable and reliable means of solving them.

It can be stated with assurance, however, that the rise of the "science of races," with formulas that have since been outmoded, debased practically every colored minority to a subrace, if not a subhuman status.

---

[27] *Op. cit.*, pp. 122-23. See also *Commission on International and Interracial Factors in the Problems of the Mexicans in the U.S.*

Religious groups early showed interest in the Negro. Later they tended to withdraw, or to curtail, or to neglect such actions, due to changes in the social weather, to the force of the mores, or the shifting sands of public opinion. Many Negroes have thought that the capitulation of religious groups to pressure and rationalization opened the way to accept the philosophies of scientific and secular groups that seem to offer them hope for their problems. Among certain of the more articulate Negroes a certain disillusionment remains as they regard the remnants of the hopes they once had—and some still have —that the Christian Church would prove the major organization to proclaim and to insist on social, economic, and political justice.

But there remains the mass of Negroes who have been unshaken by secularism and the growth of science. They still believe in God, in the church, and in the principles of Christianity. If there is any question in their minds, it is doubtless: "How long before we see the harvest of justice and righteousness for which we have so long hoped?" Meanwhile, I believe, most of them are resigned to waiting; but they still believe that if the Kingdom does come and God's will is done, it will be as a result of the activity of the Christian Church.

I confess a certain hesitancy in assessing the impact of secularism among the other minority groups already discussed. For what they are worth—and I offer them not as facts but as impressions—it seems to me that the Mexicans, for example, have looked to the Roman Catholic Church more for a philosophy of life and the hereafter than for social, political, and economic philosophies. Indeed, if the latter were given them, they would be strained through the basic philosophy of the church and would doubtless give little room for secularistic tendencies.

The Japanese and Chinese have tended to develop their own organizations in the United States, and although there has been a certain amount of missionary activity among them, I wonder if those activities have not the more been devoted to Christianization, with all that has meant, than to removal of their disabilities by direct methods. You will notice that I ask and do not state that as a fact. At any rate, no evidence was found by me to indicate that secularism has had great growth among these minorities.

The Indian has been an object of "pathos," and both religious and secular organizations have interested themselves in his advancement. Perhaps the most important agency devoted to his welfare—and that devotion has been at times seriously questioned—is the federal government, certainly a secular agency. In one of the instances where I found any comment on the impact of the Christian religion upon the Indians, the evidence was equivocal with reference to results attained. In the absence of more factual evidence I believe that we may conclude that if there has been a decay of religion among Indians, it has been due less to the rise of secularism than to a conflict of cultures.[28]

Secularism, then, due to various reasons, has comparatively preempted the field of philosophy and action devoted to amelioration of the condition of minorities in our land. Secular organizations have been apparently more active, and their activities have been received with increasing hope. The success of science in other fields has stimulated hope that it might also bring solutions in social relations. Scientists have emphasized on occasion both the duty and necessity of using science for moral ends. Lyman Bryson, for example, coins the term "scientific humanism" and defines it as the "struggle to better in every possible way the lives of all human beings."[29] F. L. Wells declares that "benign emergentism" is the "greater correlation of altruistic with aesthetic, intellectual, and other categories than now exists in human nature."[30] Robert A. Millikan sees no conflict between scientific truth and the deepest spiritual values but tends toward a naturalism that is definitely secular in tone.[31] Charles S. Johnson, assessing the problems of the South and the Negro, believes that "economic improvement will bring adjustments in race relations."[32]

As a shining light among secular organizations the National Education Association, sponsoring a program of "intercultural education," adopts as a plank in its platform the "employment of scientific method in the solution of social, economic, political, and other problems of our culture."[33]

---

[28] Laura Thompson and Alice Joseph, "White Pressures Upon Indian Personality and Culture," *American Journal of Sociology*, July, 1947, pp. 17-22.
[29] *Science and Freedom*, p. viii.
[30] In *The Unconscious: A Symposium*, pp. 201-41.
[31] *Christian Education*, Sept., 1947, pp. 271-74.
[32] *Op. cit.*
[33] *Americans All: Studies in Intercultural Education*, pp. 11-12.

Yet when observers assess the effect of secular organizations upon problems of minorities, not too great success is recorded. Donald Young says that the influence of reform organizations and individual reformers in the field of race relations "is definitely limited to particular instances of injustice . . . and to campaigns of public enlightenment concerning the basic community of interests among all peoples in the United States." [34] Walter Lippmann, however, may have touched the tender spot of failure of such theories and organizations when, comparing *laissez faire* and socialism as secular philosophies, he says that they "have ignored the chief lesson of human experience, which is the insight of high religion, that unregenerate men can only muddle into muddle." [35] J. Arthur Thompson, although scouting the idea of man assisting God in human affairs, says that men have not made too much progress in "improving the world without." Therefore he concludes that "until man has made more progress in the cultivation of his own personality, we distrust his landscape-gardening of wild Nature." [36]

If the influence of science reinforcing secularism has been unmarked by notable successes in achieving the good life, it must be due to the fundamental inability of secular philosophy fully to comprehend, and secular methods fully to attain, the ends desired in human relations, or to alleviate maladjustments which exist between minority and dominant groups.

We may take heart when we see that scientists, moralists, and philosophers express uncertainty concerning the attainments of science in problems of human relations. Indeed, Lippmann,[37] Rufus M. Jones, [38] and Irwin Edman [39] cast serious doubts on a main thesis of secularists, that "man knows the good, and his mastery of Nature gives him the power to achieve it."

Are we, then, premature or inaccurate when we suggest that the growth of secularism has changed the focus of minority problems but has offered no acceptable permanent solution? If so, the conclusion is inescapable that Christianity and the church must once again

---

[34] *Op. cit.*, p. 589.
[35] *A Preface to Morals*, pp. 250-51.
[36] *Science and Religion*, p. 226.
[37] *Op. cit.*
[38] *New Eyes for Invisibles*, p. 143.
[39] "Our Changing Moral Weather," *New York Times Book Review*, Oct. 26, 1947.

assume their places in the vanguard of amelioration of social malad-
justment among minorities and never again renounce their pre-eminence to secular philosophies or groups. For it has not yet been
intimated that Christianity and the church do not possess the genius,
power, and personnel to accomplish the spiritual regeneration and
social improvement of mankind.

Is There Any Hope?

What, in conclusion, has been the relation of secularism and
Christianity to race antipathy and minority problems? Certainly in
many respects both have sought to define and bring solution to the
problem in the best of their traditions.

If the influence of Christian attitudes has been vitiated by the
rise of man's belief in his own power to achieve the good apart from
consideration of the divine will in human affairs, that belief has not
been validated by success or remarkable achievement. If Christianity
did not achieve, and is not now achieving, a diminution of antipathies
or a solution of minority problems, it is perhaps due to premature
withdrawal from the field, perhaps to the dilution of secularism, and
certainly to lack of entire faith in the principles which have been
its very heart; or it may very well be due to a continuing hesitation
to attempt anew a task that has once been laid down, if not forgotten.

Meanwhile the problems of minorities remain with us, defying alike
solution and our faith in ourselves, through God, to achieve desired
ends. There is now, and for some time has been, lacking an indispensable ingredient in our formulas for achieving the better life for
men, under the aegis of the Christian Church and philosophy. Rufus
M. Jones has summarized this point of view:

You cannot make a better world by schemes of human betterment
that ignore basic spiritual laws of the universe. You cannot get a golden
age by merely reshuffling old leaden human units. The "acids of mod-
ernity" have eaten under many quick schemes to rehabilitate the sick old
world. We must have faith in the infinite worth and the infinite preciousness of the human soul and in its high destiny as something kin to God
himself. We must deepen the quality of life and enlarge our faith in the
scope of human destiny before any of the fine schemes will work.[40]

[40] Op. cit.

Gordon Poteat states clearly that "only the recognition that all of us depend ultimately on God for what we are can keep us from arrogance and pride. Without Christian faith man oscillates between arrogance and despair." [41]

Leroy Loemker, in his brilliant and incisive chapter on "The Nature of Secularism," has set the stage, has pointed the way to a definite return to the principles of Christianity, and has reinforced our hopes that Christians may yet accomplish enduring and important reforms in the relations of minority groups with the peoples of America:

Most of all, the church must lead men to see the narrowness of their daily loyalties, and the triviality and impermanence of much that they live for. It is our own treasures that betray us in the end. American life can achieve greater substance and durability only through a widespread transvaluation of values. . . . The church must hold aloft the glory of the gospel; it must enlarge our vision of the possibility of salvation, so that even now men's hearts may be strengthened and their resolves to live together in God's spirit clarified by a vision of the will and the power of the living God.

[41] *Can We Have the Fruits of Democracy Without the Roots?* p. 9.

SECULARISM—A BREEDER OF CRIME

J. Edgar Hoover

WE OF THE FEDERAL BUREAU OF INVESTIGATION LOOK TO THE MINIS-
ters of this nation as allies in our fight against those forces which
threaten the security of the United States. The more than 76,000,000
people who profess church membership have it in their power to
make this a more secure and better nation.

But the task is gigantic because through indifference, hypocrisy, or a lackadaisical atttiude God has been blocked out of too
many homes, schools, and entire communities. Proof that large numbers of our people have turned away from God can be found in the
sordid record of crime and in the predominance of a materialistic
way of life which has steadily become more evident each year since
the turn of the century.

Methodists point with pride to their 8,500,000 members. But unfortunately this membership is almost matched in size by another
group—7,500,000 in number—of men and women, boys and girls
who have been arrested for an offense sufficiently serious to warrant
their fingerprints being taken and forwarded to the identification
files of the F.B.I. Here is a force that represents one out of every
nineteen persons in this land, a force responsible for more lives taken
by murder in the past generation than there were Americans killed
during World War II. The same fate is predicted for the next generation.

In dollars and cents the losses occasioned by crime many times
exceed the costs of maintaining all of our religious institutions. There
is no way to evaluate the misery and suffering which follow in the
wake of crime. During the first nine months of 1947 a serious crime
occurred every time your watch ticked off eighteen seconds. Every
forty minutes a human life was taken by murder; every forty-three
minutes a rape was committed; every eight minutes a robbery occurred, often at the point of a gun; every five minutes two automo-

biles were stolen; every one and three-quarter minutes a burglary was perpetrated; and every thirty-three seconds a larceny occurred. In addition there were millions of lesser offenses which present a problem of shocking proportions.

REASONS FOR CRIME

But why? you ask. Do we not have the finest churches, the greatest educational systems, excellent means of recreation, and the highest standard of living? All these we have, but we have departed from fundamentals. We have grown physically, intellectually, and materially—but spiritually we have not kept pace.

There was a time when man began his day with prayer and ended it with thanksgiving. In that time our nation was founded with the acknowledgment that all men "are endowed by their creator with certain inalienable rights," and it was acknowledged that for every right there was a duty—the duty of a "firm reliance on the protection of Divine Providence." This nation started with God and flourished with God's help; but now that we have grown of age, vast segments of our population apparently feel that God has served his purpose and is no longer needed.

I have long realized that such agencies as the F.B.I., however necessary, are but temporary expedients. Law enforcement can apprehend the wrongdoer and bring him to justice; but we work in a vicious circle, because more than half of all persons committed to our penal institutions are repeaters.

It was not long after I was appointed director of the Federal Bureau of Investigation in 1924 that I reached the inevitable conclusion that a crime-free America means a land where God reigns, not in symbolic terms but in reality, in the hearts and minds of a majority of our people.

The extensive and erudite theories of crime causation fill many books, but this is needless because the real cause can be stated in a few words. Men and women commit crime because they lack a sense of moral responsibility. For the most part, men and women commit crime in the exercise of their free will by intentional wrongdoing. "Righteousness exalteth a nation: but sin is a reproach to any people." This bit of scripture states a truth which cannot be contradicted, because righteousness is God-given. It can come from no other source.

Sin and crime are matters of degree, but they stem from a common source—godlessness or, as expressed in terms of the theme of this book, secularism.

In its initial stages secularism is not an evil of immorality or aggressive badness. It is an evil of amorality and indifference. That is why I have said time and again that "the greatest crime is the toleration of crime."

Secularism, I have never doubted, is the basic cause of crime, and crime is a manifestation of secularism. The secular notion that whatever gets results is good, the secular preoccupation with goods and gadgets, and the secular indifference to what Paul calls "the unsearchable riches of Christ"—these ultimately find expression in the man who takes a short cut across all the moral and legal codes of humanity and grabs what he wants by force. The difference between this man and the man who, by devious practices, spends his life accumulating wealth, totally indifferent to the moral chaos around him, is merely a difference in technique. They both itch with the same greed, and both have the same goal. One becomes impatient, misses his goal, and becomes an outlaw. The other arrives, accepted by a world willing to ignore the slime through which he has waded, a world prone to shrug off the moral implications of his arrival by saying, "You can't argue with success."

This is the secular apologue. The moral that our children can draw from it is that they must not get caught, that the means do not matter as long as the end is attained. Here is the summation of secularism. Crime begins with this amoral notion of guilt.

Sometimes it starts in high places, which makes it all the more serious. For example, I have been told of a community known for its peaceful atmosphere, where gangsters are given sanctuary so long as they do not ply their trade. Certain gambling houses run to capacity in violation of the law, the affluent gambling syndicate having bought protection by paying a reported $1,500 a day to the corrupt political machine in power during the season it is in operation. I know you are asking, "Where were the police?" The officers themselves, no doubt, would have gladly raided these dens of chance, but they were powerless to act because the man who received the payoff controlled their every action.

The fact that corruption has existed in high places is distressing, to be sure. Even more distressing is the apparent quiescence of church people. The voices of the ministers of the gospel can sound the clarion call for good citizenship. The spirit of the Master rising in righteous indignation to drive the money-changers out of the temple is what is needed. The fact that a gambling syndicate pays off some public officials is as shocking as the fact that secular-minded people tolerate such a condition.

The voice of even one courageous preacher mounting his pulpit in righteous indignation with the fortitude to carry through would be all that would be necessary, unless, of course, his words fell on an audience so numbed by secularism that they had lost their Christian perception of right. Even then, I have faith that the spirit of God would manifest itself and prevail.

In another city an honest chief of police was ousted from office. He had committed the offense of securing an affidavit from the operator of a house of prostitution, alleging that two of the top city officials had been customers in her house and had threatened her with death if she ever revealed the details of their patronage. So far as I have been able to learn, the church people failed to come to the aid of this man, whom I know to be honest and God-fearing.

Gambling and vice syndicates could be driven out of business within twenty-four hours in every community in the land where they operate in violation of the law but for the protection which secularism gives them.

The crime problem is essentially a youth problem. In the first nine months of 1947 the arrests of boys under twenty-one years of age increased 13.6 per cent over the same period the previous year. The greatest increase in the arrests of boys under twenty-one was for offenses against common decency, which increased 26 per cent over 1946.

Of all persons arrested for murder in the first nine months of 1947, 12 per cent were under twenty-one years of age; so were 26 per cent of all persons arrested for larceny, 27.8 per cent of all persons arrested for rape, 28 per cent of all persons arrested for robbery, 39 per cent of all persons arrested for burglary, and 47 per cent of all persons arrested for auto theft.

The tragic aspect of these figures is found in the fact that 55 per cent of all persons arrested had records of prior arrest. Invariably you will hear these words in courts: "This is the first time he was arrested, your Honor." How false they are in spirit. It may be the first time he is before the court, but invariably he is already an old offender. These words simply mean that this is the first time he was caught. These boys and girls are products of the American home, which should be a place of learning as well as a place of living.

SECULARISM'S TOLL

Secularism has taken its toll. Too many homes consist of four walls, some furniture, something to eat, and a place to sleep. The spirit of parenthood has vanished or, to be more correct, has been superseded by one of secularism. The moral fiber of the nation has weakened. Standards of decency have been polluted. Human rights have been trampled in the slime of corruption, indifference, and selfishness. A wanton disregard for personal responsibility is growing.

The experiences of law enforcement authorities are filled with record after record of parental neglect. For example, police in one city were advised that a crying baby was keeping everyone awake. They investigated and found a five-month-old baby girl in her crib. Blisters caused by filth covered her legs; there were large bed sores on her back. A two-year-old girl was found tied to a bed. A three-year-old girl tied to the bedstead with a window-sash cord had succeeded in crawling out the window to an open porch. All three of the children were nude. The father, because of his work, was forced to be away from home considerably. The mother openly associated with other men and brought them to the home for entertainment. On the night in question, however, both parents were out "enjoying" themselves.

For the most part, delinquent children are the products of neglect and improper training, the victims of parents who either never knew or completely disregarded their responsibilities.

When homes are broken, the children are the real victims. They are the ones who suffer the consequences of secularism which manifests itself in selfishness. Incompatibility not only keeps the lives of parents in a constant state of turmoil but likewise leads to emotionally upset children who can develop rebellious attitudes.

One such case recently came across my desk. A youngster had stabbed another child. The real crime was not the boy's but his parents'. On many occasions he was forced to witness their arguments, which sometimes necessitated police intervention. In fact, as a result of their drinking and fighting they devoted little attention to the boy, who was undernourished and, resenting his home life, developed an aggressiveness which caused his attacks upon smaller children.

Criminals are made, not born. Long before a youngster is legally labeled a juvenile delinquent, his acts are mirrored by a familiar pattern of conduct which usually manifests itself in truancy, falsehoods, failure to carry out family instructions, and petty stealing. Each dereliction leads to another; and unless the youngster learns the fundamental lessons of self-discipline, trouble is inevitable.

It is all well and good to give youngsters the greatest amount of freedom in expressing themselves. But when freedom of expression transgresses common decency, it imposes upon the rights of others. It is then time to call a halt. Our prisons and reformatories today are filled with men and women, boys and girls, who have had too much freedom of expression and too little self-discipline.

Among my earliest recollections are the lessons I learned in Sunday school, supplemented by the teachings of my parents, that everyone is a child of God. I was also taught that while man is created in the image of God, he soon had what preachers call a "fall," because he did not obey the mandates of God. Then after a long span of time, when secularism was as rampant as it is today, God sent his Son to bring salvation to those who believed. The lessons laid down by the Master were not then, nor are they today, easy ones. But *if, if* the world lived by these lessons, by the Golden Rule, the Kingdom would be upon us, and the brotherhood of man would logically follow.

In this modern day, however, we often "get the cart before the horse." Therein, I think, is where secularism has been able to make its advances. We espouse the social gospel too frequently without the Christian gospel coming first. We too frequently think of the glories of heaven without realizing the inevitable consequences of perdition. We can still fear and fight the menace of secularism, but

I think we can also with profit take the affirmative approach of the Sermon on the Mount.

The experiences of our modern day prove conclusively that those who call themselves Christians frequently have had too much freedom and too little discipline. By tightening up the ranks we can present a solid phalanx through which secularism cannot penetrate.

As the lengthening shadow of despair falls across the world, we have no other place to look, except to religion, for guidance and strength. Crime is not another social or economic problem, like the housing shortage; it is a spiritual problem because it results from spiritual apathy.

Law and order are not ends in themselves; they are the means whereby we can enjoy our inalienable rights of life, liberty, and the pursuit of happiness. Law and order provide the means wherein we may enjoy our civil rights and also perpetuate our democratic order.

You know only too well how on occasions the church and the religious man are held up to scorn and ridicule by the secularist who rejects all forms of religious faith and worship, and maintains that the problems of the present life should be the sole objects of man's concern.

The F.B.I. and Communism

I feel qualified to speak on this because the organization I have been so proud to head for twenty-four years is the constant target of attack. Those whose progress we block resort to every strategem and charge. You may have heard it said that the F.B.I. is a menace to civil rights—but you have never seen the charges proved because the F.B.I. is a protector of civil rights. I grant we are a menace to those who seek civil license to rob, plunder, kill, and subvert our democratic order to a totalitarian way of life.

You have heard it said that the F.B.I. is anti-Communist. This it is; but we were also among the first in the land to move against the Nazis, the Fascists, and the hooded K.K.K., and we came through World War II with an absence of enemy-directed acts of sabotage and with espionage under control. We also came through the war without the outbreak of mob violence.

The F.B.I. today is the same organization which protected civil rights during the war years; it is staffed by the same men, who are the products of our American colleges, universities, and churches— by the men and women who can be counted upon to give the same high quality of stewardship they have given in the past. Above all the F.B.I. is an organization made up of men and women appointed and promoted because of their ability; and it is an organization where race, color, or creed has no place. If I can judge by the sacrificial efforts put forth by the men and women who do its work, I suspect that secularism has made little advance in their lives.

Secularism advances because men have little faith in God. The menace of secularism also lies in the fact that it too is a crusade. The secularists themselves have turned to a kind of religion and have become militant.

The danger of Communism in America lies not in the fact that it is a political philosophy but in the awesome fact that it is a materialistic religion, inflaming in its adherents a destructive fanaticism. *Communism is secularism on the march.* It is a mortal foe of Christianity. Either it will survive, or Christianity will triumph, because in this land of ours the two cannot live side by side.

The Communist bible is Marxianism, and its messiah is Lenin, who said:

Marxism is not materialism which stops at ABC. Marxism goes further. . . . It says: We must be able to combat religion, and in order to do this we must explain from the materialistic point of view why faith and religion are prevalent among the masses. . . . Hence down with religion. Long live atheism! The dissemination of atheist views is our chief task.

In his book *Toward a Soviet America,* which is used as a text in Communist schools, William Z. Foster, who heads the Communist Party of the United States, says:

God will be banished from the laboratories as well as from the schools. . . . The churches will remain free to continue their services, but their special tax and other privileges will be liquidated. Their buildings will revert to the State. Religious schools will be abolished and organized religious training for minors prohibited. Freedom will be established for anti-religious propaganda.

This expression of Communist doctrine does have the virtue of being forthright. But when the Communists found their views growing in unpopularity, they changed their tactics. A Trojan horse strategy was substituted for open attack. Their aim—the destruction of the power of religion and the establishment of a godless, atheistic society—has not changed. Only their propaganda line has undergone alteration. Now they, the most reactionary advocates of tyranny the world has ever known, best described by the phrase "Red Fascists," advertise themselves as the champions of liberty. They claim to stand for equal rights, for better working conditions, for the abatement of poverty, for the equitable division of the products of industry, and for the rights of racial groups and political minorities. But all those idealistic objectives for which all God-fearing people stand are but a cover to conceal their real aims of undermining democracy.

Communism is an infamous international conspiracy against Christianity and democracy—and they know it.

We Americans are at a crossroads. We will either turn and follow the road upward toward the abiding faith of our fathers and the redemptive power of the Master, or we will follow the road of secularism downward toward the familiar demigods of state and tyranny.

The churches lead us, I know, toward the upper road. The responsibility of the churches is tremendous. Of all the forces for good, the message of the church alone has the final solution to the problems of our time. Secularism springs up where Christianity has retreated, or where it has grown weak, or where it has never been.

The man who confessed, "Thou art the Christ," approaching his days of martyrdom in a world filled with false prophets and teachings, gives us an answer today as he did to his people then. Peter, I am sure, was pleading for the development of Christian character as well as trying to thwart secularism when he wrote:

Grace and peace be multiplied unto you through the knowledge of God, and of Jesus our Lord,
According as his divine power hath given unto us all things that pertain unto life and godliness, through the knowledge of him that hath called us to glory and virtue:
Whereby are given unto us exceeding great and precious promises:

that by these ye might be partakers of the divine nature, having escaped the corruption that is in the world through lust.

And beside this, giving all diligence, add to your faith virtue; and to virtue knowledge;

And to knowledge temperance; and to temperance patience; and to patience godliness;

And to godliness brotherly kindness; and to brotherly kindness charity.

For if these things be in you, and abound, they make you that ye shall neither be barren nor unfruitful in the knowledge of our Lord Jesus Christ. —II Pet. 1:2-8

PERSONALITIES—UNPRODUCTIVE, HANDICAPPED, AND NEUROTIC

Henry Lee Robison, Jr.

To SAVE LIFE, GIVE IT MEANING, ZEST, AND SAVOR ARE THE MULTIPLE functions of religion in our everyday existence.

The average man may claim that he has no place in his thinking for theology. His chief concern, he explains, is making a living and getting along with his neighbors by being honest and minding his own business.

And yet that is exactly the concern of theology. In fact theology is one of the commonest commodities on the market of civilization. It is handled daily by the people, whether they recognize it or not.

The theology by which man lives is made up of our conception of what God is like, and what man is, and the meaning of life.

In the eighth psalm the question is asked: "What is man?" The answer to this plunges us at once into life's complex and complicated realities. According to the King James Version the psalmist says: "Thou hast made him a little lower than the angels." Another version translates this: "Thou hast made him a little less than divine." A third declares: "Thou hast made him a little lower than God." Choose which you may; the problem is about the same.

Religion has always answered the question "What is man?" with this threefold explanation: In the first place man's relation to God's creation is the crown of creation. Secondly, in relation to God, man is a son made in his image. And in the third place man in relation to his fellow man is a brother.

This complicates life. If we could say some men by peculiar gifts are thus in high relationship to creation, to God, and to the human race, we could settle the matter of our responsibility to the economically unproductive, the handicapped, and the neurotic. We could use the gas chamber for some, isolate others in asylums or prisons, and send some to the faraway islands and forget them. But the problem cannot be solved so simply as long as we allow theology to complicate our lives.

It is not even satisfactory to say, "I am my brother's keeper." Sometimes the state must be the "keeper" in the form of the nurse for a tuberculosis patient, the attendant for the mentally ill, or the guard for the socially sick. But the "keeper" relationship is not satisfactory for the Christian. He must be a brother, and as a brother share the burdens of his less fortunate brothers. This means that it behooves us to seek constantly for improved ways to enrich the lives of the members of God's family.

"When the Nazis entered upon systematic extermination of all the feeble-minded in Germany, the Christian conscience was aroused throughout the world," says Dr. Seward Hiltner, executive secretary of the Commission on Religion and Health of the Federal Council of Churches. Then he adds: "What do we more than these?"

Certainly it is a virtue not to exterminate. But it is doubtful whether the crowding of 180 persons in a "cottage," 400 in a dining hall, herding large groups in a dormitory at 6 P.M. to be awakened at 5 A.M. can be considered a basis of Christian dealing. We must be grateful for the humanitarian progress on the part of our state governments, which have established seventy-six institutions in this nation for a hundred thousand feeble-minded persons. But we must yet go on to give adequate care to this group. Furthermore we must make provisions to educate and care for an additional half million persons in this country whose intelligence is too low to permit them economic independence in a complex society.

A few years ago Harry A. Bice conducted a brief study of religious education programs in mental deficiency institutions. He found a serious lack of material and planning in the programs. This prompted the convention of the American Association on Mental Deficiency to declare: "If religious and ethical instruction is a means of motivation that we should continue to use, then we should do a better piece of work with it."

Since 1945 a number of studies have been organized and authorized by the Federal Council of Churches' Commission on Religion and Health. Projects are being conducted to improve religious programs in institutions housing the handicapped, demonstrating how the Chrsitian conscience can work through our churches to help man assume intelligently the responsibilities of brotherhood in the fields of the economically unproductive, the handicapped, and the neurotic.

One Sunday morning, in the midst of the first hymn of the service, I chanced to glance down the center aisle of my church and noted a familiar face on the right about two thirds down. I could not recall where I had seen this man before. He was not a member of the church, neither had I seen him in the congregation before. When the service was over, I tried to locate him in the throng, but he evaded me. The next Sunday he was there again, and again I failed to locate him after the service. The third Sunday I made sure that I would get to meet my friend.

During the singing of the last hymn I walked down the aisle, planning to give the benediction from the rear of the church. Just as I passed this man, my mind clicked; his name came to me, and the name of the place where I had known him.

As the congregation went out, I shook hands with my visitor and asked him to wait awhile so I could talk with him. He consented. When the people had gone, I inquired where he was living; and, finding that it was in the direction of the parsonage, I invited him to ride with me. As soon as we were in the car, he said: "You know, I came to your church because I knew your father." I was pleased at hearing this and inquired about himself and his family. He told me that eight years before he became mentally ill. The family physician suggested that he enter one of our state hospitals, with the assurance that he would recover. He said that they had been helpful to him at this hospital and now he was discharged and fully recovered. His general health was good, and he had a job. But during his stay in the hospital his children had grown up and married, and his wife had become self-supporting. They were all kind to him, but they had so adapted their lives that they no longer needed him. He viewed this as the greatest tragedy of his experience.

Like tragedies go on every day in our American life. The church alone is in position to prevent them. An understanding minister in the home church, together with an understanding hospital minister, could have worked together to keep the ties strong enough in this family to have prevented this tragedy. The family could have been helped to adjust to a temporary separation, always looking forward to the day when they could be united. Instead of a breaking of ties, the ties could have been strengthened, and the lives of every member could have been enriched.

The Need for Institutional Ministers

There is a great need for intelligent and trained institutional ministers today. The relation between them and the church should be very close. This closeness can be created by the church taking the responsibility of providing ministers for this major home-mission field. The church can train, select, and provide adequately for the support of such ministers. Such a plan calls for an understanding relationship between our state institutions and the church, but it also ensures against the domination of the church by the state or the state by the church.

The institutional minister is a member of the institutional staff, but he is also independent of it. He works in close co-operation with the staff, but at the same time he is recognized by the patients of the hospital or the inmates of the prison as the minister and not an official of the state. Thus his ministry is enriched, and his relationship to all concerned is evident. If he is wise, he becomes a counselor for the staff and the patients. He remains a link between the church and the institution, being in a position to advise with the administration when he is sought, and to keep the church aware of its responsibility to the patients and their families.

Where do we find a community of fifteen hundred persons without half a dozen churches and ministers? Yet a large number of our public institutions are still without the ministry of the church.

The charge is often made that chaplains in public institutions are lackeys for the superintendent—mere handy men to censor the mail, provide entertainment for the patients, and make a good impression on the public. Sometimes this has been true. But it is a condition that need not continue. It is one of the strongest arguments for church support of institutional pastors.

The old saying that "he who pays the fiddler calls the tune" holds true in this field. When the state pays the salary and the superintendent of a public institution signs the check, the relationship of the institutional pastor to the staff and patient group is different. On the other hand, when the church pays the bills and works out a definite arrangement with the institutional authorities, a proper relationship is realized. When the pastor is charged with the responsibility of working out a constructive worship and instruction program for the community church (not the chapel) and seeks opportunity to know his people and their problems by constant checking with the physicians, psychiatrists, and social workers, he becomes a shepherd of the flock. The story of the institutional ministers' work will be different only when the pastors are chosen because of their qualifications—of the right personality, equipment, and type of consecration the work requires—and when the church adequately finances this work.

Providing adequately trained and supported pastors for public institutions is not the total work of the church, however; two more things are imperative. First, a definite program for counseling families whose members are in the institutions must be worked out. Institutional ministers are responsible for making confidential reports to the local parish pastors. At the same time a relationship of confidence with the inmate or patient must be maintained. This requires sound judgment and a special sensitivity on the part of the minister. In the second place the churches in the community have other responsibilities toward the institution besides providing for a qualified chaplain. Persons in the institution must have a wholesome attitude toward the larger community of which they are a part. The local ministers, by regular visits to the institutional church, can contribute much toward this. By serving the community at large the churches can help the institutional population feel that they belong to the society at large.

What Is the Institutional Minister's Job?

The beginning of wisdom in ministering to the handicapped in a congregation or a public institution is to be found in the pastor's conception of his calling. Just what is his job? Or is it a job at all?

Clergymen have been called by many titles. I think one of the most devastating is the title "doctor." Frequently those who designate themselves "doctor" are the least deserving of the name. When a minister answers the telephone by saying, "This is Dr. So-and-So," I cringe. Such a man is building a barrier between himself and his people. To be called a doctor by others is not the same thing as referring to oneself as doctor.

The most appealing designation for a parish minister is "pastor," which is used by the Germans and by our own American Lutherans.

The title has respect, personal affection, and indicates the office to which the minister is called, namely, pastor or shepherd, one whose high privilege it is to be a friend and a personal counselor in the name of the great Shepherd; one who guides, watches over, and feeds his flock.

This is of special importance in the institutional ministry. The most common title used is chaplain. Some object to this designation on two grounds. First, the title is one long associated with the military. Second, for too long our institutional ministers have been men grown old and worn out in useful ministry who face the alternative of retiring or accepting a chaplaincy post in some institution. Generally they choose to do both. This condition has been tragic. It has led the public, institutional officials, and patients to look upon the title and the office of chaplain with less than proper respect.

A clergyman qualifying for the institutional ministry should have training and experience similar to that of regular pastors. But in addition he must have other essential training to qualify him for the work.

College and seminary degrees are basic. To this should be added a thoroughgoing clinical training course, including resident study of at least three months in a general hospital, a mental hospital, and a well-organized prison. In each case he should be directed in his study and experience by a well-qualified institutional pastor. His work in these places should include counseling, leadership in worship and religious education, and contact with pastors and families of inmates or patients. He should be given every opportunity to know the institutional social workers, physicians, and psychiatrists. He should have access to a wide variety of books dealing with mental and physical health and some especially designed to interpret the relationship of his job to that of other professional workers. He should know something of the psychosomatic approach to medicine and its relation to the problems of religion and health. He must learn to avoid the tendency to step outside his role as a pastor and confuse himself with the psychiatrist or social worker. He is related to both, but he has his own peculiar function which is as important as either. Familiarity with a few psychological terms does not qualify one as a psychiatrist any more than the ability to recite the Ten Commandments makes one a minister.

The numerous types of social work known today have grown out of the experience of the church in its effort to minister to the handicapped. It has been quite proper, as institutions have grown and social-work technique has become specialized and enlarged, that this work should be taken over by the community. Frequently, however, this has resulted in the church and its offspring growing apart. Every effort should be exercised to help the church to continue its interest in, and to make its unique contribution to, the ministry of social work in our world. The church and the state should co-operate in every way helpful in ministering to those in need.

Institutional pastors must avoid the danger of becoming *institutionalized*. Many workers succumb to this temptation.

Bishop Francis J. McConnell tells of his first trip to the Orient to represent the Methodist Church. It rained slowly all day when he arrived in Shanghai. He saw jinrikisha boys pulling their jinrickishas for a penny a mile, getting hot, sitting down on the curb to rest, cooling off, and coughing. That night when he reached his hotel, he could not sleep, thinking of the jinrikisha boys, pulling their burdens, resting, coughing.

He remained in Shanghai a month. On the thirtieth day it rained again. Jinrikisha boys again pulled their customers for a penny a mile, perspired, sat down on the curb, cooled off, and coughed. Bishop McConnell went to his hotel that night and slept.

We must not permit ourselves to become so accustomed to human tragedy and suffering that we are no longer sensitive to the needs of men. A minister's job is to share in the experience and to identify himself with his people so that their burdens become his. Only then can he effectively reveal the gospel of God's love—a love that has not merely a sentimental quality about it but one that has healing power in it. An experience of from five to ten years in an ordinary parish will help an institutional pastor to keep his perspective, be aware, and guard against professionalism.

A Clinical Case

One morning during the depression there came a knock on my study door. In response to my invitation to come in the door opened, and a strange young man entered.

"Mr. Robison, I'm in hell. Could I see you alone?" he burst out.

I dismissed my secretary with a nod and invited the visitor to sit down. My study was small. The handsome young man refused to sit down, but paced back and forth across the room.

"I've been in hell ever since I went to church yesterday," he began his story. "Three weeks ago I came here with a woman who is not my wife. Everything went O.K. until we went to church.

"I have been married for ten years, and my wife recently had our first child. We have been happy during the years since we were married, but during her pregnancy I began going out with women. It was all innocent at first, until I fell for this cheap woman. She knew I was married and recently suggested that we come away together. I have a new truck with which I can make a living. The people in whose home we are staying insisted on our going to church with them. We declined until yesterday. As soon as I stepped inside the church, I was in hell. All that I have done became clear to me. I've been a fool. I love my wife, and I want to go back to her and tell her the whole story and ask her forgiveness. I believe she will take me back and let us start all over together."

He told me his story uninterrupted, making it clear that he had suggested to his companion that they might return home, but she had refused. He was afraid that she might cause trouble if he attempted to leave her, because he had brought her across the state line. He feared becoming involved in the white-slave-traffic law. Then I asked my first question: "Are you willing to go back and tell your wife the whole truth?"

He answered, "Yes."

Then I asked, "What do you want me to do?"

He explained that he wanted me to find out from a local judge how he could move and not get into trouble. I called a judge I knew well, and he assured me that the lad was free to go home if the girl was of legal age. Then the youth made his decision. He would get up the next day, leave enough money for his companion to return to her home, and then leave.

The decision was his. I said very little during the entire interview. He did not reveal his name, and I did not ask for it. No sermon was necessary. My part in this was being a listener. It was unnecessary to give advice or to preach. The very fact that he had come to me as a minister indicated that he wanted to find the right decision and that that decision was to be his own, based on his religious experience. There were three of us there that day. This youth, the minister, and God. The minister acted as a catalytic agent; his presence made it possible for the young man to get the courage and strength from God to do what he was already convinced was right.

One morning there was a note in my box at the state prison where I was serving as a minister. It was from Mike, who worked in the print shop. He wanted to see me. Frequently our paths had crossed on the prison grounds, but I was unable to make any sort of impression on the youth. The request surprised me, as well as his fellow prisoners. I sent for him; and when he came, I invited him to sit down.

"No, thank you," he answered.

"What can I do for you?" I asked. He was a slender, handsome youth of twenty-two. Quiet, industrious, and always minding his own business.

"Mr. Robison, don't get me wrong," he said in answer to my inquiry. "I don't go in for this religious stuff, but I thought you would help me."

The Lord endowed me with an easy smile and a sense of humor. I smiled and said: "That's all right. How can I help you?"

He took a small piece of paper from his pocket and laid it before me on the desk, and said: "You see that?"

It was a pencil drawing of a man's head made from a newspaper print.

"This is some of my work," he explained. "I have a gift for drawing. The doctor tells me that I have heart trouble and that when I get out I will have to make my living by using my head rather than my hands. I wondered if you would get me a magnifying glass like this?" He indicated a reading glass with a handle.

I assured him that I would be glad to get one.

"Of course, I shall pay for it and for your trouble," he added. And then as he turned to go, he repeated: "Now don't get me wrong. I don't go in for this religious stuff." I laughed this time and stood up as he went out.

I had a reading glass in my bureau drawer at home that had belonged to my mother. It had not been used for six years since her death, except one day when my son Jim, who was ten, had spent a day in bed with a cold and had used the glass to burn a hole in the sheet.

That night as I was preparing for bed, I recalled my promise to Mike. I slipped the reading glass into my coat pocket.

The next day was not my regular day for visiting the institution, but I dropped by and sent for Mike. When he came in, he was embarrassed, realizing that I had made a special trip to bring the reading glass. I gave it to him. He said: "Thank you, but I really didn't want you to go to any trouble over me."

I assured him it was no trouble. When he asked me how much the glass cost, I told him it would cost him nothing, but he protested. Then I said: "Mike, this glass did not cost me anything, yet I came by it honestly. It will not cost you anything if you will accept it."

He expressed his gratitude, but warned me a third time that he did not "go in for this religious stuff." Again I laughed, and this time he smiled. As he went out of the door, he looked over his shoulder and said: "Mr. Robison, I always thought you were a stuffed shirt, but you're O.K. by me."

I knew then that I had won my spurs.

From the records I learned that Mike had come from Maine, that his people were nominally Roman Catholic, and that his father had died when Mike was about fourteen. Then his mother had remarried; and although Mike had stuck it out through high school, he was never very happy over his mother's marriage. As soon as school was out, he went to sea and landed at Norfolk, where he got into difficulty with some other sailors and had come to prison.

I saw Mike a few times in the print shop, looked over his drawings. About ten days before he was to go out, I sent for him, as I did all the men to ask about their plans. This was not to give advice but to let the men, if they wanted, "just talk it over." When Mike came in, I said, "Well, Mike, I see you will soon be going out. What are your plans?"

This time Mike sat down and relaxed more than ever before. He seemed glad to talk it over.

"I am going to Washington," he told me. I asked him why he chose that city.

"Well, in the first place, it's out of Virginia," he explained. Many men said this because there is an additional year for second offenses in Virginia.

"In the second place," he said, "Washington is a big place. I want a job with a commercial artist where I can learn and earn. There ought to be some jobs like that in Washington."

I agreed with his reasoning, then added: "Mike, I have a friend in Washington who has helped a great many people. She is Mrs. Morris. Would you like her address?" He would. Then I explained that when one goes into a new place it is important to establish an address that is acceptable and that it is also important to meet people who will be helpful.

I gave him the address on the back of my card, then added, "Mike, several times you have told me that you don't go in for 'that religious stuff.' Do you mind telling me what you meant."

"Well, Mr. Robison," he began, "I find that the churches are not interested in people. They are simply interested in building up their membership and getting money. The Catholics want to get the Protestants. The Protestants want to get the Catholics. The Methodists want to get the Presbyterians, and the Baptists want to get the Methodists. They aren't really interested in helping people."

"Mike, I am a Protestant minister," I told him, "and I wouldn't walk across the street to change a man from one church to another, but I would be willing to give my right arm, if need be, to help you understand what God can mean in the life of a man."

We talked a few minutes about God, and then with a brief prayer we shook hands, and Mike left.

That night I wrote Mrs. Morris and told her that a week from Friday Mike would come to see her.

Three weeks later I received two letters. Mrs. Morris wrote, thanking me for sending Mike to see her. The other letter came from Mike, thanking me for sending him to Washington. Of course, I did not send him to Washington. That was his own idea.

In the next letter Mrs. Morris related that on Mike's third visit "just to talk" she asked him if he had a New Testament. He confessed that he did not have one. She asked, "If I give you one, a good one with readable type, will you use it?" He said he would.

The next time he visited Mrs. Morris, Mike made a confession: "I have read my New Testament every day, and for the first time in my life I have prayed."

He wrote me brief letters every two weeks, telling me of going to church with Mrs. Morris and of meeting some fine Christian businessmen. He walked about Washington for a couple of weeks, going to a few shows, stopping at the library to read some good books, and hearing some music. He enjoyed his new freedom to the fullest. After he had been there two weeks, he landed the first job for which he applied. It was with a young commercial artist who wanted a man willing to work and learn.

Mike stayed for a year, and then his employer closed shop to enter the army. Mike had no job. He applied for a place with one of the federal agencies and gave me as a reference. The F.B.I. sent a man to inquire about Mike's prison record. My reply was: "I would give Mike any job that I might have if it was in the realm of his knowledge and experience." The F.B.I. recommended him, and he has steadily moved up in the federal service since his first employment.

One day soon after Mike went to Washington I had a hunch that I should go to see him. I telephoned, went up, and met him at a well-known restaurant one Saturday afternoon. When we sat at the table, Mike unfolded his long legs, relaxed, then confided, "Mr. Robison, our chance meeting in Richmond was the turning point in my life."

I smiled, then said, "That was not a chance meeting, Mike. God was there, and his church was there because you are important."

Long ago Jesus said to his disciples, "Ye are the salt of the earth." Salt, as we commonly use it, has a double purpose. In the first place it saves food, keeps it from spoiling. And in the second place it gives flavor and tang, making food tasty and desirable.

Just so should we be and do. It is our business as brothers to our fellow men to save life, keep it from spoiling, give it flavor, zest, and meaning.

Part

V

CHRISTIANITY'S WITNESS
IN A SECULAR WORLD

THE MISSIONARY ENTERPRISE

Hugh C. Stuntz

MISSIONARY PASSION IS THE GENIUS OF CHRISTIANITY. THE CURVE OF vigorous life indicated by the expansion of Christianity has always been determined by the zeal of Christians to win men to Christ. Whenever the church has become complacent, institutionalized, ecclesiastically minded, or turned inward upon itself, the flame of vigorous life has flickered low. Perhaps the greatest danger faced by Christianity in our day is that the church, honeycombed by secular influences and facing the pressures of secularism from without, may in spite of world-wide spiritual hunger become merely a comfortable fellowship of decent citizens who mind their own business.

The health of Christianity has invariably grown from, and been reinvigorated by, the results of missionary zeal coming up from the "grass roots" of society, as in the days of John Wesley, or rebounding from the frontiers of Christian missions, as in the days of Livingstone, Thoburn, Lambuth, and Mott. During the past hundred years the source of missionary power has come, not from Mediterranean Europe, so long the center of Roman Catholic influence, nor from northern Europe, more recently the center of Protestant influence, but from Britain and North America, particularly from the United States, though less than 150 years ago our country was a frontier mission field. During the next century that source of Christian health may well move on to Asia.

The responsibility of Christianity is immediate as well as long range. We face the emergency demands of a "time of troubles," as Arnold J. Toynbee calls it, made ominous by our inability to control for human welfare the forces of nature harnessed by our secular and scientific minds. At the same time we are part of the fragmented and undisciplined body of believers, called Christians and comprising one fourth of the human race, who have the secret, but apparently lack the will, the vision, the unity and therefore the power, to lead mankind into brotherhood. We face the disintegration of a civilization that has inherited the finest conceptions of God, man, and society, but which has permitted those ideal concepts to be overlayed and smothered by the base goals of materialism. But we must look ahead, as well as serve the present age. Christianity holds no brief for any secular way of life; it survived the fall of Roman civilization and will survive, if it cannot yet redeem and purify, this Western civilization. However, mere survival is not our goal. We believe it possible for the gospel of Jesus Christ to create a new civilization. We are not thinking merely in terms of minor or major repairs to the old machine, but how we may create a new vehicle for society that shall utilize whatever is good from every culture to build one world of human brotherhood. Such an enterprise requires spiritual and social engineers who set their stakes by the centuries, who share the patience and confidence of Christ, and who do not permit immediate misfortune to turn them from the ultimate design.

HOME MISSIONS

This is the missionary enterprise as I see it: A program of sacrificial self-giving in the effort to win men to Christ, to make Christ relevant to every aspect of human life, to free men from bondage to the power of evil, and to help them comprehensively to achieve abundant life now. And it is also a long-range movement in which men share with God through Christ in the eternal task of bringing in the Kingdom of God. These are not separate goals; results of the immediate task will channel into and quicken the current of the greater movement, but too much preoccupation with immediate needs of men has at times led Christians into mistakes that the long view should correct. We need the balance of bifocal vision.

One of the greatest responsibilities of the ministry in the United States is to lead church members toward an adequate appreciation of missions. For generations millions of American Protestants have thought of foreign missions as being little more than a sentimental, soul-saving gesture toward unfortunate and unenlightened folk, "half-devil and half-child," in lands far beyond their primary range of interest. Unfortunately missions too often has been portrayed as a bit of charity, a patronizing gift from superiors to inferiors, until a large proportion of church members and a majority of adult citizens have received an entirely erroneous impression of the vital, constructive, long-range program of redemption, of building world brother-hood that really is Christian missions. If there is still a chance that we may win one world in spite of present conflicts, that chance remains largely because of what Christian missions has meant to people of every race and culture, enabling them to reach across barriers of man-made differences and enjoy fellowship in terms of a common faith. The world church is a product of missions; the ecumenical ideal is largely a product of missions; leadership toward greater co-operation and unity within Protestantism has been in many instances the result of missions. And the incontrovertible testimony of thousands who dur-ing the war saw at first hand the product of missionary effort in every part of the world adds to the evidence that Christian missions is not a sentimental bit of charity but rather a realistic movement for the establishment of human brotherhood in one world.

In the United States so-called home missions have been better able to justify their importance to American church members, for that program of service has been within reach and has been directed toward the most needy conditions of city and country life. Manifestly, com-munity churches or settlements serving various minority or disadvan-taged groups, located in overcrowded slum districts, are mission pro-jects deserving adequate support. Pioneer work among American Indians, with men in lumber camps, with people in sparsely settled areas, or among the isolated folk of the Ozarks, the Cumberlands, the Smoky and the Appalachian Mountains, is again clearly mission work. The changing problems of shifting industries that drag a huge follow-ing of workers with them, as well as the condition of migratory workers who follow the harvests, present even more compelling need for home missions.

Home missions also meets the problem of race relations and must seek not only to lift the race discriminated against to a higher religious, moral, economic, educational, and civil status, but, what is equally important, also to transform attitudes of superiority among those practicing discrimination. The task of reorganizing ingrained habits in human relationships is long and slow, but it is a major responsibility of home missions if we are to demonstrate our gospel at home and obtain acceptance for our faith in other lands.

Probably the greatest home missionary area is in rural life; for the developments of the past fifty years have completely altered the old life of rural America that centered in the farm home, the little red schoolhouse, and the rural church. The gadgets of materialism, the goals of secular society, luring country boys and girls cityward, together with the enormous advance in mechanized agriculture, have profoundly changed the atmosphere of rural life. Home missions has a tremendous challenge to make the Christ the Saviour of rural people, to bring back to rural young people the conviction that life in the country can be both splendid and satisfying. It is the attraction of secularism, of sophistication and materialism, that we face here as in city life; for the secular press, the secular radio, the secular cinema, and the secular public high school are shaping in molds of materialism the thought and life of these rural young people. Unfortunately the church has not yet fully understood the critical nature of that problem, for we continue to appoint our ablest church leaders to city churches and "supply" the country pulpits with student pastors and superannuates or with lay preachers of limited preparation, although we know that most of our church members are still in the country, that most of our churches are town-and-country churches, and that the membership of our city churches is recruited principally among country-bred folk.

The transformations in American life produced by World War II have been significant but not revolutionary. Secularism has made rapid progress during years of emphasis upon physical might. That was probably inevitable. Ten million men and women in uniform, learning to kill and practicing their skill on human beings, must suffer a deterioration of their faith in spiritual ideals. Testing those ideals in the midst of war experiences many have reacted against what they believed as adolescents, and they have become skeptical. Thousands have adopted a purely materialistic outlook upon life. These are problems for the church and for the leaders of home missions. Unless they are met, the influence of such persons in positions of national leadership may destroy any hope of peace or brotherhood.

Evils that weighed upon our national life prior to the war were magnified under the pressures of war. Crime, drunkenness, mental disease, have increased at a fearsome pace. The tension between wage earner and employer threatens our economy at frequent intervals. These and attendant evils require bold measures here at home. The church must purify and gird itself for battle on the home front.

Such home missions is an essential segment of the world-wide missionary enterprise; for only as we at home demonstrate the power of the gospel to transform life on every level, can we expect that people beyond the seas, nurtured in an ancient creed and conditioned by an age-old culture, will be convinced by our unsupported word.

FOREIGN MISSIONS

But the most profound transformations occasioned by the war appear in other parts of the world. There destructiveness has left scars never to be healed; there the survivors still suffer indescribable hardships. Long years of malnutrition have destroyed moral as well as physical fiber. In former enemy countries, where old ideals proved false, a new center of loyalty must be provided to make life worth living. In countries like China, Burma, the Philippines, the islands of the South Pacific and Indonesia, where Japanese vandals left human and material ruins behind them, psychological as well as physical conditions have been permanently changed. In India, Java, Korea, and Indo-China, as well as in Egypt, Palestine, and other countries classed before the war as colonies or mandated territories, the war has transformed a growing desire for political and economic independence into a clamor that will not be denied. India is the first to secure independent status. That transfer of authority has been accompanied by riots, massacres, looting, anarchy, and chaos, worse than any troubles in over two hundred years of India's history. The outcome for Christian missions is unpredictable, but chaos and calamity offer emergency opportunities to the servants of Christ for constructive service. And Christians must continue their aid to the afflicted everywhere.

War always enhances the appeal of materialism, since in war might seemingly makes right. And after an appeal to arms in order to settle some ideological or international issue no one need be surprised that the going is harder than ever for the leaders of a spiritual movement. That is true in every part of the world, and it means that the missionary evangelist has a more difficult intellectual as well as spiritual task before him. He must break through that crust of secularism and cynicism, of indifference or antagonism, and reach men with a presentation of the Christian revelation that is convincingly the most satisfactory explanation and solution of their problems. In lands where ancient ethnic religion profoundly affects man's every act, such reasoned presentations of the gospel are as necessary as when one faces a contemptuous cynic of our Western culture.

Evangelism needs also the witness of life that is transformed and strengthened by the power of the Spirit. Probably the greatest service missionaries and Christian nationals did for the cause of Christ in China during the war was to stand firm for Christian principles in the face of threat, violence, and death. That testimony is dynamic. Evangelism, through such examples of men and women wholly committed to Christ, will continue to make disciples.

In churches destroyed by war the remants of old congregations are reassembling; but pastors have been killed or have died; seminaries have been closed; the problem of ministerial leadership is acute. The missionary must rely upon laymen, untrained, untried in the work of the church, men like Peter and James and John and their fellow disciples when called by Jesus. But there are no others with which to re-form the scattered congregations. The strategy is to inspire these untrained leaders so that their sincerity and zeal may in some degree compensate for their lack of preparation. The present shortage of trained leaders is probably the most serious deficiency in mission strategy. Few new missionaries were ready for service when the war ended. Thousands were needed. Fewer still were the new and prepared workers among national Christians. A main effort now must be to provide condensed, brief, accelerated courses, in-service study programs, and other emergency training for national workers while long-term training programs are in progress. The situation also calls for the recruitment and preparation of missionary personnel with utmost care and in unprecedented numbers.

Another problem of leadership is the fact that so many able national leaders during the war carried major responsibilities in the absence of their missionary comrades. Many missionaries, formerly in positions of authority, were replaced during the war by nationals. Upon return of these missionaries, no matter what may be the realignment of responsibilities, the resulting relationships are bound to produce misunderstanding, frustration, and friction, unless both missionary and national can in all humility face their tasks as true co-workers. Testimony of recent observers indicates a rising feeling of frustration on the part of some missionaries returning to the Far East, due in part, no doubt, to the postwar inflation, the destruction of cherished homes and institutions, the enormous change in conditions, but also partly because of a shift in authority. To relinquish authority gracefully is a difficult test of Christian character. There is dire need for both missionary and trained national, but in many places the successful transfer of authority from missionary to national will be the key to future development.

A third problem of leadership arises from the denominational character of much missionary activity. Missionaries and nationals have been selected, prepared, and frequently supported by denominational agencies. Appeals for financial assistance to carry on their work have been made to denominational sources in the sending countries. Progress reports have been required by such agencies, and missionary education in each sending church has usually stressed the work of that particular denomination. Real intelligent denominational loyalty is admirable, and possibly no other method could have produced comparable interest and support; but unfortunately it has transferred to mission lands some of the spirit of denominational exclusiveness and separateness from which Protestantism suffers in the sending countries. Not infrequently the older missionary fostered that spirit, and some of the older national leaders have been loyal to such a fragmented view of the church. But the future certainly belongs to the forces of unity in missions, as in every other phase of international co-operation; and one of the greatest responsibilities of leadership in missions is to direct the growth of co-operation and unity so that the loyalty and zeal engendered by a denominational interest may be conserved in a more inclusive concern for the Kingdom.

Co-operation in building unity in the Church of Jesus Christ has recently been exemplified on a large scale in South India, where the British Methodist, the Anglican, the Presbyterian, the Reformed, and the Congregational Churches have united in the Church of South India, forming a religious community of more than one million people. That could happen on the mission field! But it is a lantern of hope lighted by the younger churches of Christendom guiding us all toward the goal of greater unity.

Many types of mission work abroad have already achieved some degree of unity. The colleges of the Near East, the union universities and colleges in China and other countries, union theological schools, hospitals, nurse-training schools, agricultural enterprises, industrial co-operatives, social welfare institutions, and other agencies of mission work have proved to be more effective than the exclusively denominational enterprises. Many of these institutions are preparing the leadership of tomorrow, and we may be confident that such leaders will look favorably upon interdenominational co-operation and unity.

Leadership in missions, whether "national" or "missionary," must also seek a solution for the problem of self-support. Before World War II less than 15 per cent of the 55,000 Protestant churches in mission lands were self-supporting. In some mission areas abroad self-support has gained remarkable headway; but among the younger churches of Africa and the Far East, in general, that goal is far from being realized. The human background of these churches is one of extreme poverty. Many older converts to Christianity were first attracted by the opportunities for education, the liberation from bonds of caste or prejudice, the security of being in some sense under the protection of the white man. Except in Japan these earlier converts came largely from the underprivileged mass of people at the lowest economic level. They had everything to gain and little to lose, and the missionaries who welcomed them seldom thought of urging that they support their own Christian enterprise. After all, a poor farmer in China, a low-caste man in India, or a common laborer in Africa or Asia could barely keep himself alive, let alone support a religious-educational-medical-social enterprise. Large-hearted missionary leaders felt compelled to provide from mission funds the salaries needed for national preachers, evangelists, and Bible women. Magnificent educational and medical institutions were erected with mission funds; and the salaries for faculties and staffs, as well as the money for maintenance, came principally from board appropriations of missionary funds raised in the United States and in British and European countries.

That may have been the only way mission work could have been initiated, but the result has been to encourage many of the younger churches in virtual dependence. Such congregations do not develop vigorously; they are denied the obligation to use their own powers; they have little sense of ownership and consequent responsibility, and the vast surrounding population of Moslems, Hindus, Buddhists, or other non-Christians, who support their own priests and ecclesiastical institutions, look down upon these dependent Christians as weaklings, subservient to foreign authority, followers of an alien, demoralizing religion. Recent studies made in China and India reveal that average contributions to the support of the Christian Church per member were one fifth as large as the support per member given by non-Christians to maintain their religious establishments. In India the average Christian family in rural churches of the United Provinces makes a contribution of between three and six annas per year (approximately ten cents) or three tenths of 1 per cent of its annual income! A subsidized religious enterprise seldom generates a sacrificial spirit. The marvel is that so much vigor has been displayed by these younger churches, handicapped as they have been by failure to develop greater self-dependence.[1]

Today, with the spirit of nationalism and independence rising and the prestige of the white foreigner diminishing, the outlook for a vigorous younger church is dark unless it can develop a large measure of self-support. The acceptance and use of foreign funds for the support of religious or other activities may well be banned by national governments, as happened in some countries during the war. Foreigners are now restricted as to the positions they may hold, the school subjects they may teach, the medical practice they may carry on, even the traveling they may do, in many countries; and it is quite probable that restrictions applied to foreigners will be extended to cover the use of funds contributed by foreigners to private individuals and institutions. So expediency and security, as well as the demands of self-respect and vigor, require of the younger churches immediate advance toward self-support.

Colleges, schools, hospitals, and other large institutional enterprises were usually undertaken with missionary funds on a scale comparable with similar establishments in the United States but far beyond the ability of the younger church to finance or maintain. These institutions have served most effectively in the development of trained national leadership and in the creation of an atmosphere favorable to Christian ideals. As long as they make a constructive contribution to the life of the people, and as long as governments permit, they should be maintained by missionary support. But the younger church must soon come to enjoy the dignity and power that can be possible only through

---

[1] Merle Davis, *New Buildings on Old Foundations*, p. 80.

increasing self-support. The membership must be educated to under-
take the self-discipline of systematic, sacrificial giving even in these
times of emergency if they are to attain lasting strength. We must
apply the underlying principle of the Marshall Plan for the sake of
future indigenous development.

In China at the time of the revolution some missionaries accustomed
to the old ways exhibited a reactionary attitude in the face of political
and social change. Later, during the vicissitudes of the early republic,
there was a tendency to hark back to the comparative peace of the
Manchu dynasty. Even the announced aims of Japan to develop a
"co-prosperity sphere" in Asia seemed to some missionaries to offer an
improvement over conditions in a war-lord-ridden China. The
Kuomintang, because of its original relations with Communists, was
denounced by these missionaries. The democratic aims of Sun Yat-sen,
unwelcome as they first were to many of the business interests of the
Western powers, received little sympathy from many of the missionaries. All such attitudes, common among foreign residents, created the
unfortunate impression in the minds of liberal Chinese and true friends
of a democratic China that missionaries were worshipers at the
shrine of the *status in quo*. Antiforeign demonstrations in 1927 indicated the temper of national feeling.

In India, Africa, Burma, Indonesia, and in other imperial territories
the fact that missionaries usually were admitted only on condition
that they would do nothing to disturb colonial rule put them among
those suspected by nationalists of sympathy for imperial rule. The
fact that many mission schools and hospitals received subsidies from
imperial governments added to that suspicion. The result is that not a
few nationals, church leaders among them, inspired perhaps by na-
tionalistic propaganda, but with genuine patriotic fervor, have come
to feel that the missionaries as a whole are either lukewarm or un-
sympathetic toward their democratic political and social aspirations.

THE DEMANDS OF THE MISSIONARY TASK

The missionary task is demanding. The strain and wear of long service
in hot countries, the long separation from home and loved ones, the
health hazards, the constant drain on mind and soul and body from
everlastingly giving out with little chance to fill up the reservoirs of
the spirit, and the never-ceasing massive pressure of a non-Christian

environment demand their toll of strength. To contemplate the necessity of change in social, political, and economic life is not easy for such workers, especially when that change may seriously affect work accomplished or planned. But there is no defense ever for complacency, for attitudes of reaction, for refusal to recognize the inevitable fruitage of the gospel in efforts by nationals to attain the freedom so long denied them by economic and political imperialism. Missionaries are not politicians or economists. Primarily they are evangelists. But the essence of their redemptive missionary task is to demonstrate the relevance of the gospel to the highest aspirations of the people among whom they are working. When the lives of their people are profoundly affected by changing social, political, or economic ideas, partly as a result of the very gospel proclaimed, the refusal on the part of missionaries to recognize this constructive social change, and in every legitimate way to favor, to guide, and to encourage the transformation, is bound to recoil against and invalidate their message.

The masses of men everywhere are in revolt against oppression, against paternalism, colonialism, discrimination, and every other form of exploitation. That resentment can produce chaos in which the virus of communism will spread its infection, or it may channel into and become a normal evolution toward freedom and brotherhood. Christian missions have a fundamental spiritual and social contribution to make in such a process. However, missionary leadership that lacks prophetic social vision, that looks back toward the "high and far-off times" of international white supremacy, is as vestigial and as dangerous to the cause of freedom and of Christianity as the vermiform appendix is to the health of the human body.

"Christian missions do not imply a low estimate of the culture of the people to whom they are sent." Jesus esteemed personality without distinction as to race, creed, culture, or economic condition. He believed in human beings, in their potentialities, and in their right and power to recognize and accept the highest ideas concerning God and his creation. He came into a world filled with religious concepts, among people with high ethical insight and noble ideas about God and man; yet he did not hesitate to confront them with something better. We do not think of Jesus as a negative force, seeking to destroy the faith by which others lived. He simply offered a new view of

God, a new way of life, a new means of salvation from sin and failure. When men compared his gospel with what they had, they recognized his "words of eternal life"; and, leaving the old and inadequate faith, they entered the new way of life everlasting.

The attainment of that new way of life, through the experience of individual converison, has been for more than a hundred years of Protestant missions the chief, if not the exclusive, purpose of the whole enterprise. It remains our chief aim. But there are other important changes that must be wrought in individuals and in society, transformations without which this experience of individual conversion may suffer debilitation and disintegration. The new convert requires opportunities for fellowship with others who are disciples of the same Lord. He needs frequent opportunities to widen his understanding, to realize his responsibilities, and to exercise his new faith by sharing it with others. Perhaps more than any other influence he needs an environment favorable to his new way of life. The church usually offers the opportunities for fellowship for worship and study, and should provide the tasks that strengthen spiritual life. By their establishment of churches missionaries have done this with very considerable success. But until recently the necessity to transform the environment so that newborn Christians might have a better chance to retain and follow their new way of life has not been accepted as a primary responsibility of missions.

Suppose we convert a non-Christian from an ethnic religion that has its tenacious grip on every phase of life, and then drop him back into the stream of that pagan culture with its overwhelming authority, accepted for thousands of years and adopted unquestioningly by family, friends, associates, and employers. Unless we can provide the convert with a substitute for the cohesive power of that culture, and an atmosphere favorable for his Christian development, he must be an extraordinarily powerful personality to survive as a Christian. The enveloping folds of that hostile environment are usually enough to smother his purpose. For his family turns him out; his associates leave him; his employer discharges him; his wife and children may desert him. He becomes a pariah, with nearly every door of normal life barred before him. Moral man in our immoral Western society has a hard enough time to keep spiritually alive and socially motivated for significant service, but imagine the pressure of society dominated by a primitive or ethnic religion which determines every act of life, but which lacks the motivation of high ideals, of moral incentive, of noble example, of intellectual respectability.

Missions must not only aim at the redemption of the man, but for his sake must strive to redeem the environment in which that man is compelled to live. Life is a unit. Spiritual, mental, and moral aspects of life are handy descriptions; but they do not denote real divisions. No conceivable bulkheads can successfully keep them separated. And to approach the missionary task in the spirit of "go-to-now," let us limit our service to the need of men's bodies, or to the need of their minds, or to the need of their souls, would be willful blindness. Total needs must be our target.

Wherever Christian missions have greatly prospered, one invariably finds that the non-Christian or the sub-Christian culture itself to some extent has been transformed. We have discovered that spiritual conversion, though basic to our whole enterprise, will not purify the source of drinking water that is poisoning a village. Eroded and mishandled farm land will never respond to sermons. The need there is for intelligent and scientific application of agricultural knowledge to local conditions. Exploitation of cheap labor in mill, mine, forest, or factory is overcome primarily by proof that there are more constructive and productive economic practices which also conserve the values of personality. Illiteracy that shackles the minds of half the human race retreats only before education. Disease that robs African families of eight out of ten children, that reduces life expectancy among the people of India to less than thirty years, that undermines vigor and destroys hope, must be met by prevention, sanitation, medicine, and surgery. To cure a patient of pneumonia and let him return immediately to live in filth, squalor, and undernourishment subjects him to attacks of typhoid, typhus, or other virulent bacterial disease. He is not safe until his physical environment has been cleaned up and improved. That change usually requires a complete transformation, a new way of life.

An Experiment in Bolivia

An experiment among the Aymara Indians of Bolivia, referred to by Merle Davis in his book *New Buildings on Old Foundations*, and which for a number of years I had opportunity to observe, illustrates the significance of this comprehensive, redemptive process which, I believe, should characterize the present and future program of missions to exploited or disadvantaged people.

For three centuries and more the Andean Indians have been oppressed, exploited, and demoralized. Under their ancient indigenous society land was never owned by individuals but was held by *ejidos* or communal groups and apportioned according to established custom on the basis of need. The Spanish conquistadors were extreme individualists like most Westerners, and by force or chicanery took the good land, distributed it to individuals, and made serfs of the helpless Indians, who, from that time to this, have worked the land for their masters without wages or other compensation except the privilege of occupying a miserable hut and of using a small garden plot. That system has produced poor crops of food, but a veritable harvest of hatred, which has many times burst into a conflagration of massacre. A constant fear of such outbursts is the price most white owners pay for the use of the land.

Some twenty years ago a North American visitor who had observed these conditions was taken sick and died in La Paz. Before his death he willed a portion of his estate for the purchase of a farm to be used under the direction of an interdenominational board for the improvement of Indian life. A property of twelve hundred acres bordering Lake Titicaca, about seventy-five miles from the capital city, was bought, and a schoolhouse, dwelling, and church erected, and an evangelistic missionary was appointed. Approximately two hundred Indians who were living on the farm when purchased came with the property, expecting to work for their new masters as they had for the previous ones. The missionary followed the pattern he knew, sought to bring the children into his school and the people into the church; but the farm operations, the culture of the people, their need for guidance toward a better way of daily living, were not covered by that pattern. Farm practices, left to an Indian *capataz* or straw-boss, did not improve; drunkenness, sullenness, thievery continued. Feast days, which were numerous, celebrating Indian customs as well as saints were times of debauchery. Men, women, and children chewed coca, the leaf from which cocaine is made, to deaden pain, hunger, and fatigue; and it slowly deadens the mind. Houses were miserable, filthy, vermin-ridden, leaky, and smoke-filled huts. There was no incentive to industry or cleanliness. People still feared the white man.

For a number of years the experiment dragged along, getting very meager results. A few children came to school; a few adults came to church. Then there arrived a missionary with vision. He proposed to restore pride and dignity, honor and hope to the people on the land, and he initiated a program that eventually would make each Indian family the owner of a small part of the farm. He established a dispensary and secured the services of a medical missionary. He took over the direction of the farm and began a study of crops that might be grown at that elevation, twelve thousand feet above sea level. Potatoes had been practically the only vegetable grown and frequently were the staple diet of the Indians. The missionary studied soils, crop rotation, possibilities of irrigation, and began experiments with every kind of garden product. He worked with the Indians to develop a co-operative program of operation for the main farm, paying wages in crops raised, meat butchered, wool sheared, and in cash. He helped get a co-operative buying and selling program under way to escape the high cost of the middleman. It took years of patient, persistent, and slow work to get voluntary consent to change; and that came only after years of demonstration that the new way of life offered a better way in home, farm, and community life, and could be followed by each and all even though the missionary should be removed. The school was enlarged with volunteer Indian labor. It is their school, where adults in the evening learn to read and write and children in the day time have their classes. The huts have been replaced by well-constructed cottages with Indian rugs on the floor and Indian woven curtains at the windows, with a chimney and stove, with nearby water supply and sanitary conveniences. Tables and stools or chairs are made in the community shop, where boys and men are taught the better use of tools. Weaving has been improved by introducing a better type of loom. New breeds of poultry, hogs, sheep, goats, and cattle have been brought in; and the garden truck now raised and preserved by each Indian family affords a balanced diet and lasts through the cold season. In a few more years each family on the farm will have earned its own place, of from ten to twenty acres. Illiteracy has been reduced; young people are going from the local school to the secondary school in La Paz, and the hope is that they will return to start similar programs of rehabilitation among Indians of other communities. Education in nutrition, home and family life, health and hygiene, has completely transformed the character of the community. Sullenness has disappeared; soft drinks have replaced firewater, and chewing gum has ousted the coca leaf! Now days of rejoicing celebrate Indian traditions and customs, but with games, native dances, and community picnics instead of drunken debauches. Four-H clubs, community fairs, and farmers' organizations give new opportunities for fellowship and new incentives for better rural life. The medical unit has brought science to replace superstition and serves hundreds of Indian families in the vicinity of the lake.

And possibly the most interesting result is religious. Now the church is alive, the membership active and missionary-minded. Formerly Indians would not join the church, suspecting and fearing that the white man might be seeking to gain an advantage over them. (They are considered to be among the most difficult people of the world to reach with the gospel.) But in this mission station they have taken over responsibility for church work. The missionary preaches and also trains Indians to go into other communities with the message of hope and salvation. The influence of that experiment flows out to thousands of people.

The good that was present in that stream of culture has been brought to the surface and purified by Christian ideals put to work in ways the people could understand, appreciate, and follow. The new brotherhood offers them a social cement more binding, a spiritual center more commanding, an appreciation of personality more satisfying than they have ever known. And that has happened within fifteen years among a people steeped for centuries in the poisons of suspicion, fear, and hatred of the white man.

The Call Today

Christ's redemptive process must be applied to every phase of life if the people of the world are to become one in spirit and in truth. We must promote an evangelism of the soil as well as of the soul, of the mind and body as well as of the spirit; and we must come to see that process as unitary both at home and abroad. That is our long-range objective.

The impact of our Western civilization upon the older societies of the world is enormous. Never in history has one culture spread so far and fast. It is breaking down the rigid caste system of India, the ancestral pattern of family life and loyalty in China, the hierarchical system of Japanese society, the tribal pattern of African life. Industry, trade, the press, the radio, the cinema, the world-wide dispersal of men in uniform, the exchange of students, and innumerable other agencies have speeded that process. Nothing can stop it; but unless it is accompanied by Christian forces, these secular and materialistic acids of our society will dissolve the structure of other cultures and leave nothing to serve as a basis for worth-while living. Christian forces must accompany and provide the spiritual interpretation of science, the goals of human welfare for the new economics, and replace with the binding cement of Christian love the crumbling mortar that has held together the ancient, living civilizations of the world. Without that witness the expanding force of our materialistic society will be overwhelmingly destructive. Societies integrated on a communal family, clan, or tribal basis will be atomized, and materialism offers no power that can put them together again. Resultant chaos becomes fertile soil for the seeds of anarchy, communism, nationalism, and dictatorship, that have invariably brought civilizations crashing down to ruin.

We are half way through a century already crimson with the bloodiest wars in history and threatened with further disaster. Prophets of calamity like Spengler have been justified by the facts. We Christians, who have received the gospel, who know the truth, and who therefore bear the responsibility for establishing a world order based on creative love, are called upon now to widen our horizons, expand and extend our mission of redemption, and commit ourselves to "attempt great things for God," in confidence that through the grace and power of our Lord Jesus Christ a new way of life may dawn for all men everywhere.

THE SPIRITUAL VIEW OF
SECULAR AFFAIRS

Gerald Kennedy

ONE OF THE MOST DIFFICULT DECISIONS JESUS HAD TO MAKE WAS THE one concerning his attitude toward the secular. Back of the symbolism of the temptation story there was this burning question of what was to be the relation of his Kingdom to the kingdoms of the world. It was a difficult question for him, and it is for us. The difficulty is due to the fact that Christianity is neither completely this-worldly nor other-worldly. It is both. The gospel is both in history and beyond history. Not only are we to spiritualize the material, but we are commissioned to materialize the spiritual. We shall never find any way to a truly spiritual view of secular affairs unless we have this clear understanding of the nature of our religion.

THE SECULAR IS A PROVINCE OF THE KINGDOM

Let us look at the view which regards Christianity as entirely of this world. This has been the most popular position in our time. There seemed to be such a wide gap between primitive man and civilized man that many felt we moderns had established a new kingdom on this earth. The similarities between human nature in its beginnings and human nature now were overlooked. If we had come so far, what was to prevent us from going much farther?

This imprisoned man in the historical process and made him significant only as a member of a group. Out of that belief there came the worship of the nation and the blood. This is still the only faith of millions of people. This is the new Leviathan. This is Moloch risen again. Often a Christian tinge is given to this secularism, and a modified Christian vocabulary is used. But it does not worship God.

A great many humanists never expected this emphasis to turn out as it has. They were simply men who became impatient with trying to peer into the mind of God and very often were rebelling against a dogmatic, anthropomorphic theism. To them the other world seemed in the realm of the unknowable and the unimportant. They were trying to make Christianity work without theology. Many of them were brave liberal spirits who stood for human values against the dehumanizing processes of our industrial society. They wanted Christianity's social concern without its spiritual assumptions.

What is wrong with all of this? Simply that this point of view does not do justice to the relation of each man's separate soul to God. True it is that man is a social creature, but he is not only a social creature. He is made for direct relationship with God, and he knows no rest until he finds it. Unfortunately for this point of view it is still true that man does not and cannot live by bread alone.

But what about the other extreme which sees our faith as entirely otherworldly? This does violence to the gospel, for it sees the world as completely evil. It intimates that a religious man ought to flee from society and protect himself from its stain. If the world has any meaning, this viewpoint will grant it only a negative one. The world, in the mind of the otherworldly thinkers, is beyond redemption and must one day be destroyed. But this is certainly a distortion of the gospel.

We cannot be Christians and doubt the love of God for all his creatures. What shall we do with the affirmation: "For God so loved the world, that he gave his only begotten Son, that whosoever believeth on him should not perish, but have eternal life" (John 3:16)? We cannot believe that our relations with other men are merely meaningless, temporary affairs. When we are dealing with persons, we are dealing with absolutes.

It is true that this world is not enough. But when we begin to insist that this world is for no importance whatever—that it is something to endure with what courage we can muster—we do wrong to the Christian viewpoint. It is like insisting that since bread will mold if kept too long, it is bad even when it is fresh.

Christianity is both this-worldly and other-worldly. The earth does have significance, and God is concerned with it. His presence can be observed in nature, and some of the deepest religious experiences possible will come to us there. But this is not the end of the matter. We discover that all goes wrong with us here if we are not also citizens of heaven. Arnold Toynbee described the situation as follows:

On such a view, this world would not be a spiritual exercise ground beyond the pale of the Kingdom of God; it would be a province of the Kingdom—one province only, and not the most important one, yet one which had the same absolute value as the rest, and therefore one in which spiritual action could, and would, be fully significant and worthwhile; the one thing of manifest and abiding value in a world in which all other things are vanity.[1]

For the Christian the secular world is a province of the Kingdom of God.

MEN ARE STEWARDS OF THE SECULAR

The fine concept of stewardship has been neglected by Christians to their detriment. It is much more than tithing, though that is part of it. Stewardship is a philosophy of living and a broad program of giving. It means that we do not own anything here, but are called on to administer our possessions in the name of the Owner. All of our lives will be affected when touched by this spirit. The freedom that it brings is one of the great experiences of Christianity. It brings us the joy of giving.

The futility of hoarding becomes plain to any thinking man. Why should we pile up perishable goods like a squirrel? Who wants to have happen to him what happens to the miser? I have never seen a man bent on collecting goods that I did not want to say in the words of Jesus: "Woe unto you that are rich!" No sensitive man envies such as these, but on the contrary he feels a pity at this waste of living. A man went to a wealthy citizen to obtain a gift for a community project. He was refused on the ground that the man simply could not afford to give anything at this particular time. "Joe," said the solicitor as he prepared to leave, "if you are not careful, you are going to be the richest man in our cemetery." Is that a worthy goal for a thinking man?

In contrast to that I think of my father. He never had much money, and at no time did he have an adequate financial margin. Yet at one of his lowest periods I saw him give a man a dollar. When I remonstrated with him, his answer was; "It came out of my tithe. Of course I could afford it." But I knew many a man who was a hundred times better off financially who would not have been able to afford it.

[1]*Christianity and Crisis,* June 23, 1947.

When a man becomes a steward, he looks at things from a new point of view. The Hazen Foundation has a little pamphlet with this intriguing title: *Teaching Economics with a Sense of the Infinite and the Urgent.* Can the dreary science be taught with that sense? Yes, for everything can be observed from the viewpoint of the eternal. Jesus commands us to think of treasure in heaven and not on earth. The Christian steward is the man who has learned to think of his earthly treasures in the light of treasures in heaven.

Giving is an art to be learned. In some ways it is unfortunate that we are not born with it, but we are not. Our first impulse is to get and keep. We want to fight off any who may come asking us to share. Many a man never gets beyond this stage. If he is hounded, he may give a niggardly check. But giving is always a painful thing, and only polite blackmail will separate him from his possessions. It is a sad truth that the churches are full of people who have never been taught what Jesus meant when he said, "It is more blessed to give than to receive." This is really a tragic thing, and it is an indication of one of the worst failures of our Christian education.

Consider the sponge and the spring. A sponge swells up several times its normal size in order to hold on to all it can absorb. The only way to get anything out of it is to squeeze it. But the spring is always giving out. It does not keep anything back but spills out across the meadow with abandonment. The sponge is a corpse, but the spring is alive. Men die when they keep, and the light goes out when they no longer enjoy their giving.

It is not only a matter of giving money. There are our talents and our time. The steward knows that if he wants to administer what has been committed unto him, he cannot bury his talent in the earth. The sense of having to use what we have redeems us from self-pity and gives us a sense of the dignity of our lives. Maltbie Babcock wrote: "Genuine kindness oftenest comes from self-repression, a cheerful message from a sad soul, a brave word from a trembling heart, a generous gift from a slender purse, a helping hand from a tired man. It is not your mood, but the other man's need, that determines kindness." Stewardship is a kind of insurance against selfishness and narrowness. It is the only assurance we have that, in dealing with secular things, we will not become personally secularized.

THE SECULAR IS IMPERMANENT

People who look upon the world as the end of all things have trouble in keeping up their courage in the face of crumbling hopes and defeated aims. Why is everything so impermanent? Why can't we build something that will last? It is no wonder that, in the face of the destruction of time, many a Christian looks to the other world entirely. Optimistic humanism always ends in despair because its hopes are always betrayed. Utopia may seem to be just around the corner, but it fades before us like the end of the rainbow. The worldling is always sure that a few more changes will bring about the beloved community. He believes that if we kill a few more thousand people, we can establish peace. But when at last he loses his hope that human efforts can establish the good life here, he becomes of all men most miserable. He often swings from the extreme left to the extreme right.

In his famous *History of the Persian Wars*, Herodotus comments: "The cities which were formerly great have most of them become insignificant; and such as are at present powerful, were weak in olden times. I shall, therefore, discourse equally on both, convinced that prosperity never continues long in one place."

At first sight this is a devastating picture of life in the world. Weary souls, whose paths have seemed to wind uphill always, hope for a resting place where they may find release from their exertions. The dispossessed, fighting for their rights, hope to create a society where the fight is over and the victory won. The man who is tempted almost beyond his power to resist, dreams of achieving a character impervious to temptation. We make our sacrifices in the hope of a time when the lights will come on and the darkness be ended forever. To say to such as these that there is no permanent victory and there can be none seems like announcing the futility of all striving.

But it is not so. The universe is built on the principle of growth, and it is more necessary for us to grow than it is for us to be comfortable. Men are rightly suspicious of anything which hints at the stagnation of perfection or suggests a changeless future. That is why Methodists have always had to be careful in explaining what they do not mean by John Wesley's doctrine of Christian perfection. If it meant that men could achieve a state in which they no longer needed forgiveness and judgment, it was not acceptable.

One of the reasons young people are not particularly thrilled with the idea of becoming saints is that, in their minds, the saint is one who has achieved perfection and hence can no longer grow. Yet Paul addressed his first Corinthian letter to those "called to be saints" at Corinth. But were they saints in the sense of being perfect? Read the letter and you will discover that they were worse than average church members of today. Paul knew that, but to him a saint was a man who was moving in a certain direction, not a man who had arrived. He was not a man who had achieved or already been made perfect, but one who pressed forward.

Are we then completely at the mercy of time? Is there no resting place down here? The Christian faith knows that each man's soul can be invincible and that the victories and the defeats which really matter are within. A man is always affected by his environment. It is for him an important fact, but it is not the essential fact. The Christian is in the world, but he is not necessarily of the world. There is set within us an inner fortress which none may enter unless we open the gate. Every man has the final advantage over force, for he can always say no. This is a rock upon which we stand.

We live in a world that can be either too important or not important enough. It can be something which enslaves us or something which repels us. It can be for us a prison, or it can be a fool's paradise. It will put its mark on us. No matter how spiritual may be our desires, we must still use material things. The secularist has no satisfactory answer to his problem. Neither has the otherworldly dreamer. But for the spiritual mind the world is neither frightening nor enslaving. It is under the loving rule of God. Possessions are to be administered in his name. In the midst of the impermanence of the world God has established man's eternal soul, and he has made man's spirit undefeatable.

Handel wrote *The Messiah* in twenty-four days. Critics say that perhaps this has never been equalled as a record for great musical composition. He hardly left the house during that time. His servant said oftentimes he would take a meal up, put it on the table, and come back an hour later to find it untouched. When the servant came into the room after Handel had finished Part Two, which contains the "Hallelujah Chorus," he saw the composer looking out of the window with tears shining in his eyes. Said he, "I did think I did see all

Heaven before me, and the great God Himself." It is this which the Christian sees shining through the secular. This province of his Kingdom is marked with the glory of our God. The spiritual mind knows how to live in the world and be free.

SECULAR QUESTIONS DEMAND SPIRITUAL ANSWERS

The attempt to build an earthly paradise has been a noble one, and for a time it was an acceptable one for many men. The conquest of disease made rapid strides, and it was confidently expected that a time would arrive when most of the pain and suffering of life could be eliminated. Life was getting longer, and perhaps one day in the future we might expect to live twice as long as men live now. This was not too encouraging for those who were about to die, but at least it was a goal that promised better things for the future generations. Today, in contrast, we sit waiting for the first diabolical use of germs to destroy life wholesale, and it is a picture more horrible than we have ever considered. Now we wonder if a few more years would make any appreciable difference in our existence anyway.

All these things were proposed on the supposition that life is quantity and not quality. If we had enough things and a few more years, then we hoped to be satisfied with this world as the end of all. But the human spirit is not satisfied with just quantity. Life is a kind of experience and not a number of them. Men sometimes live longer and more profoundly in five minutes than they do at other times in five years. It is the inability of the world to provide the kind of experiences we hunger for that made this aim too small.

Count Hermann Keyserling once remarked that the greatest American superstition is belief in facts. If we can state our knowledge in a series of precise descriptions, we assume we have achieved truth. This is the secular viewpoint. But who is to determine what a fact is? Well, you may say, a fact is what anybody can see and what can be proved. Be careful! You cannot live one day in this world on that basis. I cannot take one step forward without believing things I cannot prove and trusting people I do not even know. We try our best to live factually, but it will not work. The facts are never enough. Man does not live by facts alone.

We are told that we must accept the fact that we will die. So we must. Then we are told that we must accept the fact that death is the end of us. Who said so? A materialist said so. But he began with a philosophy that cannot be proved and must be taken on faith. Why should I be asked to believe something he cannot prove? Besides, there is a great body of testimony to the effect that death is not the end of us. Says the materialist, "You cannot prove it." No, I cannot prove it, and it too must be a matter of faith. It would appear, then, that the only choice is between one faith and another faith. It is never a choice between faith and facts. I must find the faith that answers the most questions and fits best my experience. It will be the part of wisdom to observe what kind of fruit is produced by any particular faith. The final test is its effect on persons. Does it enlarge life?

Paul says death is a great enemy, which is to say it is a great evil. It is the great symbol of the incomprehensibility of the world. If personality is the supreme thing, then it is a shabby way to treat the supreme production. Every human relationship becomes a trap for misery and final defeat if death is final. So much of the dignity of life becomes triviality and vanity if death has the last word. We cannot escape this feeling of defeat for any length of time. Life might otherwise make sense if death was not a denial of any glimmer of purpose.

One of the things that seem to be true of all life is its power to produce what the environment demands. What we need, we develop; and through the years there is going on a constant process of adaptation to our surroundings. Animals develop what they need to live where they are supposed to live. On this basis, how do we explain the spiritual life of man?

There is such a wide variation between the mind and the body. There seems to be no balance here that will help man be at peace with himself. On the contrary there is a constant tension. While the body grows weak, the spirit may grow strong. The spiritual side of a man's life so often reaches its zenith at the very time his body is growing weaker. Why should it be if this world is all there is?

In the words of James Martineau, we seem to be overprovided for, if life is to be terminated by death. We do not need this spiritual equipment for our overnight stay on the earth. As a matter of fact it is often the very thing that makes it difficult to be at ease on our journey. It would seem as if man is equipped for something beyond this world and that his experience here is a preparation for something even greater. Martineau went on to say that "we do not believe immortality because we have proved it, but we forever try to prove it because we believe it." This is an important distinction. It is our spiritual nature that cannot settle down here as if this were our home. We are driven to seek reasons for the mind because the spirit is already convinced that there is more to come. The root of the matter is not in any philosophy but in the nature of man himself. We are as travelers on our way to a destination beyond the stars. We always lay our heads in a foreign land when the day is done.

Much criticism has been made of the spiritial viewpoint as an excuse for social unconcern. We are familiar with the revolt against a promise of "pie in the sky." A very imposing case has been built against religious institutions which fail to act in the interest of social justice now. They have been portrayed as contemplating a time after death when each man will get his just deserts. The supposition is that the other world is an enemy of this world. These critics believe that if we could only destroy the whole idea of the other world, then men would spend their time and energy reforming this one. It is a convincing idea until you follow the implication of the argument.

No one wants to justify the appeasement of evil in the name of the comfortable doctrine that assures us everything will be set right after death. But the falsity of the secular point of view is shown by the fact that the struggle for justice here is not intensified by denying immortality. The only way to promote justice is to ground it in the faith that there is something owing to creatures who are ends in themselves. But when the secularist tries to make that assumption, he finds himself cut off from any logical support. If men are here for a short time only, does it make any final difference how they treat one another? Does the treatment of men seem to be of eternal significance if men are not eternal creatures? The foundation of social concern is a religious assumption about the nature of men.

Codes of ethics or moral pronouncements all stand or fall on their answer to the question "Why?" If we say a man must be free, again the question to be faced is "Why?" If a man is an automaton, is there any convincing reason why he should be free? Am I supposed to be just to cattle? Have I a right to kill them for food? We say "Yes" to that because cattle are of this world only. But if a man is regarded as of this world only, what sense does it make to talk about a vast distinction between my treatment of a man and my treatment of an animal?

The realization is finally driven home to us that to maintain what we would call decency in our society, we must treat men as creatures of eternity. Whenever a society forgets that, the most horrible things can be done to men. When men cease to believe in immortality, they cannot even make things work here. So if a man says it is inconsequential, or at least secondary, whether he believes in immortality or not, he is wrong. It is a matter of first importance. The world has been going from bad to worse ever since it took its eyes off the next world. Instead of being a matter of interest to theology alone, this is a matter that ought to be the concern of any realistic person. Our life here is not enough and cannot make sense. Men are such creatures that only when their eyes are beyond this world can they live in this world. Men are so made that until they can believe the last enemy has been vanquished, which is death, they are half alive.

Let us summarize and conclude. In the first place the spiritual mind does not regard secular affairs as inherently evil, or as something to be escaped from and ignored. They are not necessarily contaminating to spiritual life. In the words of Arnold Toynbee, the world is a province of God's Kingdom. Secular affairs have the marks of God upon them. Secondly, the spiritual man will not allow himself to think of secular objects as things to be owned. That always leads to an enslavement in the worldly scheme of things and results in the gradual secularization of the human spirit. A man is a steward of the material values, and he administers them in the name of God. Third, the spiritual mind regards secular affairs as impermanent and, if taken as ends, inevitably disillusioning. Secular values, therefore, must never be regarded as eternal. Material treasures have value only when they are shared and not hoarded. Finally, secular affairs demand spiritual foundations. There is implied in every human activity a spiritual answer if the activity is to have more than a passing significance. Once you begin to ask the secularist "Why?" he is driven either to a confession of futility or to a confession of faith in God.

HOW CHRISTIANITY CHALLENGES SECULARISM

Gerald O. McCulloh

SECULARISM MAY BE THOUGHT OF VERY SIMPLY AS "BELIEVING AND behaving as though man were an end in himself; as though humanity existed in its own right and for the sole purpose of its own power and glory."[1] This view, which holds that the present world with its problems and possibilities is "all the reality there is," has a long history in human thought. Plato was confronted with a secularist atheism. Amos reflects the secular attachments of the tradesmen whom he denounces for their yearning that the new moon and the sabbath be soon gone so that they could return to their businesses wherein short change and short measure were the common practice. The epistles of Seneca contain his recommendations to the secularists of his day that they should call upon the help from above which alone could free them from the hopelessness of their worldly concerns. Jesus pointed to the obsession of a successful young man who could see no farther than his bulging barns. The thoughtful men of every age have seen to their sorrow that

> The world is too much with us; late and soon,
> Getting and spending, we lay waste our powers.

A feature of secularism that has not always been clearly recognized is its self-imposed limitation. As a philosophy secularism has historically borrowed its frame of reference from a more inclusive world view. It has come to have meaning only as it has been projected against a view which regarded this world, this span of time, the present value judgments, as part of a more comprehensive reality. Aristophanes' famous quip, "Whirl is king, having cast out Zeus," shows the daily affairs to have usurped a throne that belonged rightly to a greater king. Walter Lippmann, in the chapter on "Lost Horizons" in his *Preface to Morals*, exhibits the delimitation of meaning

[1] D. R. Davies, *The Sin of Our Age*, p. 33. For a fuller statement of the essential ideas of secularism, see John Baillie, *What Is Christian Civilization?*, p. 26.

which is characteristic of contemporary secularism. The wider horizons, while being known, are yet denied.

Today's secularist has become so fascinated with the present world, with its new techniques of discernment and manipulative mastery, that he has apparently forgotten that one of the committments of the method being employed is to a reductionism. The word "secularism," coming from *saeculum*, meaning one age among many ages, has lost its proper humility. The present age with all its engagements is regarded as the whole of reality instead of but a part of a larger, richer, more intricately related whole.

Secularism leaves man's needs unmet, not by what it does but by what it fails to do. Man has experiences which are not accounted for and needs which are not fulfilled by a secular concern with this world alone. For man's life, present and future, secularism is inadequate, philosophically and religiously.

The inadequacies, which we shall discuss specifically, are the following: (1) secularism provides the basis for what is at best a partial and distorted evaluation of human personality (human nature); (2) it proffers no saving help which man can seek in time of trouble and in which to ground a final hope; (3) it affords a tentative rather than an ultimate authority for value judgments which, in claiming as its essence revisability, gives man no certainty at all; (4) it offers man as a vocation only the adjustments and adaptations of temporal expediency as a basis for the investment of his life; and (5) it proposes no spiritual community in which man may find fellowship, for spirit is not one of the categories in the secular view of reality.

Christianity, on the other hand, meets the felt needs of man in these five areas by proclaiming a God in whom he may have faith and with whom he may enjoy fellowship. God is the giver of life and the final authority for all true value judgments. The Christian faith centers in Jesus Christ, the incarnate Revealer of God, man's Lord and Saviour in the Kingdom community. The Christian life continues in the communion of the Holy Spirit, man's Convictor, Comforter, Counselor, and Companion. It is a way of life under the law of love, which begins here and now and extends beyond history in the hopeful assurance of personal immortality.

BASIS OF SELF-EVALUATION

One of the most serious inadequacies in contemporary secularism is its failure to take account of the various dimensions of life in terms of which man must evaluate himself. There has been no lack of evaluative statements, but these have been tediously uniform in stating the ultimate supremacy of man. The Protagorean dictum, "Man is the measure of all things," has been the secularist's gospel.

In comparison with the other tenants and orders of beings of this space-time world, man is the highest being. However, man is aware also of his limitations. He finds himself drawn by ideals which are above him. He knows his shortcomings. But short of what? What do his valuations, negative as well as positive, take as their ground? This sense of finiteness is puzzling if man is truly the measure of all things.

Christianity meets man's confusion and his need by providing the basis for seeing himself in proper perspective. Man is aware of his shortcomings; he is drawn by ideals because he is a spiritual being. Man is personal, responsible to a personal God. As a self-conscious spirit he is capable of fellowship with higher spirits. Man measures himself against a dimension of reality that the rest of the earthly order does not know. In this realm, says Christianity, *God is the measure of man*. In comparison with God man sees himself as independent, derivative, incomplete.

Man, by taking thought, cannot add one cubit to his stature. But man, enlightened by the Christian faith, can discover that there is another measure, "the measure of the stature of the fullness of Christ." Herein man sees himself coming short of the glory of God. Man discerns himself to be sinner, an insight available only to a spiritual being. The real truth about man is that he is spirit, born of God.[2]

In practice and precept Jesus regarded the whole man. He saw men sinning. Indeed, it was because of man's lostness in sin that he came to seek and save that which was lost. But concerning the sinners to whom he preached, among whom he moved, and at whose hands he suffered the final earthly violence, he always preached and acted as if they were capable of hearing the word of God and responding

[2] See John Bennett, *Christianity and Our World*, p. 13.

to it. Their deafened ears were due to their hardness of heart. It was to men as spiritual beings, though turned by their own wills away from God, that Jesus' call to discipleship was given.

The Christian faith provides the only adequate basis for man's evaluation of himself. Man is of more value than a sheep or many sparrows, of more worth than earthly institutions, even the Sabbath. As sinner he is lost in outer darkness, perishing in spiritual poverty away from the Father's house, in bondage to Satan. But he is capable of "coming to himself," of turning to answer the call of the Father's love. He is spirit, restless with a divinely imparted dissatisfaction. Having responded to the call of his high spiritual destiny, he is capable of entering into fellowship, here and hereafter, with God.

Upon this basis contentment with mediocrity is impossible. The insight of faith is the ground for radical criticism and correction. When the infinite goodness of God is the basis of self-evaluation, the demands of righteousness and holiness outstrip man's highest achievements. "Be ye therefore perfect" is the familiar phrasing of the Christian imperative from Jesus' lips. Thus Christianity issues in the lifelong call to man to sanctify himself, to make himself holy unto God.

SAVING HELP

In keeping with secularism's making man the measure of all things there is the further assumption that man is "on his own." The secular view acknowledges no revelation whereby man may come to know that which is otherwise hidden wisdom, no strength beyond the mustering of his own resources to aid him in achieving the difficult goal, no direction beyond his own preferences for his guidance. In short there is no God who will teach him, uphold him, or save him in his time of need.

The practical result of this assumption in the life of the individual has been the embrace of some will-o'-the-wisp "ism" promising saving deliverance from present frustration and hopelessness, or the consulting of the purely secular psychological counselor when personal problems arise. But the help has not been adequate. Frustration and a sense of impotence remain. In the social order also there is hopelessness in the face of chaos and confusion. The desperate need of food and the growing fear of the disappearance of freedom at the hands of new tyrannies are exceeded only by a lack of faith. Social deliverances promised through faith in imperialist nationalisms have failed to materialize. In the United States even our fanatic faith in progress has disintegrated. Man feels the need of spiritual help, a saving faith.

Christianity finds the answer to this longing, individually and socially, in the fact of God and his concern for his creatures, in the promise of "a saving help from a higher source." [3] Throughout the centuries of the Judaeo-Christian faith the hand of God reaching down into history to come to man's aid has been clearly seen and deeply trusted. The word of Jesus to those beset by hunger under the niggardly harvests of the Palestinian hills, enslaved by Roman imperialism, and ravaged by centuries of the crosscurrents of war was an exhortation to faith in an everlasting Kingdom. He brought a way of life which offered salvation through him who had already overcome the world. Throughout the intervening centuries our fathers have found in their faith deliverance beyond the reach of "dungeon, fire, and sword." Christian salvation has recently been described by Harris Franklin Rall as "the reach of God's help down into the depths of man's life in the transformation of man, the making of new men." This newness of life is the saving help. Herein is man's salvation.

One wonders why confessing Christians have so widely lost this sense of saving help. Has the trumpet of the church's voice given forth an uncertain sound? Perhaps we preachers and teachers have feared to recommend and proclaim it. Or perhaps the difficulty has lain in the manner in which the help has been understood and hence sought. True saving help is operative within the consciousness of the person as the life of faith. We may properly seek God's aid, not in an influence on or deliverance from the external event, but in the faith and inner strength wherein the event is met. In God's help man finds security and strength. As it is unto faith in the fellowship with God that we are called, it is in this faith and unto it that we are saved. Christian faith is thus both the means and end of man's deliverance. The avoidance of the valley of the shadow of death was not given to God's own Son, but deliverance from its bondage into continuing life came to him in full measure. That was Christ's victory,

[3] William James, *A Pluralistic Universe*, p. 307.

just as it is the victory always wrought for the Christian through God's saving help. Faith will not bring the island to the raft-borne seaman, but it will sustain him through the vicissitudes of anxiety and waiting unto the island or unto the end. When the function of faith is thus understood, man need not fear the pragmatic test, for God has been the "strength in time of trouble" to all those who have called on him in faith. Thus, in prayer and worship, devotion and self-denial, as ways to saving faith, Christianity offers man salvation in an area of need where secularism fails.

AUTHORITY FROM ABOVE, CERTITUDE WITHIN

When man has accepted God's saving help, when he has found that he can live above himself by "surrendering himself to the lifting power of a higher love," [4] he finds that Christianity strengthens him at another point where secularism is weak, namely, in the realm of authority and certitude.

In its analysis of the ethical problem secularism has erected the twin pillars of revisability and relativism to support the arch of the moral life. All judgments, secularists say, must be regarded as tentative. Truth is real only as a proposition becomes true in experience and persists for that experience alone. All judgments, ethical and valuational, are subject to revision in the next instant when the tastes of the judger or the circumstances surrounding him may have changed. Since all value judgments are relational judgments of preference or choice, they are at best creatures of contingency. To the thoughtful observer of human morality, individual and social, it is not surprising that the arch of the moral life resting upon these pillars is seen to be falling, for the columns themselves are not of marble but of clay. They have been unable to withstand the weather and weight of human passion.

Christianity offers for man's strength and stability a dynamic response of inner certitude to an authority which is beyond himself. The requirements upon man are grounded in the eternal goodness of God. The great ethical monotheism of Israel saw God as the inescapably authoritative giver of the moral law. In Christianity this abiding authority from above is complemented by the inner witness of the spirit within man, whose response is one of trust and certitude.

[4] James Martineau, *The Seat of Authority in Religion*, p. 616.

This conviction comes not as a result of logical coercion, nor as the expedient adjustment of enlightened self-interest. Nor is it the whip-lashed obedience of the frightened slave. Man's certitude springs up as his eager response to abiding obligation, his answer to God's call.

Jesus taught that the assurance of man is within his own being, at the springs of his actions, as clearly as he taught the lofty authority of God. He emphasized the internal seat of man's response by pointing to the heart of man as the source of both his defilement and his devotion. Evil thought, fornications, murders, coveting, pride, and foolishness proceed from the heart (Mark 7:21-23). It is from the fullness of the heart that the mouth speaketh to make confession (Matt. 12:34). Love to God proceeds from the heart and then goes on to captivate the mind and strength (Mark 12:30). Nicodemus had kept the law, but behind his questions Jesus saw a searching heart, so he challenged him to inner renewal, the new birth of the spirit (John 3:3-6).

The Christian life is not just the acceptance of truth on the ground of an external authority. The authority concerning the good, the true, the beautiful, the holy, and the loving, coming from above man, is yet accepted by him as his inner treasure. The man who lives "in Christ" finds the strengthening of his certitude in the assurance of the Spirit. This is not a mere taking of oneself in hand and a muster-ing of the "will to believe." It is a responsive certitude, belief grown sure and certain because it cannot help believing.

Upon the Christian basis man's morality, his knowledge, his sensi-tivity to beauty, his consecration of himself to holiness, his pouring out of self in unselfish love are not the timorous uncertainties of the merely tentative, nor the expedient exploitations of the momentary circumstance. His life grows in joyous confidence when he embraces as his fixed purpose obedience to the will of God. Life grounded on the revisability and relativism of the secular mood crumbles. Life grounded in the authority of God and responding in the certitude of the inner witness of the spirit stands secure.

VOCATION

Having gained the assurance which comes as the divine authority sparks the fire of certitude in the soul, man looks for an oppor-tunity to invest his life. His sense of high calling is a part of his awareness that he is more than the sum of his animal appetites. Man's sense of vocation to live for something beyond himself has been appealed to by the secularist. But the secular philosophy affords no basis for this sense of call. Even the altruism upon which secularism depends for its idealism has been defined as "enlightened self-interest."

The term "vocation" is widely used in educational and job-counseling circles in the secular sense. In keeping with this usage a vocation is determined by a series of tests designed to discover interests and aptitudes. The statistical results disclose the vocation for which the person is suited. It is scarcely surprising that vast numbers of people who have arrived at their occupational decisions by this or the alternative "survival of the fittest" techniques face their daily tasks without any clear sense of the importance or relevance of what they are doing.

Significant living, the abundant life, is to be achieved as man finds himself responding to a vocation in the higher sense of a call from above. Paul Scherer recently made the vivid suggestion that the world has not been changed as significantly by those who have had both feet firmly on the ground as by those who have had "one foot in heaven." The consciousness of having invested powers and abilities in tasks that are holy is the daily reward of the man who has heeded the call of God.

Dr. Homrighausen, in the third volume of the Interseminary Series, says: "What is needed today is a renewed emphasis upon the vocation of man in the service of the living God, a recovery of the meaning of individual life in the community, . . . the basic duties and disciplines of the common man in the pursuit of his daily life and work." [5] Such a sense of divine vocation has run like a golden thread through the tapestry of Christian history. It was the precious possession of the medieval Christian, layman and cleric alike. Though Calvin's Geneva was excessive in its ecclesiastical legalism, which governed all phases of life from the price of meat to the hour at which the hosteler was to put his guests to bed, yet the thread is traceable in Calvin's words: "God has appointed to all their particular duties in different spheres of life." A similar awareness characterized the daily piety of the New England Puritans in their doctrine of divine calling, whether to sea captaincy, farming, or the

---

[5] *The Gospel, the Church, and the World,* p. 195.

ministry.[6] One has but to compare this tradition to the attitude of the present day to see how clearly Christianity challenges the contemporary secular sense of vocation—or the lack of it.

Jesus' words about the stewardship of various talents, and his healing and restoring men to their places of useful service in the community, bespeak his attitude toward the rightful investment of human life. His own sense of earthly mission was fulfilled within the daily life of the world. The selection of the common elements of bread and wine for the sacrament of remembrance shows how fully he believed in the high spiritual usefulness of the commonplace when it is rightly consecrated. Paul urged the Corinthian Christians to continue in their respective callings (I Cor. 7:17-24). To the Romans he pointed out that the many members in the Christian body have various offices (Rom. 12:4-8). The vocation of the Christian is to make his livelihood the implement and occasion of Christian devotion.

The confrontation of man with the holiness of every gift of God has been peculiarly lacking in our preaching. We have spoken of stewardship, but it has hardly warmed men's hearts. The sense of stewardship rightly viewed should bring men joy instead of pain, for at its best it acknowledges a gift, a trust from God. Beyond our failure to catch the spirit of stewardship there is the insistence in the gospel that life must be lived in response to the divine vocation.

To exploit life for oneself is to lose it. Life given unto God is saved unto life eternal. Christianity offers unequivocally a call to eternally abundant life beginning in the dedication of the tasks of every day.

SPIRITUAL FELLOWSHIP

The last of man's needs which we shall consider is apparent in the urge for fellowship in a spiritual community. This tendency has been secularly described as a gregariousness or the desire to participate in a public. Modern society has witnessed the breakdown of the family and parish units of social organization. These primary and homogenous units were of great importance in the transmission of the Christian heritage. In their place there has appeared a welter of groups or publics of which man finds himself perforce a member. Urbanization and industrialization have played significant parts in this transition.

---

[6] William W. Sweet, *The American Churches*, p. 118.

Today man dwells in a residence community among people with whom he may have very little in common. He works in the specialized system of industry with another group at tasks of an impersonal sort. With the achievement of more leisure he may become a member of a recreational or leisure public, such as a club or a hobby group, which differs from his residence community and his business associations. None of these social units supplies man with a community of spirit such as was represented in the closely knit family and parish relationships of an earlier day. For all man's present lack of aloneness his need for spiritual fellowship is left unfilled in modern secular society.

There are those who voice serious doubt "as to how far the spirit of Christian neighborhood can ever be infused into the life of such an industrial society as now exists. For it would seem that the displacement of the primary by the wider social groupings is inevitably accompanied by a great and growing dissipation of the spirit of community itself." [7] Far from viewing this possibility apprehensively, John Dewey has expressed satisfaction at the breakdown of the units wherein the "superstitions of supernaturalism" and the hope of immortality were transmitted.[8] More recently, however, we have seen a growing concern at the crumbling of the ethical structure of society and its spiritual controls on the part of certain of the more socially idealistic of the secularists. They have appealed to the churches to provide the moral guidance for the control of the monsters of modern scientific devising. For the rebuilding of the moral structure of society the Christian faith demands the re-establishment of a spiritual community as the foundation for any vital social ethic.

The social ethic constitutive of the relationships of faithful men and women has its ultimate moral authority in God, whose will for man's society is the Kingdom. The Kingdom of God is timeless, but its timelessness does not exclude history. Jesus spoke of the Kingdom in the present as well as the future tense. He sought to establish among earthly men his Kingdom of love and righteousness. He taught his disciples to pray to God: "Thy kingdom come. Thy will be done in earth." This society with the spiritual, timeless quality of a heavenly Kingdom is to begin here in the community of men of faith.

[7] John Baillie, *op. cit.*, p. 29.
[8] *A Common Faith, passim.*

In contrast to the failure of secular social morality the unity of the world Christian fellowship has withstood with amazing vitality the shocks and divisiveness of the recent war years. The world Christian fellowship is not a fiction or merely a hope. It is a fact. And that the emergence of the spirit of Christian unity has not waited upon the mechanism of some organic union of church institutions gives added evidence of the inherent strength of the Christian brotherhood. For this evidence points beyond the churches to a unity of spirit in the community of the Kingdom of God. In entering into the Kingdom community the Christian finds the ground for a catholic and universal loyalty great enough to embrace all mankind.

A final word should be said about the church. I believe profoundly that the church can be, and ought to be, the earthly instrument or focal point of the Kingdom community. The church has the charge to preach, proclaim, organize, and implement the spiritual community among men. However difficult the problem, it must be met by providing the fellowship for man's spiritual life and nurture. The church is fallible, as all of us who are near the center of her institutional life know. Yet she can be cleansed continually as we who are churchmen repent of our sins individually and corporately, and seek anew the spirit of her Lord within the body ordained to establish the community of the Kingdom.

In so far as it is possible to analyze a way of living, I have sought to do so in contrasting the secular with the Christian way. The secular life is inadequate in depth, length, height, and breadth. The Christian life begins in man's awareness of being a child of God, convicted of sin, and in need of help. It continues in the assurance of salvation, a divine gift. Its issue is in living up to a high spiritual calling, individually and socially, in the tasks and relationships of every day. In knowledge of self, God, the world, and one's fellows, man's life "in Christ" is abundant.

SECULARISM AND CHURCH UNITY

Alexander C. Zabriskie

IN THIS CHAPTER I SHALL DEAL BOTH WITH SECULARISM AS AN AGENT of church disunion, and also with the necessity of the reunion of the churches if secularism is to be combated effectively. May I add two other assumptions I have made: first, that we all agree with Dr. Loemker's discussion of the nature of secularism, and second, that we all agree that the chief requirement for combating secularism is a deeper and more intelligent faith in God, deeper personal commitment, and a closer relationship to God on the part of professing Christians. It is probably needless to add that what I say reflects my own views only and is not an attempt to commit any group with which I happen to be connected.

If an effective witness to the Christian gospel is to be borne in our secularized world, it seems to me imperative that Christians generally should acquire a more adequate understanding of the church, and that a truer embodiment of its authentic character be attained by the reunion of existing denominations. This is not the place for a detailed discussion of the doctrine of the church, but one aspect of it is central to our problem.

Both Paul and John think of the church as constituted by the exalted Christ and those who are his. Let me illustrate this doctrine first in a totally nonbiblical figure. A horseshoe magnet attracts and attaches to itself particles of iron, tacks, nails. Furthermore, the particles in juxtaposition to each other on the magnet become attached to each other so that sometimes it is as hard to separate them from one another as to pull them from the magnet. Lastly, objects attached to the magnet, if it is strong enough, become themselves conductors of the magnetism so that through them other objects are attracted. I remember seeing a magnet, one end of which was so completely covered by very fine iron filings as to be invisible, which still drew other objects to itself through this covering layer. Magnet and filings had become one magnetic force. In terms of this analogy one thinks of our Lord attracting people to himself; those attached to him he attaches to one another; through those thus attached to him he draws still others. He and his disciples constitute a redemptive unit, and this is the church.

In a better figure, because drawn from living objects, John wrote of the vine and the branches. The trunk of a vine is not one object and the branches totally distinct and separate ones; rather taken together they constitute a living, growing unit, putting out more shoots, leaves, blossoms, fruit. Paul used the figure "the body of Christ" in two slightly different ways. In Ephesians he wrote of the church as the body and Christ as its head, distinguishing between the two; in I Corinthians he wrote of Christ and his followers together forming one body: "For as the body is one, and hath many members, and all the members of that one body, being many, are yet one body: so also is Christ" (12:12). It is not the church, mind you, that despite many members with different functions is yet one body, but Christ. However, Paul's two uses are not really in conflict; for the head is part of the body, albeit the controlling part. Christians are so joined to Christ, and to each other in him, that he and they together form one living body, he being the controlling head and his Spirit the informing, integrating force.

This seems to me the most profound thought of the church in the New Testament: that it consists of Christ and those who are attached to him, and thereby to one another.

The Church Today

On the basis of this conception of the church let me make two comments on the existing situation in our churches.

First, in point of fact our existing ecclesiastical structures contain a goodly proportion of those whose attachment to our Lord, and therefore to their fellow Christians, is very tenuous. They are like tacks very loosely attached to the magnet; like sick members of a body, unresponsive to the brain and un-co-ordinated with each other. That is to say that secularism—i.e., the spirit of this world which opposes the spirit of Christ—has made deep inroads into our communions. We know that these people—and who will say he is not of this number?—are a negligible factor so far as bearing effective Christian witness against secularism is concerned. The effective witness-bearer to the gospel and the Christian understanding of life in any community is now, as it has been for generations, the minority group of Christians who are so closely attached to Christ that his Spirit controls their outlook and attitudes and actions; for it is only these people who have the firmness and clarity of faith, the strength of ethical judgments, and the spiritual power that are necessary to overcome the power of secularism.

Furthermore, we all know that the experience of generations of Christians shows that those so attached to Christ often are discovered to one another and are bound together in a fellowship that transcends all barriers of race, color, language, nationality, and denomination. It seems to me that one of the most important questions of our day is how to give more effective expression to this group, this "church within the churches" as someone called it, and to articulate its voice Godward in worship and manward in witness.

Second, you will recall also that Paul wrote to "the church of God which is at Corinth," and again to "the saints and faithful brethren in Christ which are at Colosse." The church in Corinth, in Paul's mind, was that part of the total Christian society that lived in that particular city. If we were to think in a similar fashion, we should speak of the church of God which is in Chicago or Alexandria or Fairfax Court House; that is to say, the part of the total Christian society which lived in those places. We should probably go further and speak of the church of God which is in the United States or Great Britain or France or China. And this seems to me a very important point. For as F. D. Maurice argued a century ago, and Augustine long before him, people function and develop in a number of organic human communities—the family, the village or town or section of a great city, the nation—and the subdivisions of the church of the living God should correspond to these organic human communities. I used to fear national churches lest they become infected by unredeemed nationalism; but increasingly it seems to me that international denominations are not any more immune to this virus, or to any other form of secularism—think, for instance, of German Lutheranism or Italian Romanism—and also that a truly national church has more opportunity to infect the life of its country with Christian faith than a number of denominations, just as a single strong church can more deeply affect its community than a number of denominational congregations.

Yet in point of fact the great bulk of Christians belong to international denominations—Methodist, Anglican, Roman, and the rest. We have practically lost Paul's conception of one body of Christ in the world, functioning in subdivisions which correspond to the organic human communities, and its recovery demands the reunion of the denominations. I incline to think that the existence of the denominations is a striking manifestation of the extent to which "the spirit of this world," to use John's phrase, has permeated those who bear the name of Christ; and I sympathize deeply with Bishop Charles Henry Brent, who, in. his later years, was increasingly unwilling to speak of the "Methodist Church," the "Anglican Church," the "Roman Church," and so forth, because he thought that the word "church" could properly be used only of the whole body of Christians or its representative in a particular area.

ECUMENICAL REFORM

The influence of the spirit of this world within the Christian groups obviously extends to every phase of their activity, and therefore every phase of their activity needs to be cleansed and reoriented. It is for this reason that the most important and hopeful fact today seems to me to be the nascent ecumenical reformation.

History is the story of the conflict in the hearts of men between the Spirit of Christ and the spirit of this world. This is true of church history to only a slightly lesser degree than of secular history; for churchmen, being human, are exposed to their own *Zeitgeist* and to all the temptations of their fellows. But at various epochs God has raised up men who have striven against secularism in the church with uncommon effectiveness, and their efforts have brought about the great reform movements. As I see it, they have always engaged the enemy on three fronts sooner or later: ethical norms and practices, basic theology, the conception and organization of the church.

Consider the Reformation of the sixteenth century. Luther began with an attack on the ethical evils that seemed to him to be polluting the church. The sale of indulgences, the profits from which were supposed to go to glorifying God by finishing St. Peter's, but which were really going to the Amsterdam banking house of Fugger in order to repay the loan it had made to the archbishop of Branden-burg to enable him to pay the pope the sum required for permission to violate the canonical prohibition of pluralism, seemed to Luther peculiarly obnoxious; and the sale of propitiatory masses but little better. The spirit of this world had infiltrated the body of Christ to a terrible degree, and had polluted it morally. So in the name of the Lord he fought the ethical battle.

The refusal of the pope and his agents to discuss this matter from the biblical point of view, commanding Luther merely to obey the order to keep quiet, convinced him that the spirit of this world had permeated and captured the ecclesiastical organization. Its gov-ernment was hierarchical and authoritarian to a degree that made it entirely different from the New Testament idea of church govern-ment; its actions were based on the expediencies of power politics and on a legal system copied from the Roman Empire rather than de-duced from biblical teaching. So, in the name of the Lord, he fought the ecclesiastical organization.

Furthermore, whatever might be the church's official doctrine—and Luther objected to it because it was Scholastic rather than bibli-cal—the Church's practice taught the common people an unchristian faith. The sale of indulgences and propitiatory masses conveyed the idea that God's favor could be bought, that God was one who could be bribed or cajoled or controlled. This was a denial of his sovereignty, his righteousness, his grace. It made the Atonement of no real effect and changed faith from the commitment of the total personality into obedience to the priest's commands to believe this and do that. The spirit of this world had perverted Christian faith. So in the name of the Lord, Luther fought the contemporary theology.

Other reformers joined the fray. Romanists replied, not only by fighting them but also by the decrees of the Council of Trent. The total result in the areas of ethics, the doctrine and organization of the church, and theology constituted the sixteenth century reforma-tions.

But the spirit of this world never ceased its warfare; and in the course of three hundred years it again infected very deeply Protestant and Roman ethics, their doctrine and organization of the church, and their theology. About a century ago other men were raised up for a new effort to purge the Christian forces of secularization in those same three areas; and these efforts, now becoming co-ordinated, constitute the ecumenical reformation, something which in God's providence may have as far-reaching results as did the Protestant Reformation. But though the struggle is in the same three areas, the precise issues are different.

In the field of ethics the main point since the days of F. D. Maurice in England (1805-72) has been Christian teaching and practice in corporate life. From Maurice to Archbishop William Temple, and from Gladden to Niebuhr, Christian leaders have fought against the spirit of this world which maintained that public policy, wages, hours and conditions of employment, governmental actions, and so forth, were no business of the church, and that Christians should accept conditions as they found them or, like pagans, should act on the basis of enlightened self-interest, which meant the interest of the more powerful groups.

In the field of theology reformers have been contending against the spirit of this world's insistence that science is the only reliable source of knowledge, that "natural law" controls the world, that men, by their own knowledge and skill, can so arrange things that all will be well in the world, that sin is an outworn notion, and the like. Maurice fought the mid-nineteenth-century version of these assertions as strenuously as Temple and Niebuhr and others have fought the contemporary formulations of the same ideas.

In the area of the doctrine and practice of the church the ecumenical reformers became convinced that the atomization of the church into innumerable sects stemmed from this-worldly influences such as exaggerated individualism, the denial of any objective truth, the assertion that a man's religion is his private affair and that the churches are associations of like-minded individuals. With increasing persistence they have been trying to recover for the non-Roman world the true biblical teaching of the church and to bring the existing ecclesiastical organizations into co-operation, federation, and union. As medieval secularism had shown itself in the church as too authoritarian and totalitarian, recent secularism has made itself felt in the Protestant world as too libertarian and individualistic. Therefore those who in recent years have fought against the spirit of this world have striven for a true doctrine of the church and for the reunion of the denominations.

In the last decades the people fighting secularism in the churches have seen that the battle in the three areas was really one struggle, and now the ecumenical movement—or, as I prefer to call it, the ecumenical reformation—is seen as a single reform movement operating on different fronts. Archbishop Temple synthesized this many-sided struggle more than any other man of our time, and the World Council of Churches is its most conspicuous organizational manifestation. The attempt to make the churches more Christian, and therefore more adequate in fulfilling the mission entrusted by our Lord to his followers, has made men realize both the theological and pragmatic necessity for the reunion of the denominations. We can now see that the struggle for church unity is a major part of the struggle to enthrone the spirit of God and to overcome the spirit of this world.

The picture is not all dark. One very important and hopeful development in this century is the extent to which earnest Christian scholarship has distinguished between barriers to unity that spring from cultural or sinful causes—such as, for example, preferences in forms of worship or antipathy of national, racial, and economic groups —and those which owe their strength to genuinely religious or theological considerations. So far as I know, every responsible Christian leader thinks that the former sort of obstacles, however great their power because of our limitations and sinfulness, must be resolutely exposed for what they really are and fought till their influence is broken. In addition, reverent Christian scholarship has shown us that often what we thought to be differences in basic Christian faith are really differences in language. Different groups mean the same thing by different words, and some words have quite varying connotations to sundry groups. As we grow into better understanding of each other's meaning, still further barriers to reunion will be eliminated. It is important also to note that there has been a very important growth in understanding and co-operation among the non-Roman Churches: Protestant churches have recognized increasingly the values of Catholicism and vice versa, and the number of denominations belonging to the Federal Council and the World Council is very impressive.

In proportion as we are driven to our knees and to our Bibles we can become the kind of people out of whom God can make a spiritually powerful and united church; and meanwhile the organs of co-operation—like local councils, the Federal Council, the World Council—can draw us together and form a structure through which the united church of the future can function locally, nationally, and internationally.

ORDERS AND CHURCH REUNION

The most stubborn barrier to reunion is, of course, the ministry. Here too we should recognize a significant advance in recent decades. On the one hand there is a widespread recognition that there is a real difference between the ministries of those communions which have preserved the three orders that characterized the pre-Reformation Catholic Church from the very earliest days, and of those communions which in one way or another have altered that ancient form and have employed a different organ for ordinations. They may be complimentary; they may be equally of God; but they are different. On the other hand, most churches of Catholic order now recognize frankly that the ministries of the great nonepiscopal churches have manifestly been owned and blessed by the Holy Spirit, and that their sacraments have been used of God as means of bestowing his grace upon men. What God has so owned cannot be other than real ministries of the word and sacraments. Speaking as an Anglican who values both its Catholic and its Protestant heritage, I believe that at the Holy Communion celebrated by a minister of one of the great nonepiscopal denominations the Lord is really present and communicates himself to the faithful, and that the minister's offering of the memorial Christ commanded us to make—and the congregation's self-oblation in unison therewith, together with their money, their praises, and prayers—is an offering acceptable to God.

Behind this view lies an interpretation of the Reformation. I am bound to think that Luther's protest was divinely inspired. To make it good he had to organize his forces ecclesiastically. To do that demanded a ministry; and since bishops did not join him, he had to find some other way of admitting men to the ministry. The Lutheran and Reformed ministries, as I see it, were raised up by God as a judgment on the then Catholic one. Ordination into a ministry that God originated and has continuously used must carry a gift of grace.

What is needed is some way of fusing these two different, divinely originated and divinely blessed ministries.

There appears to be but two ways of effecting such fusion. One is that of mutual reordination. The presupposition of this is that each ministry is a real and divinely recognized one, and that the members of each could receive a further gift of grace by ordination at the hands of the proper authority of the other church. For myself, I have no doubts whatsoever about my own ordination; but I should certainly expect a further gift of grace if I were ordained by the authorities of, say, the Presbyterian Church, with whom my communion is now negotiating; and by the same token, I think Presbyterian clergymen would receive a further gift of grace if ordained by an Episcopal bishop.

The other way is that of extension of ordination. If this is conceived as meaning a further gift of grace, it is indistinguishable from mutual reordination. If it is simply a matter of extension of jursdicton, it seems to be tolerable as an interim measure in a plan of organic union, but even then distinctly less desirable than the other way because all of us manifestly need further gifts of grace to exercise the ministry in the quite new situation and under the new problems and responsibilities of a united church.

This does not mean that I think of grace as a certain "quiddity," to use Hooker's phrase, conveyed by ordination as through a pipe line. Grace is always the impact of God on man, the activity of the Holy Spirit. That is why I find all attempts to define precisely what capacities are conveyed by any gift of grace so unsatisfactory. The Holy Spirit acts through bishops of the traditional ministry and through the ordaining authorities of the other great churches.

STEPS TO TAKE

It seems to me that several important steps need to be taken as quickly as possible in order that we may advance toward a united church, toward what Theodore O. Wedel called "the coming great church."

1. To formulate and teach widely in every communion a true biblical view of the church, so that people may understand that they have been incorporated into a divinely originated organism rather than think that they have merely elected to join a voluntary association of like-minded people.

2. To find ways of giving more adequate expression and scope to the total community of Christians in any community by great

joint services and by common enterprises, and also to those trans-denominational fellowships of people closely attached to Christ and by him to one another.

3. To find ways of making the great bulk of professing Christians understand how much they have in common with the members of other denominations, that is, to make them appreciate the extent of their existing unity in Christ.

4. To strengthen the interdenominational organs which unite us in common tasks and which can be powerful agencies for drawing us closer together toward organic unity.

5. To carry on experiments in unity at the grass roots level. One illustration of my meaning must suffice. In a suburb of Cincinnati, a Presbyterian and an Episcopal parish decided it would be both a waste of human and material resources and also a weakening of Christian witness if they were to build separate plants and develop separate programs. So a governing board was formed, drawn equally from the two congregations. This board, with the approval of the local presbytery and Episcopal bishop, called a clergyman to minister to the combined parish; a united service, church school, and total parish program were initiated. The contributions for benevolences outside the combined parish are sent to the presbytery and diocese in proportion to the number of Presbyterian and Episcopal members of the parish. The bishop of the diocese makes an annual visitation to administer Confirmation, and the moderator of the presbytery comes to admit qualified candidates into full communicant status in the Presbyterian Church. There are more details, but this will indicate the general scheme. It seems to me that such combined parishes, if wisely and strongly led, will grow together; they will be potent forces for bringing together their constituent denominations in their areas; they can be powerful factors for church unity, and so a far more effective witness to Christ in this secularized age.

Church Unity Is Imperative

I began this chapter by pleading the importance of "the church within the churches" in combating secularism and also of organizing the subdivisions of the Christian Church along the lines of organic human communities. Because of the extent to which secularism has infected all our Christian groups, it seemed necessary to mention again the ecumenical reformation which appears to be slowly making itself felt, and to view the movement toward church unity as one phase of that total effort to counteract the ravages of the spirit of this world within our ecclesiastical structures. That led us to consider possible ways of dealing with the most difficult barrier to church unity, the ministry. Then we considered certain steps which are important for uniting the denominations. In conclusion, let me try to sum up what I have already partly suggested, namely, why this unification is so imperative, both doctrinally and pragmatically.

First, I think any candid student of the New Testament will agree that a multiplicity of churches is entirely contradictory to its teaching. In the Gospels and the epistles the followers of our Lord are thought of as forming one society. This society might have many congregations, and these congregations might be organized differently and might display variations in ministry and cult, for there is nothing stereotyped in the New Testament. But the members of all these congregations formed the body of Christ, the ecclesia, the fellowship of the Spirit, the new Israel. All of them owned one Lord, one faith, one baptism, one God and Father; all were within the new covenant; all of them together formed the church of the living God; all were in communion with one another, both in the sense of partaking together of the sacrament and in the sense of forming a community. Our present situation negates this idea of the church.

I am not arguing that the church should be a highly centralized organization, with an authoritarian world government; the papal system negates the idea of the church as much as Protestant divisiveness does. Nor do I plead for a dead level of uniformity; different temperaments and cultural traditions demand different modes of organization and forms of worship and ways of formulating the Christian attitude toward God and man.

I am arguing that church demands that all churchmen be free to participate in each others' sacraments; that they hold a common faith, of which the Bible is the source and the norm, and of which the Apostles' Creed is the best brief summary; that they proclaim, and try to live by, a common ethical standard; that they have a ministry recognized by all as having both the inward call of God and the proper ecclesiastical authentication; that they are so organized as to avoid reduplication and competition, and as to make their common work and witness effective. To accomplish this demands the reunion of the denominations. Let me repeat again that New Testament teaching calls for one branch of the Holy Catholic Church in each country, rather than international communions; for the nation is a basic human unit, and the universal church should be subdivided according to fundamental human communities, the nation and the local area. The church of God in the United States, in Great Britain, in France or Germany or China, subdivided into the church of God in Chicago or Fairfax, is a truer concept than the international Methodist or Anglican or Presbyterian branch of the Holy Catholic Church.

Second, it seems so obvious as not to need discussion that our present denominationalism vitiates the influence of Christianity in our secular world. In innumerable American towns there are four or six small struggling congregations, each unable to support an adequate program or to maintain a permanent minister, whereas they could support one strong, well-staffed congregation carrying on a program that would influence the entire town. In the struggle to survive these pitiful congregations often misrepresent and malign each other, to the scandal of Christiantiy; and their competing, discordant versions of the gospel bewilder and disgust men of good will. In the mission fields the rivalries are even more serious; for in lands where Christianity, especially Protestant Christianity, is a very small minority group, it can have influence only if it presents a united front and a common program, and makes the best possible use of its total resources.

Again, please note that I am not pleading for bureaucratic control or complete uniformity. In large cities there is need for several congregations with different forms of worship, and there is need for such flexibility of organization and procedure as will permit the Christians in each particular area to fulfill their mission in that area. I am pleading for a visible demonstration in every community that all Christians therein obey the same Lord, profess the same faith, worship and commit themselves to the same God and Father, live by the same ethical norms, serve their fellows in the name of the same Master. To accomplish this the union of the existing denominations is imperative.

God has brought the Christian Church to a time when it must become truly Christian and truly church. That is his demand. The alternative to obeying it is his condemnation: its withering away because it is irrelevant, futile, useless as his agent in the world. If such be his judgment, he will raise up a new and truer body of Christ. On the other hand, if we fulfill his demand, we do not know the issue in world history, but we can be assured that our struggles and pains and prayers will be vindicated.

SECULARISM IN CONTEMPORARY LITERATURE

Edwin Mims

I KNOW OF NO BETTER TEXT FOR MY PART IN THIS SYMPOSIUM ON secularism than the words of T. S. Eliot in his essay on "Religion and Literature," in which he refers to "the gradual secularization of literature during the past three hundred years." Novelists like Dickens and Thackeray took faith for granted; novelists like George Eliot, Meredith, and Hardy "doubted, worried about, or contested the faith; others never heard the Christian faith spoken of as anything but an anachronism." Eliot continues: "What I do wish to affirm is that the whole of modern literature is corrupted by what I call secularism, that it is simply unaware of, simply cannot understand the meaning of, the primacy of the supernatural life; of something which I assume to be our primary concern." Then he adds in words that express the fundamental change that came over his thought in the midyears of his life:

We feel convinced that our spiritual faith should give us some guidance in temporal matters; that morality rests upon religious sanction, and that the social organization of the world rests upon moral sanction; that we can only judge of temporal values in the light of eternal values. We are committed to what in the eyes of the world must be a desperate belief, that a Christian world order, the Christian world order, is ultimately the only one which, from my point of view, will work. . . . The modern world separates the intellect and the emotions. Human wisdom cannot be separated from divine wisdom—without tending to become merely worldly wisdom, as vain as folly itself.

However one may disagree with Eliot's adoption of the Anglo-Catholic faith, I suppose there is no more authoritative critic of literature in our time. In *The Waste Land*, "Gerontion," and "The Hollow Men" he gave poetic expression to the disillusionment, restlessness, and blank despair of modern thought. Some of his lines, as well as the title of his most widely known poem, may well serve to express what has happened in modern thought. In *The Waste Land* there are no roots that clutch, nor do branches grow out of this stony rubbish.

> A heap of broken images, where the sun beats,
> And the dead tree gives no shelter, the cricket no relief,
> And the dry stones no sound of water.[1]

It is not physical but spiritual death when he exclaims, "I had not thought death had undone so many." There is no silence or solitude in the mountains, "but red sullen faces sneer and snarl from doors of mud-cracked houses." The empty chapel has no windows and is only the wind's home. Gerontion, "an old man in a dry month," a "dull head among windy spaces," is symbolic of many types of futility and despair. Was there ever a severer indictment of many of our modern writers than the Hollow Men who live in a dead land, a cactus land, "the broken jaw of our lost kingdoms"? It is no wonder that they anticipate the end of the world and that they go down "not with a bang but a whimper."

William Butler Yeats said that when he edited *The Oxford Book of Modern Verse* he could find few poets, and those minor ones, who were at all interested in religion; and in his own poem "The Second Coming" he summed up the general intellectual situation as he saw it:

> Things fall apart; the centre cannot hold;
> Mere anarchy is loosed upon the world.
> .   .   .   .
> The best lack all conviction, while the worst
> Are full of passionate intensity.[2]

He himself rebelled against the odor of blood that was characteristic of Christianity. He preferred the rose rather than the cross as the symbol of life. E. E. Cummings, the most radical experimenter with the forms of poetry, speaks of certain Cambridge ladies who believe in Longfellow and Christ, "both dead." Philip Horton says in his life of Hart Crane: "In the late '20's and '30's to confess religious emotions in New York literary circles was far more damaging to whatever went by the name of 'poetic prestige' than the confes-

---

[1] Used by permission Harcourt, Brace & Co., Inc., publishers.
[2] From *Later Poems*. Copyright 1924 by The Macmillan Co. and used with their permission.

sion of any number of sexual or moral irregularities." Another poet, John Peale Bishop, wrote:

> There was One might have saved
> Me from these grave dissolute stones
> And parrot eyes. But He is dead,
> Christ is dead. And in a grave
> Dark as a sightless skull He lies
> And of His bones are charnels made.[3]

These quotations and citations might continue indefinitely. There is another side to the picture which is well expressed by C. Day Lewis in *A Hope for Poetry*. He uses the parable of the prodigal son to illustrate what he considers the value of the experiments in technique and content in contemporary poetry:

The younger son, fretting against parental authority, weary of sentimentalism, suspecting that the soul needs a rest, has packed his bags and set out for a far country. Rumors of his doings come to our ears; they are generally unfavorable and always distorted, for they have had to pass across seas. He is flirting with foreign whores or with ghosts; he has wasted his fortune; he has forgotten how to speak English; he has shamed his father; he has gone much in the desert. Only his father smiles indulgently with secret pride, amused at the vigor of his seed. Then the younger son returns, not a broken prodigal, but healthy, wealthy and wise. He has many acres under cultivation over there; he has money in the bank, strange tales to tell us, and some fine children already.

Some of these prodigals, like Eliot, W. H. Auden, and others, have returned to the faith; but their apostasy has been excoriated by many of the contemporary critics. Edmund Wilson, for instance, characterizes Eliot's change of heart as "a desire to believe in religious revelation, or that it would be a good thing to believe, rather than a genuine belief." And another one of the most frequently quoted critics writes that "the religionist in Eliot has gained on the critic as he has gained on the poet," and then adds: "Had Mr. Eliot only served his literature with half the zeal he served his religion," all would have been better. It never seems to occur to the critic that Eliot might have a maturer, a richer mind and a fuller heart by worshiping in a cathedral rather than wandering aimlessly through

[3] From "Ode." Used by permission Charles Scribner's Sons, publishers.

the desert. Another young critic laments the fact that Auden has gone from Freud to Paul and has thereby forfeited his claim to be a leader of poets. The determinism and communism of Auden's early days have been "transfigured by Christian optimism" and obedience to authority.

So much needs to be said, although much more might be said, of the situation in contemporary poetry. The same is true of contemporary fiction and drama. Henry S. Canby, who, as editor of *The Saturday Review of Literature* and as chairman of the Book of the Month Club, has read as much contemporary fiction as anybody in the United States, has felicitously summarized the progressive stages in the life of a typical member of the younger generation as portrayed in a typical novel:

> At seven he sees through his parents and characterizes them in a phrase. At fourteen he sees through his education and begins to dodge it. At eighteen he sees through morality and steps over it. At twenty he loses respect for his home town. At twenty-one he discovers that our social and economic system is ridiculous. At twenty-three his story ends because the author has seen through society to date—does not know what to do next.

He might have added that somewhere along the road he sees through religion and abandons it, or, as a contemporary writer graphically expressed it: "All gods dead, all wars fought, all faiths in man shaken." Or, as Hemingway expressed it: "There is no remedy for anything in life."

SECULARISM IN FICTIONAL DRAMA

Eugene O'Neill is certainly the most widely known and perhaps greatest contemporary American dramatist. With few exceptions, and those not the best of his dramas, we are confronted with disillusionment, extreme naturalism, determinism as the only explanation of life's tragedies, and with behaviorism as the explanation of psychological crises. One feels at times that O'Neill's tortured soul is yearning for some kind of faith that lies beyond the horizon, but his most typical characters express their ideas of God in such words as the following from *Anna Christie:* "Don't babble about it. There ain't nothing to forgive, anyway. It wasn't your fault, and it ain't mine and it ain't his neither. We're all poor nuts, and things happen, and we just get mixed in wrong, that's all." And again, in *All God's Chillun Got Wings*—a clinical study of miscegenation and racial hatred—the hero cries out: "Maybe He can forgive what you've done to me, and maybe He can forgive what I've done to you, but I don't see how He's going to forgive—Himself." In *Marco Millions*—a dramatic denouncement of modern commercialism and imperialism —the hero says: "My hideous suspicion is that God is only an infinite, insane energy which creates and destroys without other purpose than to pass eternity in avoiding thought." In *Strange Interlude* the stream of consciousness is the dominant theme; the asides and soliloquies reveal a married woman with three lovers, the Oedipus complex, the father-daughter fixation, all leading to insanity or despair. *Dynamo* reveals the power of the modern machine—the death of an old god and the inability to find any satisfaction in a new one. When O'Neill wrote *Days Without End*, he seemed to find a way out of the chaos of the modern world by a return to the Roman Catholic faith, but the play is generally regarded as a failure. Many who hoped that he would, after his long silence, present a more hopeful dramatic representation of life were disappointed when in his production of *The Ice Man Cometh* he used as a background a saloon and as types of characters the defeated who reach satisfaction only in their illusions.

O'Neill's influence is found in many of his contemporaries. Robert Sherwood, in *The Petrified Forest*, symbolizes in his "dead stumps in the desert" the passing of Platonism, patriotism, and Christianity. In his *Idiot's Delight* one of the characters exclaims: "We don't do half enough justice for Him. Poor, lonely old soul. Sitting up in heaven with nothing to do but play solitaire. Poor, dear God. The game that never means anything, and that never ends." No man in the United States has followed contemporary drama more assiduously and more critically than George Jean Nathan, who, in a chapter on "The New Morality" in his *Land of the Pilgrim's Pride*, gives expression to the current revolt in morals as illustrated in the contemporary drama:

The virgin does not stand as good a chance to get a husband as her lax sister. . . . Other qualities than chastity are demanded—vastly more important. A woman who has had experience is better than the average immaculate maiden. . . . Virtuous heroines of fiction and the drama have today become a laughing stock. It is slang that has broken down the barriers of reserve. . . . Sex, once wearing the tragic mask, wears now the mask of comedy. . . . Sex is really of little importance—less so than tobacco or the wine cellar. . . . Sin is rather jolly—when frailty becomes sufficiently general it becomes its own court, its own judge, and its own jury.

The success of marriage in these latter days of Caucasian civilization must be looked for very largely outside the cities and in the small towns, villages, farms, and other such places, where life is relatively drab and uneventful. Morality is a species of disease, of weakness. In comedy we find most of the true, deep, biting intelligence that has come down to us through the history of the drama. Comedy has made the human race wise. It is comedy that has purged men of their delusions.[4]

THE CULT OF SMARTNESS

Nathan and his partner H. L. Mencken dominated the critical opinion of most of the sophisticated intellectuals during the twenties. For a decade or more there were groups in Chicago, New York, and Paris who gleefully announced the dawn of a new day of liberation and emancipation. They denounced puritanism as leading to inhibitions and suppressions that had been obstacles in the way of the civilized minority, the pioneer spirit with all its crudeness and mediocrity, and, above all, the commercialism and mechanization of American life and thought. A wisecrack became the acme of human wisdom.

Harry Hansen, in his *Midwest Portraits*, has given certain sketches of the Chicago group and excerpts from their conversations in Schlogl's restaurant or tavern. The decision to write the book came one night at two o'clock when "the merry and leisurely company that gave no signs of going home" were in the full swing of "odd banter on the trivialities of existence." Ben Hecht was exclaiming: "Our architecture, our streets, typifying after all nothing but energy. We have just emerged from barbarism. We are taking the first steps in civilization, . . . only heat with energy. Utilitarian masses. No ideas, only energy, . . . barbarism." Maxwell Bodenheim is represented as "giving birth to epigrams with a deep frown on his forehead, a cynical smile on his lips." "I have a healthy contempt for the whole human race." Another quotes Sandburg's "The Past Is a Bucket of Ashes." He is an editor who has found out that "the editorial code demands on his part a certain amount of asperity and cynicism." A promising young novelist hopes to become a new Fitzgerald, while another has the psychology of the Russians at his fingertips. Now and then there are visitors who add to the gaiety, revelry, and cynicism of the occasion—notably Sinclair Lewis and a certain English novelist. Ben Hecht is represented as really the dominating personality, a combination of street urchin and skeptical intellectual, with some of the elements of the acrobat and mountebank. He characterizes himself in a passage that suggests well many contemporary novelists and dramatists:

Born perversely. Out of this perversity, a sentimental hatred of weakness in others, an energetic amusement for the gods, taboos, vindictiveness and cowardice of my friends, neighbors and relatives; a contempt for the ideas of man, and infatuation with the energies of man, a loathing for the protective slave philosophies of the people, a determination not to become a part of the mind which the swine worship in their style. A delirious relief in finding words that express any or all of my perversities. Out of this natal perversity I have written my books.

After enduring and becoming satiated with the "cursing matches" of some of these parties, Sherwood Anderson tells us in his autobiography of a visit to New York, where he met the smart fellows of the American intelligentsia who sat about in restaurants and wrote articles for the political and serious literary weeklies. We read of a party consisting of Scott Fitzgerald, Mencken, Carl Van Vechten, Ernest Boyd, Rebecca West, and others. Mencken made schoolboy jokes and talked schoolboy talk with a kind of boisterous bonhomie. Miss West seemed to be "abusing her talents and originality for the satisfaction of obtaining a certain reputation for smartness in modish literary circles."

Out of such a group came the determination to write a symposium entitled *Civilization in the United States*—a comprehensive survey of life and thought in America by thirty of the younger critics, the general conclusion being that there is no civilization in this country. The scheme of the book, according to Burton Rascoe, one of the Midwest wits who had come to join the wise men of the East, was evolved over a table in Greenwich Village one evening, when, in a group of young writers, the common discontent with things as they are in this worst of all possible worlds was crystallized into a flaming resentment. . . . Young, sanguine, and exuberant, for all their intellectualism, they set forth.

But neither Chicago nor New York satisfied the extreme left wing of American critics. H. E. Stearns himself, the leader in the enterprise just referred to, hied away to Paris, where he carried on the fight with his fellow expatriates—Hemingway, Gertrude Stein, and others. Sinclair Lewis has given a highly satirical account of the group of American artists and writers who gathered about the Cafe Dome, which he characterized as "the perfectly standardized place to which standardized rebels flee from the crushing standardization of America." He meets a young author who, by his description of vomiting and the progress of cancer, has "entirely transformed American fiction," and a woman who has "demolished Thomas Hardy, Arnold Bennett, and Goethe." "The skinny lady who has gone out for vice with the same relentless grimness with which her sister back home exploits virtue" is said to belong to "the Salvation Army of compulsory sin." "I first learned from them," says Lewis, "that it was imperative to adore, though not necessarily to read, Mr. James Joyce's *Ulysses,* who had used all six of the unprintable Anglo-Saxon monosyllables and had thus ruined their own chances of shocking people."

I have chosen such groups in order to emphasize certain fundamental ideas that are characteristic of contemporary literature. It is very evident that there developed a cult of smartness, whose official organ was the *Smart Set,* edited by Mencken and Nathan. They, like Scott Fitzgerald, sought to be "as clever, as interesting, and as brilliantly cynical as possible about every man, doctrine, book, or policy." They identified dullness with respectability, with orthodoxy of any kind, and, above all, with a faith "that lifts up heart and voice alike to view a parasite infesting the epidermis of a midge among the planets, and cries, 'Behold, this is the child of God Almighty and all worshipful, made in the likeness of his Father.' " Man seems like "a bird striving to nest in a limitless engine, insanely building among moving wheels and cogs and pistons, an intruder, a temporary visitor in the big, moving, soulless mechanism of earth and water and planets

and suns and interlocking solar systems." Or as Mencken puts it at
the end of one of his most characteristic *Prejudices:* "Man is a sick
fly on the dizzy wheel of the cosmic universe, revolving twenty
thousand miles a second, and religion teaches us that the cosmic universe is made for the fly." The end, therefore, of the long story of
man is nothing but disaster; such men look forward complacently and
sometimes gleefully to the end of the dream.

If we discount much contemporary fiction and drama and even
poetry as a rather superficial expression of smartness and as motivated
by a desire to shock people, we cannot so lightly discount the influence of science and of the philosophy that has grown out of
science. We know now that the main influence in Theodore Drieser's
intellectual development was his reading of Darwin and Huxley;
that Sherwood Anderson once said that if you want to know human
nature and human life you must consult Freud; and that the one hero
of Sinclair Lewis' novels is the doctor and the scientist in *Arrowsmith.*
Whether we think of psychology or sociology or philosophy, we
must see that they have exercised a deep influence on contemporary
literature. It is little wonder that the amazing triumphs of modern
science have led to what a brilliant American essayist has called
"the idolatry of science."

It has challenged the supereminence of religion; it has turned all
philosophy out of doors except that which clings to its skirts; it has thrown
contempt on all learning that does not depend on it; and it has bribed
the skeptics by giving us immense material comforts.

One has only to read the writings of Harry Elmer Barnes, James
Harvey Robinson, John Watson, Freud, and Jung to realize how
many modern writers have been influenced by deterministic philosophy and behavioristic psychology.

The Modern Distemper

In many ways the most complete and devastating analysis of contemporary thought is found in Joseph Wood Krutch's *The
Modern Temper.* Here in one volume, written with real distinction
of style and with abundant knowledge of all phases of contemporary
thought, is the mood generated in the author by the intellectual convictions current in his time. The masters of the modern mind found

in him a sympathetic and even submissive disciple. All the disillusion-ment, the skepticism, the debunking of traditions and sentiments, the deterministic philosophy, the futility of the search for any abiding faith, find adequate and felicitous expression. Here is the pessimism of Bertrand Russell's *A Free Man's Worship* or of Santayana, without their belief in creative art as a refuge from the cruelty of an alien cosmic order. The cycle theory of history expounded in scientific terms by Spengler is unrelieved by any conception of the role that a man may play in accommodating himself to an era of civilization rather than of culture. Science, whose conclusions on many matters he accepts so unreservedly, leaves Krutch without any faith in ra-tionality as the basis of progress; it has brought neither happiness nor wisdom. The freer handling of sex by contemporary novelists and psychologists causes him to look upon love either as an "obscene joke," or as a primitive physiological urge, or as the greatest of il-lusions. He posits both a godless and a loveless universe. Philosophy, the search for "the phantom of certitude," has no word of wisdom, for it ends either in blank materialism or in an attempt—witness James and Whitehead—to justify mysticism upon inadequate grounds. Meta-physics may be, after all, only "the art of being sure of something that is not so—logically, the art of going wrong with confidence." Religion has disappeared with all its supernatural machinery and its anthropomorphism. And the conclusion of the whole matter is that we are now waiting for some fresh invasion of the barbarians—the Russians perhaps—who believe because they do not know, and that with a stoic resignation individuals must "live like men rather than die like animals."

Such, in substance, is the latest expression of the modern temper, or, if one prefers, the modern distemper. It is the prose version of Eliot's *Waste Land*, with all its symbolism of a chaotic world. The author might well have taken as the keynote of his volume Dante's inscription over the gates of hell: "All hope abandon, ye who enter here." The fact is that in a great deal of contemporary literature we have hell but neither a purgatory nor a paradise. God himself seems reduced to an infinite eternal energy, symbolized in the dynamo as used by Henry Adams and Eugene O'Neill—the Frankenstein that may destroy civilization. In one of the most tragic autobiogra-phies ever written William E. Leonard has presented the "Locomotive God" as a symbol of the fear that haunted his imagination since he was a child. It is the demonic force that pursued him—"The Face, the Jaws, of an Aboriginal Monster, shining from the Black Circle, ready to swallow him, to eat him alive." It is the machine God of steel and fire and smoke, constructing and unmaking man, a symbol of material dominions, of the delusions of a raucous America. With something of the same forces Waldo Frank has represented the chaos of modern life as a jungle in which machines take the place of the monsters that tear each other in their slime. The machine is "an anarchic mindless master in place of God to trample us and rule us."

Now many of these ideas are implicit in contemporary literature. Unquestionably naturalism has been the most characteristic mold in which this literature has been shaped. One should draw a distinction between realism and naturalism, both of them arising as a reaction against romanticism. Realism presents the good as well as the bad, the sunshine as well as the darkness. Naturalism, as defined and illustrated by Zola, sees life from the darker side entirely. Dreiser, as he watched a lobster devour a squid at the fish market, concluded that things live on each other, and so must men. He became convinced that great mental and physical force was the prime requisite in business. Something chemical and hence dynamic was uppermost in his representation of certain titans of finance. All the qualities of an artist were lacking in Dreiser except genius, and this genius was used supremely in *An American Tragedy* to portray the darker side of American life. He and O'Neill had had experiences that caused them to see life and to form a philosophy not dreamed of by earlier American writers. Hemingway, Scott Fitzgerald, and John Dos Passos had suffered all the disillusionments of World War I; they were hardboiled because they had seen so much violence and suffering. One may not agree with their point of view, but one has to take into consideration that world which they knew by experience as well as by imagination. In the next decade James T. Farrell, Erskine Caldwell, and William Faulkner added to the naturalistic interpretation of human life in wave after wave of the most naturalistic language and treatment.

I have, I hope, been realistic in presenting the topic assigned me. If it is asked what is the use of even considering some of these extreme aspects of modern life and thought, the answer is that as teachers and preachers we need to know that such books as we have been considering have been among the best sellers and have had a profound influence on American public opinion. These authors who a generation ago would not have attracted attention have become the favorite authors of publishers, have won the praise of hitherto conservative critics, have through the lecture platform received the plaudits of men and women, and have been treated in literary courses given in colleges and universities. The poor devils of Grub Street battering at the forts of folly have been transformed into successful giants, wielding their battle-axes and beating their tom-toms. You cannot ignore them; you cannot censor them; you must even recognize their importance.

I have left out of consideration the elements in our contemporary literature that tell another story. The philosophy of Whitehead, the scientific and philosophical ideas of some of our great art scientists, the poetry of Robert Frost and Vachel Lindsay, the essays of Stuart Sherman, the later plays of Maxwell Anderson and Robert Sherwood, the novels of Willa Cather and Ellen Glasgow, the biographies and autobiographies of great Americans, the series of historical writings by Van Wyck Brooks—all these are indications of the more constructive and better balanced writing of our time. They anticipate, let us hope, a new age of faith in the years that lie ahead of us.

SECULARISM AND THE HOME

Hazen G. Werner

SOMETHING IS SMOTHERING OUR LIVES, COARSENING US AND OUR homes. The demoralization of personal and family life is the fruit of present-day secularism. Irwin Edman describes it as the "noisy dominance of the second-rate"; Arnold J. Toynbee calls it "a blended indiscriminate vulgarity"; and Lecomte Du Noüy speaks of it as "the cult of novelty."

Secularism, this modern materialistic way of life, is doing something to us and to our homes. Under its shadow the institution of marriage and the family are changing—changing in structure, organization, and function.

In the days of "plowing the south forty" and riding "a bicycle built for two" the family existed to reproduce the race, prepare commodities for its own use, train children, and teach them how to live in community with life.

Today we are witnessing the rapid progress in the transfer of family economic functions to the community. This is dramatically evidenced by such services as the launderette and precooked frozen food, everything from scallops to Brunswick stew, ready for use. Soon entire meals cooked to your taste, frozen, and packaged to your door will be an actuality. Not much of the laundering, canning, clothing repair will be performed in the home of the future; half of the housing constructed at present is of the nature of apartment dwellings. Likewise, physical care, personality development and behavior training have become community responsibilities. The existence of child guidance centers, maternal health bureaus, marital clinics, day nurseries, as well as public relief, mother's aid, foster care, and hospital maternal care evidence the same trend.

Some of the structural and organizational changes within marriage and the family are for the better. There is a change from authoritarian to a more democratic form of family organization. Children are regarded not so much for the economic help they can give but for themselves as individuals in the fellowship of the family. Sex life is seen, not restrictedly as a means of procreation, but as a source of mutual enrichment.

Some of the changes, however, add to the peril and accelerate the decline of the home. There is a growing tolerance of the departure, on the part of family members, from standards of morality. Propriety and good taste have been interpreted as approving acts of moral deviation. Nice reasons are accepted for premarital and extramarital experiences that stand in violation of moral law. Living together as a family has definitely decreased, resulting in emotional disturbance and insecurity on the part of its members.

In the main, secularism is to be charged with exteriorizing our values, glorifying the physical, dissolving our checks and restraints, inflating the ego, robbing us of our moral sensibilities, atrophying our sense of meaning. Secularism as naturalism, as humanism, as individualism, is thus indicted.

SECULARISM'S ATTRITIONAL EFFECTS

These accusations necessitate a more definitive statement concerning secularism. What are its characteristics? First, secularism provides evil with disguise since there is a mixture of the good and the bad in its activity. Secularism is the Trojan horse that enables evil to carry on its deadly work at the center of our lives, in our homes. Secularism, of course, makes the labor of the home easier and more pleasurable, adds to the efficiency of domestic routine, and beautifies our dwellings. Secularism has enlisted the intelligent will and the creative mind, and moves in the good company of science. It possesses respectability and exercises benevolence. Second, secularism has no self-consciousness. As a culture it has no faculty for the appraisal of its own directives or its deprivations, no instrument for the adequate measurement of the very spiritual values it negates. Ernest R. Groves observes: "The heart of our social troubles, hurting not only home life but every sphere of spirit-experience, is clearly a civilization that has been so captivated by its rapid material progress, that it has lost not only its sense of spiritual values, but even any realization of its deficiencies." Third, secularism is so interfused with all that we are, even at our best, as to make it utterly elusive. Secularism is like a fog closing us in, and you can't fight a fog. It has become bone of our bone, life of our life, and mind of our mind. It begins to look as though, as creators of our own culture, we are to be the perpetrators of our own death. Secularism inhabits our conceptual thinking, looking out of our minds with us at the very distress it creates.

William M. McGovern, in his book *To Lhasa in Disguise*, chronicles the amazing tale of his entrance to the forbidden city. His disguise was effected by staining his body and squirting lemon juice in his eyes. When finally lodged in a house in Lhasa, he did the daring thing of sending word to the Tibetan monks that he was there. They descended on the place in a horde, hurling rocks at the house where he was in hiding. However, quietly stealing through the back door, McGovern went out, joined the mob in the attack, and thus escaped detection. This same maneuver has been the genius of secularism, and this genius we must understand if we are successfully to combat its hostilities.

Fourth, secularism offers other than spiritual answers for spiritual needs. "Happiness comes to the home that purchases So-and-So's linoleum." "She's just the girl for you," says the beaming mother to her son, further observing that "she serves the right kind of tea." An article in the *Atlantic* described a husband living in "imminent terror of losing his job. He's tired, cannot make those snap decisions. His wife saves the family future in the nick of time by changing to a new kind of breakfast food." But when he is still a defeated person, his thoughts wandering from his work, "although she fills him as full of bran as a prizewinning hog, it is only iced coffee that can save him now." We try to nourish our emotions and our minds with the thing, the life in which we are caught. A camera, we are told, will give us what is tantamount to the immortalization of a loved one. The movies quiet an occasional haunting apprehension about life after death with a caricature of eternal life in which phantom forms glide about on a floor of clouds, in unconcerned continuance of earth's routines, including an occasional tap dance and wisecrack. Death can't be so bad!

There are two end products of this amazing accomplishment of answering spiritual needs with material means. First, there is a self-sufficiency providing a false sense of security. "I don't see where either my family or I need religion," said a church member to a pastor. "We have everything we need, a home that leaves nothing to be desired, a winter place in Florida; our health could not be better; my business is bringing fabulous returns; what else do I need?" The Christian pulpit today is being challenged to preach a message that will disturb the undisturbed. We had better interpret the gospel as salvation from that greatest of all sins, the sin of presumption, the sin of those who think that they do not need God. Second, there is a deceiving unconcern. We can sit at the movies or observe a stage play depicting an episode of moral decay and find ourselves amused or curious, not realizing that we ourselves are involved in that moral decay. A young couple, seeking a minister to marry them, blandly declared that with marriage as temporary as it is, they intended not to invest in furniture, but to content themselves with owning a car. So deep have been the penetrations of secularism. Such an incident can be brought to our attention, but we are not shocked.

"Secularism," reads a recent statement issued by Roman Catholic bishops, "has debased the marriage contract of its relation to God and therefore its sacred character. It has set the will and convenience of husband and wife in the place of the will of God." The statement continues: "What hope is there unless men bring God back into the family life and respect the laws He has made for this fundamental unit of human security?"

Christianity, on behalf of its ally the home, is in conflict with the materializing and demoralizing processes of secularism. Evangelical empowerment must come to the aid of education and psychotherapy. The deteriorations of personality and family life outrun the operatives of therapy and the teaching of family techniques. The National Council of Family Relations reports that there are 657 courses on marriage and parental education in 550 American schools and colleges. There has never before been a time when such an attempt has been made to educate people in regard to the facts of sex and family life. And yet the rate of marital and family failure mounts ever upward. According to Eric Hutton, three out of twenty children suffer serious mental and emotional disturbances. Of the young girls from our finest homes, 50 per cent are toying with the idea of premarital adventure, says one of our able authorities. Of 772 college women interviewed, 64 per cent accepted the idea of extramarital relations, is the report of Dorothy Bromley and Florence Britten in their study. Add to this such facts as one abortion to every two or three pregnancies, two divorces for every five marriages, twelve divorces granted in seventeen minutes by a Philadelphia court.

In spite of all our education, attempts at liberation from ignorance frequently seem self-defeating. A tenth-grade class in hygiene, Henry Link tells us, when given a choice, voted as a majority for the discussion of the subject of how to have intercourse without risk of pregnancy. Link observes: "The more people are taught about the psychology of sex, the more likely they are to exploit sex for purely selfish reasons."

One thing we can do is to desist from the current practice of explaining the whole biological life of man to a six-year-old who innocently asks a question or two. To presume to tell the story of the physiological process of sex to a child who does not yet know a simple multiplication table is a bit absurd. It would be better if he were to receive his sex knowledge as he receives his general knowledge, in a growing way, a little at a time.

It may be salutary, likewise, for us to remind ourselves, as well as others, that sex compatability, based on full sex knowledge, is no guarantee of a happy and lasting marriage. Marriage requires more than harmony in the physical life. Basic to the failure to achieve sound marriage and parenthood through education is the fact that we are attempting to build upon a too slender foundation.

An ideological change concerning family life has come about through a conditioning to materialism. The chief principle of this conditioning is that material values are supreme in any gradation of importance. The unspoken inference is that moral and spiritual values are secondary.

There is a relation between our high standard of living, the best in the world, and our high record of broken homes. As a single factor, consider the place of money and the related maintenance of a standard of living in the experience of marital failures. Hornell Hart tells us that in one study 69 per cent of the women questioned in regard to the cause of marital quarrels said that they were due to money questions. The cause rating the next highest—18 per cent—was jealousy.

The most obvious effect of the supremacy of the material is seen in the increasing mechanization of the home. Technology is exhausting its resources and its genius in providing for the comfort and convenience of home life. Instant eggs, cooked by electronics, are to be commonplace. Screening electrified to kill insects will be standard equipment. A crib, operating electrically by the mere pushing of a button, will elevate a baby so that grandparents may pick up the child without bending over. A clock will start the radio at a given hour, enabling a family to rise simultaneously and greet the new day with a smile. This same clock will, at the right moment, turn on the lights at night, making for a warm and hospitable welcome as people enter the home.

Said Wesner Fallaw:

We observe that our culture is surfeited with gadgets that have driven from the home any need for the parents gathering children around them, for chores and household art, thus forming a self-sufficient family economy. Once the family could stand on its own, in details ranging from preparing the ground for seed all the way to harvesting, grinding the grain, and baking the bread. But now the household is thrown out of order if the toaster won't work.

One father quite seriously suggested that he was not interested in an oil burner, explaining that "the last discipline-forming duty that can be assigned to my boy is the carrying out of the ashes on Saturday morning."

It is fallacious to claim that the mechanization of the home makes for more leisure. One hundred and twenty-eight mothers, educated women, in answer to a carefully worded inquiry, noted as a principal discontent that modern homemaking involves too much of "the fragmentation of time," and allows too little time for continuous creative work. George Lundberg comments: "In the suburbs a woman's place seems to be neither in the home nor in the office, but behind the wheel." As far as women are concerned, the possibility of added leisure has proved disappointing.

MATERIALISTIC INFLUENCES

Materialistic conditioning yields a philosophy that weds the idea of the supremacy of the material to selfishness. The offspring of the two is individualism. For one thing, present-day individualism, as far as the home is concerned, is to be found in the ever-diminishing size of the family. The reasons may be seen in such facts as the cost of living, apprehension in regard to giving a child a fair economic and cultural opportunity; the feeling that every additional child limits the parents in their freedom to enjoy life, the unconscious effect of the evaluation of life outside the home as being of equal if not greater significance than the home itself.

What is the consequence for marriage and the home? An Illinois court found that in one year 76 per cent of the divorces granted involved husbands and wives who were childless. Likewise, individualism has had its effect upon the increase in the gainful employment of women. The 1940 census revealed that women were employed in all but 9 of the 451 occupational classifications. From 1900 to 1940 there was an increase of four million in the employment of women of the ages 25-44, representing an increase of 500 per cent. During World War II, five to six million women were added to the nearly thirteen million employed in 1940.

In 1940 more than one third of the employed women of the United States were married women. The employed woman is less likely to feel the necessity of depending on her husband for security. The resulting influence on her thinking regarding marriage is obvious. The economic independence of women is not unrelated to the increase of divorce. And when personal desire for divorce is blocked by the limitations of the law, every subterfuge conceivable is exercised in order to get a decree. "It is apparent," said one authority, "that divorce lightly asked for and lightly granted is individualism gone mad!"

These materialistic and individualistic influences are also responsible for the emotional immaturity that so thwarts the possibilty of happy marriage and home life. Children are brought up under the aegis of parents who shield them from every encounter with life, since these parents are committed only to values of material and physical well-being. Experiences that might prove distasteful, unpleasant, tiresome, or annoying are kept at arm's length from the child. The emotional growth that would normally result from achievement following struggle at each age level is absent. Consequently there is an emotional vitamin deficiency. At twenty-one a young man reaches legal adulthood; physical and intellectual maturity comes at a slightly later time. The great question is the matter of his emotional maturity. If he remains a child emotionally, his adjustments to his mate, to his parental responsibilities, are bound to result in unhappiness. His emotional immaturity causes him to bring to his marriage more emotion-voltage than his marriage can stand. One woman, writing about her problem, said: "I have three children—four counting my husband." A man or woman of forty can have tantrums as well as a child of four. Parents whose goals are exclusively those of material plenty, material success, and personal comfort are building soft lives for a hard world. These soft lives, the end products of secularism, remain unadjusted and unadapted to the responsibilities of marriage and family living.

Individualism reinforced by emotional immaturity leads to doing what one pleases in preference to doing what one ought. The attritional effects of this philosophy are seen in the dramatic fact of divorce. The latter is our major disturbing social tragedy. From 1900 to 1940 the population increased 73 per cent; marriages increased 128 per cent, and divorces 374 per cent. Our divorce rate has increased 600 per cent since the Civil War. There are close to four million divorced persons in the United States, more ex-husbands and ex-wives than the number of inhabitants in our land during Revolutionary times. The devastations of divorce must be seen not only in terms of marriage breakdown, but also in terms of the effects on the lives of children—"the displaced persons" of the broken home.

We are committed to attempt an understanding of divorce in reference to the influence of secularism. Must we grant that marriage failures are likely, and that our preconceived ideas and ideals do not always work? Is divorce the excrescence of a modern way of life, a product of its emotional insufficiencies, and its emphasis upon the material? Mary Langmuir, in an article in the Ladies Home Journal, in March, 1947, suggested that "the prevalence of divorce does not mean more unsuccessful marriages." The increase in the number of divorces, she says, like the increase in the number of appendectomies, is due to more diagnosis.

When we think of stemming the tide of divorce, we must realize the limitations of legislation as an instrument. Severity of the law, beyond what our moral and social culture will sustain, merely makes for hypocrisy. We can well afford, however, to wage the cause of legislation in behalf of uniform marriage laws involving the following: physical fitness, the granting of a license only after three to six months have elapsed from the time of application, the passing of a test following a course of study preparatory for marriage and parenthood. Ironically enough, we grant a driver's license only after an examination following the study of a manual. Can marriage and parenthood be less important?

Divorce and the problems that create it, however, cannot be seen aside from the emotional and physiological involvement of domestic life. The regrettable fact of marriage failure must be faced on the threshold-side of marriage. The deterioration that leads to breakdown is to be found in the contractual view of marriage. Marriage is seen, on the one hand, as an eternal union, into which the participants must fit their individualism, personal notions, and independence; on the other hand marriage is seen as a structure of relationship, relative in its claim and accommodating itself as best it can to one's own desires and notions. Brunner, in *Justice and the Social Order*, says:

Marriage like the state is only possible because each party to the contract foregoes part of the freedom due to him in order to fulfill the common purpose of procreation and the satisfaction of the sexual instinct. The parties to the contract themselves determine the substance of the marital union. The steady increase in divorce has its main source in this individualistic conception of marriage, though many people may not be fully aware of the fact.

A chaplain tells of a G.I. who came inquiring about the possibility of marriage by proxy. When the story was fully told, it developed that this boy and girl knew one another through six weeks of correspondence and planned to marry. They had decided that if, at the time of his release from the service, they did not care to continue the relationship, they could at least divide the accrued allotment money. David Cohn, in a recent magazine article entitled "Are Americans Polygamous?" expresses the feeling that when parties enter into the marriage contract with an escape clause in their minds, "it is a marriage market place, as when one buys a stove on thirty days trial."

Ministers can help marriages to succeed by establishing, as an inevitable practice, the premarriage conference, in which realistically and spiritually both partners face up to the likelihoods and responsibilities of marriage. They can further aid the situation by interpreting to youth and those entering the marriage relation the pricelessness of that experience when it is seen as something eternal. Marriage must be viewed as a relationship that can be dissolved and yet cannot be dissolved; it is the spiritual indissolubility that must be stressed. In *Understanding Marriage and the Family*

DeRougement is quoted as arguing for monogamous loyalty as an act of faith. He bids us to be faithful "by virtue of the absurd," that is, for the simple and only reason that we have taken oath to it. Yet he goes on to give a more substantial reason, namely, that such loyalty, by such conscious choice, creates a value whose security enables the couple to develop other interests and values and to solve their problems constructively.

DISTRACTION AND ABSORPTION

Secularism works its disastrous effect upon the family by means of distraction and absorption. Like a modern pied piper, the secular way of life lures us to an extroversion of the life of the family, detaching each member from that core of family interest and life. By means of its multiplied goals, on various age levels, secularism lures the members of the family ever farther from the home base. We know intuitively that the happiness of any of us is bound up with home life. We turn to the family experience expecting to find a world there that is warm, varied, exciting, only to find that this varied, exciting world is outside. We are intrigued by the thrilling, exhilarating experiences possible outside of the home. The school consumes an ever-increasing amount of the child's day; the movies draw the growing mind into a world of romance, wealth, and big times. They vie with the church and home in forming concepts for youth. The activities of the young are more segregated from those of adults. There is a loss of identity of children and youth with adults, in serious work as well as cohering pleasures. Adults feel that children are alien to their interests and activities. In Dayton, Ohio, there were operative at one time 2,783 different units of social and civic activity. All about us are millions of homeless people who have homes but do not inhabit them. We are living our lives outside the home. In all of this we must see the resultant atrophy of spiritual life. Secularism is taking us further and further from spirituality and the experience of inner renewals of family solidarity.

Marriage and family life are an achievement. The interweaving of the family fabric, so desperately needed to sustain us in the midst of present-day tensions, is achieved by living together. A family is hardly a family until it has lived together, thought together, met responsibilities together, and shared together its elations and its sorrows. By co-operation with one another, the exercise of consideration calling for self-denial, there grows up an intimate something compounded of respect and affection. This is an achievement, a matter of maturation. A marriage grows to be a marriage; a family grows to be a family. It is this that secularism precludes. On our farm in Vermont one summer for a few days the four of us in our family worked for one hour each morning clearing up scattered boards and materials after the barn had been taken down. We all felt that something assuring and compensating came into our relationship from that experience, limited as it was.

One mother said that she did want the convenience of a modern home but not at the price of the rare intimacies that came in sharing the tasks of the home. She did not want an electric dishwasher, for she would not for all the world surrender the priceless experience of the confidences which her children exchanged with her over the dishpan. A family feeling is an achievement.

It is precisely these spiritual insights, the confirmation of our ideals, the spiritual deepening that can come only from living together in vital rapport, that are being overpassed in our response to the multiple goals outside the home. It is precisely at a time when more of the inner life so uniquely engendered by family fellowship is deeply needed to support us in the face of the uncertainties and strains of our social and political crises that we are being increasingly extraverted to life outside the family.

WE NEED EMOTIONAL SECURITY

The achievement of living together gives a sense of dependability and integrity that makes for a feeling of security. A child, a husband, a wife, feels undergirded with an affectionate concern, a strength beyond that which comes from friendship or fraternal fellowship, one that derives uniquely from a sacred partnership. By it all rebuffs are tempered, and depletions yield to renewal.

Emotional security is particularly necessary to a child; the child belongs to the family, knows himself wanted, regarded, and respected by the other members. Something out of the depths of this emotional normality answers the hunger for recognition, for value.

The absence of this essential emotional security is the chief basis of delinquency. Delinquency derives mainly from the emotional disturbances of the family. William Healy and Augusta Bonner, in their work *New Light on Delinquency*, report that 90 per cent of 105 delinquents studied had been the victims of emotional disturbances in family relations:

Dr. Leo Kanner, noted psychiatrist and head of the Harriet Lane Pediatric Hospital, Baltimore, Maryland, is quoted by *Newsweek* as follows: "Psychosis, usually regarded as an adult ailment, is increasingly becoming recognized as a childhood disease. In children as young as one or two years, psychiatrists can see signs of these disturbances."

Employed mothers, homes lacking an affectional warmth, parents consumed with community activities, unwanted children—all these factors play their part in the distressing situation of delinquency. Emotional insecurity is seen manifesting its power in the following facts and figures: Attorney General Tom C. Clark stated that from 1939 to 1945 arrests of girls under eighteen increased 198 per cent. Arrests of boys under eighteen increased for robbery, 39 per cent; for rape, 60 per cent; and for drunkenness, 102 per cent.

While we need to exercise care in conclusions formed from separated instances of errancy, still a marked delinquency trend is indicated by the following cases listed in a recent issue of *Magazine Digest*, in an article by Eric Hutton entitled "Children with Nervous Breakdowns": A fourteen-year-old boy, arrested for hanging an eight-year-old playmate, calmly told the police: "I just decided to hang the little fellow." A sixteen-year-old adopted son of a minister murdered the church sexton and nonchalantly confessed: "I had an urge to kill —it didn't matter who." An eighteen-year-old youth murdered his sixteen-year-old girl friend and then delivered her body to the nearest police station. "We decided to commit suicide because we were fed up with life," he said, "but after I killed her I lost my nerve." A seventeen-year-old Chicago boy murdered a woman in her apartment and scrawled on the wall with lipstick: "For Heaven's sake catch me before I kill. I cannot control myself." But he had committed his third murder, the strangling of a six-year-old girl, before police complied with his wishes.

In one city a children's protective association reports that one of every four cases it is asked to investigate is concerned with juvenile intoxication.

What Is the Answer?

Intelligence, accountability, and dedication are needed if monogamy and the family are to be saved. Youth must know that successful marriage will make exceptional demands in the way of self-discipline and will make serious inroads upon personal rights. The family will need to outwit the inevitable mechanization of the home, protecting its aims and development. Parents, open-eyed, must major in home living. Hartshorne and May tell us that 54 per cent of the influence upon a child's life comes from the home. Harry Emerson Fosdick has said:

> It is not difficult for parents to hand down to children the things we manufacture; the new generation takes to them like ducks to water. But not so simple is it to hand down to our sons and daughters a rich spiritual culture, the greatest heritage of Christ's faith and ethics, and we are not doing well at that. Many families in America are paying little heed to that, and in our schools that is commonly not even permitted.

Part of the answer is to be found in the growth of a family consciousness, a sense of the family as an entity, a family tradition, a feeling of family destiny. The Browns must realize themselves as the Browns, each Brown seeing himself as an integral part of the Browns, a feeling of corporate life participation. Instead of the laissez-faire idea of marriage, with the church and clergy looking on, we must actually indoctrinate our youth with a sense of vocation in homemaking.

All that has been suggested is predicated upon one fact: the importance of God in the home. Here we come upon our prime failure. God is not important in our homes—our church homes. If you were to hide a recording device in any one of our church homes, capable of recording all that is thought as well as spoken in the home, what would a week's recording reveal in regard to God as central in the life of an average church family?

If we are to save marriage and the home, Christianity will have to bore from within, set up its life and its supremacy within the structure of the home, undergirding it with a living experience of God. That is the answer to secularism.

The summons to the home is to re-establish family religion—alive, accountable, pervading, conditioning young and old to dependence on God in every circumstance and incident of life.

SECULARISM AND THE CHRISTIAN FAITH

G. Bromley Oxnam

CONTEMPORARY DISCUSSION OF SECULARISM TOO OFTEN MAKES A FALSE distinction between the sacred and the secular. Leroy E. Loemker, in his penetrating and thought-provoking paper, tells us: "Secularism is practical atheism. . . . It has become the supporting atmosphere of our culture." It is like the air about us, he says. He makes it clear that secularism is not iniquity, immorality, nor is it indifference. It appears to root in "the modern emphasis upon man's ability to achieve his salvation through his own efforts." Loemker turns immediately to religion, and, seeking to define its essential nature, says:

> Religion is the surrender of the person to God, and the commitment of life's goods to God's will, or God's plan, or the course of God's activities. The center of its reference is objective and ultimate; it calls forth reverence and worship. . . . Religion may operate in either of two contrasting ways upon the attitudes of men. Salvation may be regarded as the supreme good apart from all other values of life, the pearl of great price for which man . . . will sell all he has. But it may also be considered as the release of the whole man, and all of his valid interests and needs, from evil. . . . A Christian is one who, in common with like-minded persons, finds in the historical influence and present action of Christ's spirit a channel by which divine power is mediated and his life unified and given purpose. A Christian society is one in which such persons, living in communion with each other and with God, impart to social structures the spirit by which our common life is infused with justice and love, the power of science is directed toward human good, and art and other creative human efforts are given a content ennobling to man.

It is apparent that the fruit of a society composed of Christian persons is found in social structures infused with justice and love, in science directed toward human good, and art and other creative human efforts that ennoble man. We speak of contemporary society as secular, and in the strict use of the term that is correct. Nevertheless there is a false distinction present. Which society, as we evaluate group life in terms of Christian judgment, is secular—the God-fearing,

God-acknowledging, God-reverencing society of feudalism or contemporary democracy? In which of the two societies is there more of
practical atheism? In feudalism we see an aristocracy exploiting a vast
serf base. If we can think of atheism as a denial of God in refusal
to recognize human beings as brothers, the whole issue is vividly set
forth by Charles Dickens in *A Tale of Two Cities*. He is describing
the callous nobility of prerevolutionary France:

With a wild rattle and clatter, and an inhuman abandonment of consideration not easy to be understood in these days, the carriage dashed
through streets and swept round corners, with women screaming before
it, and men clutching each other and clutching children out of its way.
At last, swooping at a street corner by a fountain, one of its wheels came
to a sickening little jolt, and there was a loud cry from a number of
voices, and the horses reared and plunged.

But for the latter inconvenience, the carriage probably would not have
stopped; carriages were often known to drive on, and leave their wounded
behind, and why not? But the frightened valet had got down in a hurry,
and there were twenty hands at the horses' bridles.

"What has gone wrong?" said Monsieur, calmly looking out.

A tall man in a nightcap had caught up a bundle from among the feet
of the horses, and had laid it on the basement of the fountain, and was
down in the mud and wet, howling over it like a wild animal.

"Pardon, Monsieur the Marquis!" said a ragged and submissive man, "it
is a child."

"Why does he make that abominable noise? Is it his child?"

"Excuse me, Monsieur the Marquis—it is a pity—yes."

The fountain was a little removed; for the street opened, where it was,
into a space some ten or twelve yards square. As the tall man suddenly
got up from the ground, and came running at the carriage, Monsieur the
Marquis clapped his hand for an instant on his sword-hilt.

"Killed!" shrieked the man, in wild desperation, extending both arms
at their length above his head, and staring at him. "Dead!"

The people closed round, and looked at Monsieur the Marquis. There
was nothing revealed by the many eyes that looked at him but watch-
fulness and eagerness; there was no visible menacing or anger. Neither
did the people say anything; after the first cry, they had been silent,
and they remained so. The voice of the submissive man who had spoken,
was flat and tame in its extreme submission. Monsieur the Marquis ran
his eyes over them all, as if they had been mere rats come out of their
holes.

He took out his purse.

"It is extraordinary to me," he said, "that you people cannot take care of yourselves and your children. One or the other of you is for ever in the way. How do I know what injury you have done my horses. See! Give him that."

He threw out a gold coin for the valet to pick up, and all the heads craned forward that all the eyes might look down at it as it fell. The tall man called out again with a most unearthly cry, "Dead!"

When I compare feudalistic society, in which kings ruled by divine right and brazenly announced "I am the state," with contemporary society in which I behold a traffic officer lift his hand and stop all the traffic of the busiest thoroughfare of New York in order to allow a tiny child to cross the street, I find it very difficult to refer to one society as secular and to the other as sacred. Personally I prefer democracy with its free men, its concept of the dignity of the human person, democracy with its new doctrine of the worth of woman, the place of the child, or to use another illustration, its criminology, in which all the resources of modern science are brought to bear upon a human being who is thought of as a patient to be cured, rather than as an offender to be punished and upon whom society is to levy its revenge.

The rigorous religionist of early capitalism, who prayed to a sovereign God and exploited the children of the Father of all, was one who did not repudiate God as the source of spiritual unity and power, but, I fear, was a person essentially secular in spirit, since no one would call these brothers secular as far as theism is concerned, nor sacred as far as humanity was concerned.

I am simply trying to stress the fact that there is danger in surrendering the field as we cry "Secular." Our task is to co-operate with all those who know the worth of the spirit and seek to build a society in which the spirit may live.

But my task is to deal with Christian objectives in a secularized society. I desire to think of objectives in terms of faith, social justice, and the indivdual.

A Christian Objective in Faith

In introducing this objective I would like to quote several paragraphs from Arnold J. Toynbee's *A Study of History*, particularly from that section entitled "Schism in the Soul."

"The Jews require a sign and the Greeks seek after wisdom; but we preach Christ Crucified—unto the Jews a stumbling-block and unto the Greeks foolishness."

Why is Christ Crucified a stumbling-block to futurists who have never succeeded in eliciting a sign of divine support for their mundane undertakings? And why is He foolishness to philosophers who have never found the wisdom for which they seek?

Christ Crucified is foolishness to the philosopher because the philosopher's aim is detachment, and he cannot comprehend how any reasonable being who has once attained that forbidding goal can be so perverse as deliberately to relinquish what he has so hardly won. What is the sense of withdrawing simply in order to return? And *a fortiori* the philosopher must be nonplussed at the notion of a God who has not even had to take the trouble to withdraw from an unsatisfactory World, because He is completely independent of it by virtue of His divinity, but who nevertheless deliberately enters into the World, and subjects Himself there to the utmost agony that God or man can undergo, for the sake of a race of beings of an order immeasurably inferior to His own divine nature. "God so loved the World that He gave His only begotten son"? That is the last word in folly from the standpoint of the seeker after detachment. . . .

The Kingdom of God, of which Christ is King, is incommensurable with any kingdom that could be founded by a Messiah envisaged as an Achaemenian world-conquerer turned into a Jew and projected into the future. So far as this *Civitas Dei* enters into the time-dimension at all, it is not as a dream of the future but as a spiritual reality interpenetrating the present. If we ask how, in fact, God's will can be done on Earth as it is in Heaven, the answer, given in the technical language of theology, is that the omnipresence of God involves His immanence in This World and in every living soul in it, as well as His transcendent existence on supramundane planes. In the Christian conception of the Godhead His transcendent aspect (or "person") is displayed in God the Father and His immanent aspect in God the Holy Ghost; but the distinctive and crucial feature of the Christian Faith is that God is not a Duality but a Trinity in Unity, and that in His aspect as God the Son the other two aspects are unified in a Person who, in virtue of this mystery, is as accessible to the human heart as is He incomprehensible to the human understanding. In the Person of Christ Jesus—Very God yet also Very Man—the divine society and the mundane society have a common member who in This World is born into the ranks of the proletariat and dies the death of a malefactor, while in the Other World He is the King of God's Kingdom, a King who is God Himself.

But how can two natures—one divine and the other human—be both present at once in a single person? Answers, cast in the form of creeds, have been worked out by Christian Fathers in terms of the technical vocabulary of the Hellenic philosophers; but this metaphysical line of approach is perhaps not the only one open to us. We may find an alternative starting-point in the postulate that the divine nature, in so far as it is accessible to us, must have something in common with our own; and, if we look for one particular spiritual faculty which we are conscious of possessing and which we also can attribute with absolute confidence to God—because God would be spiritually inferior to man (*quod est absurdum*) if this faculty were not in Him, but were nevertheless in us— then the faculty which we shall think of first as being common to man and God will be one whcih the philosophers wish to mortify; and that is the faculty of Love.[1]

One day when Louis Untermeyer was in my home, in attempting to give a definition of poetry he said: "Poetry is describing the indescribable in terms of the unforgettable." It is our high task to describe the indescribable mystery that lies at the heart of the Incarnation. The words of Toynbee will never reach the mind or the heart of the common man. The terminology is beyond him. It is difficult for us to follow such thought when read. It pays rich rewards when studied. But we must discover some way by which the central doctrine of our faith can be made known to our people. The Word did become flesh and dwell among us. God was in Christ reconciling the world to himself. I fear that if we were to ask our people what is meant by the Incarnation, the answers would disturb us and reveal that we have failed in making our faith known to our people.

It is for that reason that I made bold to propose to the Council of Bishops of The Methodist Church, when it was considering a program for the coming quadrennium, that we set aside a quadrennium in which the major emphasis would not be raising vast sums of money but grounding our people in the faith. This does not mean that we are to disregard our duty in an hour of crisis, when relief funds must be secured. But it does mean that we shall put first things first. The proposal very simply was this: Let us give the first year of the new quadrennium to a consideration of our faith. This will be largely a matter of teaching and of study. But teaching and study must be expressed in action. Thus in each year of the crusade, in

---

[1] From the abridgment by D. C. Somervell. Copyright 1946 by Oxford University Press, New York, Inc. Published under the auspices of the Royal Institute of International Affairs.

which primary emphasis shall be in the realm of thought, a secondary and vital emphasis will be in the field of application. If in the first year we stress our faith and prepare booklets in attractive format and large type, dealing with the essentials of our faith, so that across the nation our laity may be studying together, we can move as one. If in the first month or two we should study together "I believe in God the Father Almighty," then in the second period "And in Jesus Christ his only Son Our Lord," in the third a consideration of the Holy Spirit, on through the fundamentals of our faith until at last we consider the life everlasting, we should have done something for our church sorely needed in this hour. The logical expression of such study would be in the field of evangelism, and the study should be paralleled with an evangelistic effort of great significance. Our second year should be given to a study of our church. the nature of our church, the history of of our church, the meaning of our church. The proper expressional activity here should be church extension. Literally thousands of new communities are unchurched. Into them we could move. The third year would consider our ministry, and it might be that from such a study of the call to the ministry and the meaning of ordination that the present tendency to nullify ordination by granting its privileges to anyone would pass. In that year we could recruit the ministers necessary for the service of the church. That would be the applied aspect of the year emphasizing our ministry. The fourth year would consider our mission. This would be our mission throughout the world and might involve substantial sums of money to undergird those who represent us in the mission. Throughout the quadrennium we could have special days when we might receive sacrificial offerings for overseas relief, and we could, of course, lift our world service giving materially. But the primary emphasis would be in faith.

An Objective in Social Justice

I can do no better here than to restate the definition of the Kingdom of God, phrased by a committee soon after World War I. It is not a comprehensive definition of the Kingdom, but it is in the speech of the common man, and the general term becomes specific. As we realize the ideals stated in the definition, the so-called secularized society becomes a spiritual community. The definition follows:

It would be a co-operative social order in which the sacredness of every life was recognized and everyone found opportunity for the fullest self-expression of which he was capable; in which each individual gave himself gladly and wholeheartedly for ends that are socially valuable; in which the impulses to service and to creative action would be stronger than the acquisitive impulses; and all work would be seen in terms of its spiritual significance, thus making possible fullness of life for all men; in which differences in talent and capacity meant proportional responsibilities in ministering to the common good; in which all lesser differences of race, of nation and of class served to minister to the richness of an all-inclusive brotherhood; in which there hovered over all a sense of the reality of the Christlike God, so that worship inspired service, and service expressed brotherhood.

When our people have been grounded in our faith and lay hold upon the power the faith promises, they can do no other than to move into the social order, resolved to transform it until it becomes an expression of the faith.

An Objective in Individual Action

When I took luncheon with Louis Fischer, the distinguished correspondent and author, we discussed his new book *Gandhi and Stalin* He stressed a point of considerable significance. Gandhi, he said, while making use of great political forces, never believed that the primary matter is to secure a legislative act. The fundamental question has to do with the individual. He was more interested in getting an idea into the mind of an individual or a desire into the human heart than to secure the passage of a bill in a legislature, because he held that when the millions think in a certain way, or feel in a certain way, action in that way is inevitable. The corollary of this is that each individual who holds the idea or cherishes the desire must become an active unit wherever he is, translating the idea and desire into reality in the circles in which he lives. This, I think, becomes a vital matter when we think of Christian objectives in a secularized society. A secularized society can be transformed into a spiritual society when individuals live the life of the spirit wherever they may serve. This is to lay hold upon spiritual forces that are more powerful than political or social or economic forces. This is to recognize that when the Kingdom of God is within us and living within us and expressed by us, society itself can become the Kingdom.

I have tried to suggest that the church must inaugurate a move designed to make our faith clear to our people, that it must become active in translating that faith into the realities of the common life, and that it must give to our people an understanding of the fact that there is no more powerful force in the world than the individual possessed of the spirit, and who serves in the name of the spirit wherever he may be. As these individuals are increased, and their numbers become legion, the secularized society itself becomes spiritual.

At the beginning I tried to suggest that there is a false distinction made between sacred and secular by all too many who consider these things. But I did not mean to suggest that there is no distinction between the secular and the sacred. I meant that we should approach much that is called secular in an appreciative and understanding spirit, and bring to the so-called secular so much of the spiritual that the secular is indeed changed.

Perhaps I can make it vivid by referring to the ancient poet Omar. You will recall that one morning he stood in the darkness before the sunrise. Has anyone anywhere in literature ever brought the meaning of the morning more beautifully than did he? Do you recall his words?

> Wake! For the Sun, who scattered into flight
> The Stars before him from the Field of Night,
>   Drives Night along with them from Heaven, and strikes
> The Sultan's Turret with a Shaft of Light.

I do not wish to· call this man's description of the sunrise secular because he thought solely in materialistic terms. I prefer rather to look upon the sunrise, to share in the beauties he apprehended, and bring to him a deeper understanding of the universe so that he might join with me in the words of Henry van Dyke:

> Joyful, joyful, we adore Thee,
>   God of glory, Lord of love;
> Hearts unfold like flowers before Thee,
>   Opening to the sun above.
> Melt the clouds of sin and sadness;
>   Drive the dark of doubt away;
> Giver of immortal gladness,
>   Fill us with the light of day! [2]

[2] From "Hymn of Joy." Used by permission Charles Scribner's Sons, publishers.

BIOGRAPHICAL NOTES

BERTRAM W. DOYLE was born in Alabama and educated at Wiley College, Ohio Wesleyan University, and the University of Chicago. He has taught at Samuel Huston College, Claflin College, Clark College, Paine College, and Fisk University. He has also served as pastor of churches in Tennessee and South Carolina. Since 1937 he has been general secretary, General Conference Board of Education of the Colored Methodist Episcopal Church, and is author of *The Etiquette of Race Relations in the South*. He has served as administrative dean of Louisville Municipal College since 1942.

SHERWOOD EDDY, author and executive secretary for Asia of the Y.M.C.A., was born in Kansas and educated at Yale. He served in India as a national secretary of the Y.M.C.A., working among students there between 1896 and 1911, and with the British and American armies in the first world war as Y.M.C.A. secretary. Some of his many works are: *India Awakening, With Our Soldiers in France, Religion and Social Justice, The Challenge of Russia, Russia Today, Revolutionary Christianity, Pathfinders of the World Missionary Crusade, God in History*, and also books published in India and England.

PAUL F. HEARD is executive secretary of the Protestant Film Commission. He was educated at the University of Minnesota and has been a teacher, radio continuity writer, announcer, and newspaperman. He has served in the visual education department of his alma mater and has held a similar position with the Board of Missions of The Methodist Church. During World War II he was war orientation film officer for the Navy Department and was in charge of the Navy's educational service film program to retrain men, psychologically and emotionally, for peace.

J. EDGAR HOOVER has been director of the Federal Bureau of Investigation since 1924. He was born in the District of Columbia, received LL.B. and LL.M. degrees from George Washington University, and holds honorary degrees from numerous universities and colleges. He has been admitted to practice law before the bar of the District Court of the United States for the District of Columbia, the United States Court of Claims, and the United States Supreme Court, and entered the Department of Justice in 1917. He is a trustee of George Washington University and of the National Presbyterian Church; a member of the board of directors of the Central Dispensary and Emergency Hospital, Washington, D. C.; a member of the board of directors of the Boys' Clubs of America; member of the National

Committee on Public Relations of the Boy Scouts of America. Holder of the Distinguished Service Medal of the American Legion, he was appointed an honorary Knight Commander of the Civil Division of the Most Excellent Order of the British Empire by King George VI. In 1946 he was presented the Medal of Merit by President Truman. He is the author of *Persons in Hiding* and is a contributor to numerous magazines, law reviews, and police journals.

F. ERNEST JOHNSON is executive secretary of the Department of Research and Education, the Federal Council of the Churches of Christ in America. He was born in Ontario, Canada, and was educated at Albion College and Union Theological Seminary. He has served pastorates at Holly, Michigan, and St. Paul's Church and James Church in New York. Professor of education in the Teachers College of Columbia University since 1931, he is the author of *The Church and Society*, *Economics and the Good Life*, *The Social Gospel Re-examined*, and other works.

GERALD KENNEDY has been pastor of St. Paul Church in Lincoln, Nebraska, since 1942. Born in Michigan and educated at the College of the Pacific, the Pacific School of Religion, and Hartford Theological Seminary, he has also been a lecturer in religion at Nebraska Wesleyan University since 1942. In addition he conducts three radio programs: "The Methodist Hour," "Voice of St. Paul's," and "Adventures Along the Bookshelf." He is a trustee of Iliff School of Theology, Nebraska Wesleyan University, and Bryan Memorial Hospital, and is the author of *His Word Through Preaching*, *Have This Mind*, and *The Pause for Reflection*.

LEROY E. LOEMKER was born in Wisconsin and attended the University of Dubuque. After teaching and some graduate study in mathematics he received his theological training at Boston University School of Theology and did further graduate study at the University of Berlin and Boston University, where he was awarded the degree of Ph.D. in 1931. He has been professor of philosophy at Emory University since 1929 and dean of the Graduate School there since 1946.

DON D. LESCOHIER has been professor of economics at the University of Wisconsin since 1918. He was born in Michigan and educated at Albion College and the University of Wisconsin. He has served as special agent and chief statistician for the Wisconsin and Minnesota departments of labor and industry. During 1911-18 he was professor of social sceinces at Hamline University. He has also been lecturer in economics at the University of Minnesota and collaborator in farm labor investigation for the U. S. Department of Agriculture. He is a coauthor of *Population Problems*, *Can Business Prevent Unemployment?*, and *The History of Labor*.

GERALD O. MCCULLOH is professor of systematic theology at Garrett Biblical Institute. He was born in Kansas, the son of a Methodist minister, and was educated at Baker University, Boston University, and the University of Edinburgh. During 1934-36 he served as minister of the First Congregational Church in North Hampton, New Hampshire. He later served as professor of philosophy at Hamline University (1938-42) and as minister of the Hamline Methodist Church (1942-46) in St. Paul, Minnesota.

JOHN THOMAS MCNEILL, professor of church history at Union Theological Seminary since 1944, was born in Canada and holds degrees from McGill University; Westminster Hall, Vancouver; the University of Chicago; and Queen's University, Kingston, Canada. He was ordained in the Presbyterian Church in Canada in 1913 and served as a member of the faculty of Queen's University and Knox College, Toronto. In 1927 he became professor of church history at the University of Chicago, where he remained until 1944. His latest book is *Books of Faith and Power*. He also contributed a chapter to *Protestantism*, the 1944 Evanston lectures.

CARL W. MILLER has served as professor of physics at Brown University since 1924. Born in Massachusetts and educated at Harvard, he was a Shelton Prize Fellow from Harvard at the University of Zurich and the University of Paris 1915-16, and served as instructor of physics at New York University 1922-24. During 1930-31 he was on sabbatical leave at the University of Leipzig. His most important scientific contributions have been to the mathematical theory of color reproduction, for which he was elected a fellow of the Royal Photographic Society of Great Britain in 1943, and in the field of physiological optics. He is a fellow of the American Physical Society and of the American Association for the Advancement of Science, an associate of the Photographic Society of America, a member of the New York Academy of Sciences and of the American Association of University Professors. He has written *An Introduction to Physical Science*, *Principles of Photographic Reproduction*, *A Scientist's Approach to Religion*, and a number of research articles dealing with thermionics and optics.

EDWIN MIMS was born in Arkansas and educated at Vanderbilt and Cornell universities. He taught at Trinity College and the University of North Carolina, and served as head of the English department at Vanderbilt, 1912-42, and as chairman of the division of humanities, 1928-42. In addition he has been professor of English at many summer schools in this country and has lectured in Great Britain. He is a member of the board of electors of the Hall of Fame, a contributor to many magazines, and the author of a biography of Sidney Lanier, *The Advancing South*,

The History of Vanderbilt University, Great Writers as Interpreters of Religion, and *The Christ of the Poets.*

G. BROMLEY OXNAM, a bishop of The Methodist Church, was born in California. He was educated at the University of Southern California and Boston University and continued graduate study at Harvard University and the Massachusetts Institute of Technology. He was pastor of the Church of All Nations, Los Angeles, California, from 1917 to 1927; served as professor of practical theology and city church at Boston University, 1927-28, and was president of DePauw University 1928-36. He was elected to the episcopacy in 1936. He is the author of *Labor and Tomorrow's World, Preaching in a Revolutionary Age, By This Sign Conquer,* and other works.

PITMAN B. POTTER has been Grozier professor of international law and chairman of the Department of International Relations and Organization at The American University, Washington, D. C., since 1944. He was educated at Harvard University and served there as instructor in government, 1914-16; as instructor in history at Yale, 1916-17; associate in political science at the University of Illinois, 1919-20; professor of political science at the University of Wisconsin, 1920-31; and professor of international organization in the Graduate Institute of International Studies at Geneva, 1930-41. He was director of the Geneva Research Center, general reporter for the International Studies Conference, legal adviser to the government of Ethiopia, and served on the Italo-Ethiopian Arbitration Commission in 1935. He is a member of the American Political Science Association, the American Society for Public Administration, and the American Society of International Law, of which he has been secretary since 1944, and is managing editor of the *American Journal of International Law.*

HENRY LEE ROBISON, JR. has been executive secretary of the Virginia Council of Churches since 1945, prior to which he served as director of religious work in state institutions in Virginia for seven years. He was born in West Virginia and was educated at Randolph-Macon College, Yale, the University of Virginia, and Boston University. He was president of the Richmond Ministerial Union in 1943, secretary in 1944. One of the organizers of the Protestant Ministers' Association (Interracial), he has been one of its officers since 1945. Formerly president of the Virginia Conference of Church Social Work, he is a member of the board of directors of the Richmond Community Council and has served as a member of the National Preaching Mission of the Federal Council of the Churches of Christ in America. He is a member of the Federal Council's Department of Christian Social Relations and of its Commission on Religion and Health. He is also a member of the executive committee of the Virginia Conference of Social Work and was recently appointed to serve on the program committee of the National Conference of Church Social Work. In 1947 as a member of a group of twenty Protestant churchmen he traveled in eleven European countries to observe the administration of Overseas Church Relief.

LUMAN J. SHAFER, secretary of the Board of Foreign Missions of the Reformed Church in America, was born in New York and educated at Rutgers University and New Brunswick Theological Seminary. In 1912 he was ordained minister and appointed missionary to Japan, where he served until 1935. He is now chairman of the Japan Committee of the Foreign Missions Conference of North America. He was editor of the *Japan Christian Year Book* in 1931 and is author of *The Christian Alternative to World Chaos* and *The Christian Mission in Our Day*.

GEORGE N. SHUSTER, author and educator, was born in Wisconsin and attended the University of Notre Dame, the University of Poitiers, France, and Columbia University. He served as head of the Department of English, University of Notre Dame, 1920-24; instructor in English at Brooklyn Polytechnic Institute, 1924-25; professor of English at St. Joseph's College for Women, Brooklyn, 1924-35. He was associate editor of *The Commonweal*, 1925-29; managing editor, 1929-37, and now is contributing editor. He was a fellow of the Social Science Research Council of Columbia University, 1937-39; dean and acting president of Hunter College, 1939-40; and has been president of that institution since 1940. He is the author, coauthor, and translator of a number of books, some of which are: *Catholic Spirit in Modern English Literature*, *The Catholic Church and Current Literature*, *Religion and Education*, *Pope Pius XI and American Public Opinion*, *Germany: A Short History*, *Mein Kampf*, *The World's Great Catholic Literature*, *Jesse and Maria*, *Job the Man Speaks with God*, *The Vatican as a World Power*.

HUGH C. STUNTZ has been president of Scarritt College, Nashville, Tennessee, since 1943. Dr. Stuntz was born in India and was educated at Wesleyan University, Cornell University, Garrett Biblical Institute, Union Theological Seminary, and Columbia University. During 1919-20 he served as secretary, Personnel Department, Board of Foreign Missions of the Methodist Episcopal Church. He was secretary and director of religious education for the Methodist Episcopal Church in South America, 1920-32; director of the American Institute in Bolivia, 1934-37; director of religious education, East South America Conference of the Methodist Episcopal Church, 1937-39, director of public relations for Scarritt College, 1940-43. He is the author of *Predecessors of Jesus* and *The United Nations Challenge to the Church*.

JAMES E. WARD was born in Norforlk, Virginia, and educated at the University of Virginia and Harvard University. He has taught at the University of Virginia, Clemson College, Peabody College, and is now head of the Department of Economics at Peabody. He is an active member in The Methodist Church, for a number of years was lay leader of Upper South Carolina Conference, and is a member of the Board of Publication of The Methodist Church.

HAZEN G. WERNER has been professor of practical theology at Drew University since 1945. He was born in Michigan and educated at Albion College, Columbia University, Drew University, and received honorary degrees from Albion College and Ohio Wesleyan University. He has served pastorates in Detroit and Flint, Michigan, and Dayton, Ohio. He is the author of *And We Are Whole Again* and *Real Living Takes Time.*

GOODRICH C. WHITE, president of Emory University, was born in Georgia and educated at Emory, Columbia University, the University of Chicago. He has served as professor at Kentucky Wesleyan College, Wesleyan College in Georgia, and Emory University. During 1923-38 he was dean of the College of Arts and Sciences of Emory; dean of the Graduate School, 1929-42; and vice-president, 1938-42. Since that time he has served as president. He is a member of the Senate of the United Chapters of Phi Beta Kappa and of the University Senate of The Methodist Church, and was secretary of the Commission on Institutions of Higher Education of the Southern Association of Colleges and Secondary Schools, 1940-47. He served as a member of the President's Commission on Higher Education in 1946-47.

ALEXANDER C. ZABRISKIE has been dean of Virginia Theological Seminary since 1940. Prior to that time he served there as professor. He was born in New York and received degrees from Princeton University, Virginia Theological Seminary, Kenyon College, and the University of the South. He was ordained in New York, served as secretary of the Executive Committee of the Forward Movement Commission of his denomination, and now is a member of its Commission on Unity. He has been a deputy to several General Conferences of The Methodist Church.